MAKING THE WEATHER

VERNON BOGDANOR

Making the Weather

Six Politicians Who Changed Modern Britain

Published in 2024 by
Haus Publishing Ltd
4 Cinnamon Row
London SW11 3TW

Copyright © Vernon Bogdanor, 2024

A CIP catalogue for this book is available from the British Library

The moral right of the author has been asserted

ISBN 978-1-914979-08-8
eISBN 978-1-914979-09-5

Typeset in Sabon by MacGuru Ltd

Printed in the United Kingdom by Clays Ltd (Elcograf S.p.A.)

www.hauspublishing.com
@HausPublishing

The reasonable man adapts himself to the world:
the unreasonable one persists in trying to adapt
the world to himself. Therefore all progress
depends on the unreasonable man.

– Bernard Shaw, *Man and Superman*

Contents

Introduction

In *Great Contemporaries*, a series of prose portraits primarily 'of British statesmen who shone at the end of the last century and the beginning of this', published in 1937, Winston Churchill wrote that 'one mark of a great man is ... to have handled matters during his life that the course of after events is continuously affected by what he did'.[1] One such great man, he believed, was Joseph Chamberlain, colonial secretary from 1895 to 1903, a politician who 'made the weather'.

Although Chamberlain never entered Downing Street, nor did he even hold one of the three great offices of state – the Exchequer, Foreign Office, or Home Office – he exercised greater influence on the history of the country than many of those who did. He set an agenda which others followed. In the late nineteenth century, as mayor of Birmingham, he was the first to champion civic improvement and the first major politician to call for state intervention to modify social ills. His commitment to the Union with Ireland led him to split the Liberal Party over the question of home rule for Ireland. Then, in alliance with the Conservatives, he was the first to confront the economic decline of Britain and propose measures to combat it with his idea of a unified empire protected against competitors by a tariff wall.

This book, developed from lectures I gave at Gresham College some years ago, discusses the political careers of six post-war British politicians who 'made the weather'. Three are from the

---

1 Winston Churchill, *Great Contemporaries* (Odhams Press, 1937), 43, 54.

left – Aneurin Bevan, Roy Jenkins, and Tony Benn – and three from the right – Enoch Powell, Keith Joseph, and Nigel Farage. These six have altered our lives more than most prime ministers.

Aneurin Bevan was the prime spokesman of his generation for the ideals of democratic socialism. He helped create the National Health Service (NHS), one of the most enduring and distinctive policies introduced by any British government in modern times, which he regarded as an example of socialism in action.

Enoch Powell was the most prominent post-war exponent of the idea of the sovereignty of Parliament and indeed of English nationalism, opposing as he did mass immigration, a multiracial society, devolution, and Britain's entry into the European Community (EC) – as the European Union (EU) used to be known. Popular in the country and amongst Conservative Party members, he was seen as too extreme and as racist by many leading Conservatives. He left the Conservative Party in 1974. Some regard Powell as a prophet before his time, while others see his influence as almost entirely harmful.

Roy Jenkins, who was home secretary under Labour governments from 1965 to 1967 and 1974 to 1976, instituted changes of permanent significance, sponsoring the reform of laws prohibiting homosexuality and abortion, as well as legislation outlawing racial discrimination. During the 1970s, his support for European unity put him at odds with many in his party, and in 1981, he helped found the new but short-lived Social Democratic Party (SDP), which came within an ace of destroying the two-party monopoly of power in Britain. He also played a leading part, as president of the European Commission, in launching the idea of European economic and monetary union.

Keith Joseph was the most articulate and powerful exponent of the market economy during the 1970s, a time when it was distinctly unfashionable. It was he who provided the ideological dynamic for what came to be called Thatcherism. Through his speeches in the mid-1970s, he paved the way for Margaret Thatcher's momentous premiership and for a very different kind of Conservatism than had been prevalent before 1974.

Tony Benn was the most prominent modern advocate of the idea of participation in post-war Britain. It was he who secured the right of hereditary peers to renounce their titles, something now taken for granted, but it came about only after a bitter struggle between 1960 and 1963. Benn was the first leading politician to call for the referendum to be used in Britain, something now accepted as part of the constitution. He also pioneered the selection of party leaders by members as well as MPs, something that again is now taken for granted in all major parties.

Nigel Farage is the only one of my six never to have held government office. Yet since 2010, Conservative governments have been in fear of him, and he is arguably more responsible for Britain's departure from the EU than any other politician. He is also the only one of the six who is still alive, and in the 2024 election, he led Reform UK to five seats in the House of Commons.

The influence of the other five did not flow only, or even primarily, from their time in government. One of my six, Powell, was a Cabinet minister for just fifteen months. A second, Joseph, while he was a Cabinet minister under four prime ministers – Harold Macmillan, Alec Douglas-Home, Edward Heath, and Margaret Thatcher – was widely regarded as ineffective. Only two, Bevan and Jenkins, had significant achievements in government to their credit. But they too exerted influence as much through what they said as through what they did.

One of my six, Benn, once told me that he had put down a bill for debate in the House of Commons which would, at a stroke, have repealed every single legislative enactment passed by Margaret Thatcher's governments. But, even if such a measure could have been passed, he went on, it would have had relatively little effect, since Margaret Thatcher's influence came, Benn believed, not primarily from what she had enacted but from what she had taught.

Benn, of course, believed that much of what she taught was harmful. But there could be no doubt that she had been a powerful teacher. Speaking to students from a sixth-form college in November 1982, he was surprised to discover how many Thatcherites were among them:

> She has armed a lot of bright young people with powerful right-wing arguments, and, although I enjoy discussing them, I realise I am no longer dealing with the old consensus but with a new breed of right-wing concepts. It confirms me in my belief that there will be a hard inheritance which will never be forgotten, even when all Thatcher's legislation has been repealed.[2]

Benn also told me that what the left lacked was a teacher. It had not had a teacher, he told me, since Bevan. A similar point was put in a different way by another of my six, Joseph, who told the Conservative Party conference in 1976, 'Strategy matters. Policies matter. But behind them all stands the vision. Scorn not the vision; scorn not the idea. Mao said that power grows out of the barrel of a gun. A gun is certainly powerful, but who controls the man with a gun? A man with an idea.'[3]

All of the six portrayed here were successful teachers at different levels of political activity and discourse; like all good teachers, they were wonderful communicators. Bevan and Powell in particular could mesmerise their audiences both in the Commons and in the country. Communication, of course, is a

---

2 Tony Benn, *The End of an Era: Diaries 1980–90* (Hutchinson, 1992), 257.
3 Quoted in Andrew Denham and Mark Garnett, *Keith Joseph* (Acumen, 2001), 298.

prime requirement for a politician, for political leadership consists in large part of moulding opinion and mobilising support to secure legislative measures that will reach the statute book. Support must be secured amongst the voters, but also amongst party members, MPs, and the Cabinet. Bevan was able to mobilise support at all these levels for the NHS. He was less successful at mobilising support for his vision of democratic socialism amongst the wider electorate, although he did enjoy widespread support amongst members of Labour constituency parties. Jenkins was skilled at mobilising support within the governmental elite at Cabinet level, but less so in the wider reaches of the Labour Party or amongst Labour voters. Benn, on the other hand, could mobilise opinion amongst the grass roots of the Labour Party, but not amongst MPs or the Cabinet. Powell had tremendous support in the country and amongst Conservative Party members, but much less in Parliament or Cabinet. Joseph's base lay within a section of the Conservative elite which, led by Margaret Thatcher, secured power in the Conservative Party by means, in effect, of a coup in 1975, displacing Edward Heath, who had enjoyed the support of the party establishment. Farage enjoys tremendous grass-roots support, and a great deal amongst Conservative Party members, but little in Parliament and even less in the Cabinet.

All six of my subjects were, I believe, important teachers. There is of course huge disagreement as to whether what they taught was good or bad; indeed, no one can agree with the teachings of all six, since their views were so very different and conflicting.

It is because they were such good teachers and such good communicators, that the six remain so strikingly relevant today. Indeed the issues they raised lay at the very heart of the political agenda for the 2024 election.

Aneurin Bevan's NHS is at the forefront of debate, with many asking whether it is still fit for purpose.

Enoch Powell's concerns on immigration are the concerns of many voters today, with net immigration in 2023 being 745,000, compared to a yearly average of around 50,000 in his day.

Roy Jenkins's Europeanism no longer appears particularly relevant, but perhaps our relationship with the EU has not yet been finally set in stone; Jenkins's advocacy of proportional representation and party realignment is now championed, ironically, by someone opposed to almost everything that Jenkins stood for – Nigel Farage. But Farage, by contrast with Jenkins, seeks a realignment on the right rather than the left.

Keith Joseph's advocacy of a market economy still excites many Conservatives, while Tony Benn's belief in referendums and participation continues to influence many on the left and the right, including Nigel Farage who, since 2020, has frightened the Conservatives with what amounts to an alternative agenda of the right.

A number of books have been written on the theme of *The Prime Ministers We Never Had* – the title of a recent work by the political journalist Steve Richards.[4] *Making the Weather* is not another such book. None of the six, except perhaps Jenkins, came remotely near to being prime minister, and Jenkins's political position as a pro-European on Labour's right when the party was moving towards what later came to be called Euroscepticism made it unlikely that he could ever be a consensual candidate for the Labour leadership. Much political history consists in the study of prime ministers and those who just missed being prime minister. A good deal less is written on those who made the deepest imprint upon the country. The focus of *Making the Weather* is on the influence exerted by the six, not their proximity to power. Others who came nearer to No. 10 – Rab Butler, Denis Healey, Neil Kinnock, Michael Heseltine, Kenneth Clarke,

---

4 Steve Richards, *The Prime Ministers We Never Had* (Atlantic Books, 2021).

David Miliband, and Ed Miliband, all discussed by Richards – exerted comparatively little long-term influence. There have been Bennites, Jenkinsites, and Powellites, but hardly any Butlerites or Kinnockites – or if there were, they have been largely forgotten. Some of those alleged to have exerted great political influence, such as Rab Butler and Anthony Crosland, used that influence not to alter the political agenda but to accommodate their parties to the political consensus. The six whom I discuss all challenged that consensus. They were all in a sense contrarians. That perhaps is one reason why none of them reached No. 10. It may be indeed that the exercise of long-term political influence is inimical to the pursuit of power. Clear-cut policies, after all, tend to divide, while ambiguity often unites – as both Macmillan and Wilson understood so well. Even Margaret Thatcher, so often seen as a prime minister of great boldness and clarity, was far more cautious and ambiguous in opposition before 1979 than she was in office. Before entering Downing Street, much of her agenda was being staked out not so much by her but by Joseph, her 'John the Baptist'.

Nor is *Making the Weather* intended as a series of potted biographies. There are already good biographies of all six. There would be no point in merely attempting to summarise them. As Auden says, a shilling life will give you all the facts. Instead, I seek to pinpoint the influence exerted by the six and try to discover how it was that they were able to exert that influence so that they remain live figures even in the political debates of today, when so many of their contemporaries have been forgotten.

In writing this book, I have had the great advantage of consulting the papers of my late friend and colleague David Butler, founder of psephology, in the David Butler Archive at Nuffield College, Oxford. These consist of summaries of interviews which he undertook with leading politicians and officials from the end of the 1950s. They constitute a gold mine of material on post-war British politics and cast much light on four of those I discuss – Powell, Joseph, Jenkins, and, above all, Benn, who had been David's tutorial partner as an undergraduate at Oxford and remained a lifelong friend, even though David dissented from most of Benn's political views.

I have also had the advantage of having known, albeit not well, all of those discussed in this book except for Bevan. My closest acquaintance was with Jenkins, although I was never one of his intimates. I have to confess that I liked all five of those whom I have met, though disagreeing with much of what Benn, Powell, Joseph, and Farage said. Benn and Powell each went out of their way to be helpful to me in my research even though they knew that I was far from sharing their views. Farage was generous enough to discuss his views with me on the telephone, even though he knows that we do not see eye to eye on Europe or a number of other issues. Parts of Chapter 6 have been informed by our conversation. Joseph I once heard speak at a dinner discussion. Like many who met him, I found him a somewhat awkward figure. He made a factual error in the talk he gave, an error which tended to undermine his central argument. In the discussion, I ventured to point this out – courteously, I hope. Characteristically, but rarely for a politician, he did not try to bluster his way out of the error or adopt sophistical arguments to explain it away. He admitted that he had made a mistake. Equally characteristically, he apologised profusely for his mistake – far more than was necessary. Jenkins was one of the few politicians who could laugh at himself, as he often did. Once, during his years of retirement, I mentioned that I disliked a certain Tory politician.

'Why?' he enquired.

'Well,' I responded, 'he is just a former future prime minister hanging around.'

'There are rather a large number of us, you know,' he responded with a twinkle.

Jenkins was also a man of great – perhaps excessive – courtesy. I first came into contact with him when, out of the blue, he wrote to me as a young and unknown don, to say how much he had admired a book I had written on electoral reform and the role of the referendum in British politics. Many years later, I was to have a disagreement with him on an aspect of the Maastricht Treaty. He argued forcefully against my view and convinced me that I had been wrong. A couple of days later, I received a handwritten note from him, declaring, quite unnecessarily, that he hoped I had not been upset by the force of his argument, but it was something he felt very strongly about. Jenkins was also the last of the civilised politicians. Who else could discuss the novels of Anthony Powell with the same assurance and expertise as the problems besetting the EU? He is the figure I most admire among the six whom I discuss. But all six sought seriously to confront the problems facing Britain. All made important contributions to the debate about Britain's future and to the vibrancy of British democracy. All were and perhaps still are regarded as mavericks. But all have deeply influenced our lives and continue to do so.

1

Aneurin Bevan and Democratic Socialism

I

Aneurin Bevan (1897–1960) was a man of government as well as a teacher. He was the most creative member of Clement Attlee's post-war Labour administration, which held office from 1945 to 1951, the first Labour majority government in British history. The only comparable man of government amongst the other five analysed in this book was Jenkins.

Bevan's significance is twofold. There is, first, his achievement in creating the NHS, 'the first experiment in socialised medicine to be undertaken by a major western industrialised nation' and 'the most ambitious publicly provided health service to be established by a major western democracy'.[1] There is, second, his teaching. He was the prime exponent in post-war Britain of the idea of democratic socialism. He not only tried to make people think, but also to make them feel. And in that he had something in common with Churchill – for Churchill in 1940 owed his enormous popular support not only to the strength of his arguments, but to the power of his rhetoric, which expressed the underlying feeling of the British people that they were not going to give in to Hitler.

---

1 Charles Webster, *The Health Services Since the War: Volume 1, Problems of Health Care: The National Health Service before 1957* (HMSO, 1988), 2, 397.

Bevan's early years gave no hint of what was to come. He was born in 1897 in Tredegar, in South Wales, to a mining family, and was one of ten children, four of whom did not survive into adulthood, something not wholly unusual in those days. He was certainly poor by modern standards, but his family was not amongst the poorest in the community by the standards of the time. They did not live in a slum, and in 1906 his parents were able to buy a small house of their own. Bevan's father was a miner, a Welsh-speaking member of the chapel who enjoyed choral singing, and a voracious reader, but he developed pneumoconiosis and died prematurely. Bevan inherited his father's love of reading and, to some extent, his interest in music, but unlike his father he never learned Welsh. Bevan indeed was particularly hostile to Welsh nationalism, which he regarded as an instrument for dividing the British working class, though in 1959, shortly before his death, he did come to support the idea of a Welsh secretary with a seat in the Cabinet.

Bevan's education was rudimentary, and he was certainly not regarded as the intellectual of the family. Even his admiring biographer, Michael Foot, had to admit that 'not even his ambitious mother proposed that he should try for the secondary school. No one believed that he would pass an eleven plus examination', as one of his sisters had done.[2] Aneurin left school at thirteen, after an undistinguished school career, and became a miner like his father at a wage of ten shillings a week. He worked in the mines for nine years, and was later to be unemployed for around three years.

Part of the reason for Bevan's undistinguished school career was his stutter, something he had in common with George VI, and which was to prove a bond between them when Bevan

---

2 Michael Foot, *Aneurin Bevan: A Biography: Volume 1, 1897–1945* (Four Square Books, 1966), 19.

became a minister. He also had a lisp, something he had in common with Churchill. Perhaps for this reason he was bullied, both by his schoolmaster and by his fellow pupils. But despite these impediments, he forced himself to learn to speak in public. Michael Foot once asked him, 'How did you cure the stutter, Nye?' The reply was, 'By torturing my audiences.'[3] To avoid the embarrassment caused by his stutter, Bevan would consult a dictionary and a thesaurus to discover synonyms for words that he could pronounce only with difficulty; that in part accounts for the wide vocabulary which he employed in his speeches. In February 1949, in a debate on the NHS estimates, he declared that the Tory Party 'used to represent itself as a jocund party'. Honourable members responded with 'What?' Bevan's riposte was 'They do not understand English now. I will give them a clue: "How jocund did they drive their teams afield".' Having shared this quotation from Thomas Gray's 'Elegy Written in a Country Churchyard', he explained that it meant sprightly, light-hearted.[4]

Bevan would use his stutter to great effect. Once, following Churchill in a censure debate, he declared, 'I welcome this opportunity of pricking the b-b-bloated bladder of lies with the p-p-poniard of truth.'[5] In 1957, speaking as shadow foreign secretary at Labour's annual conference and attacking the idea of unilateral nuclear disarmament, he declared that it would send a Labour foreign secretary 'naked into the conference chamber'. He added, 'You call that statesmanship. I call it an emotional s-s-spasm.'[6] The effect was considerable.

Bevan's overcoming of the stutter and the lisp were early signs

---

3 Ibid., 31.
4 Hansard, House of Commons, 17 February 1949, vol. 461, col. 1459.
5 Hansard, House of Commons, 29 September 1949, vol. 468, col. 310.
6 John Campbell, *Nye Bevan and the Mirage of British Socialism* (Weidenfeld and Nicolson, 1987), 337.

of his remarkable willpower. In due course, he became a fine speaker, second only to Churchill as a parliamentary orator – some would say equal to, or even better. When he spoke, he commanded the Commons. Bevan, like Churchill, was self-educated. Neither had been to university. On the one occasion I met Harold Wilson, who had resigned with Bevan on the issue of health-service charges in 1951, he told me that Bevan was the best self-educated man he had ever met. Bevan was very widely read, his favourite authors being Thomas Jefferson, Jack London, Stendhal, and H. G. Wells. But he also knew a great deal about Shakespeare. One weekend in 1950, he went to Stratford with Michael Foot to see John Gielgud in *King Lear* and Peggy Ashcroft in *As You Like It*. After the performances, he gave a talk to the theatre directors, headed by Anthony Quayle, on the errors made by some critics of Shakespeare.[7] As a young man, he wrote a thesis on Kant's categorical imperative which the senior tutor at Jesus College, Oxford said was the best thing he had read on Kant for many years.[8]

As a young man, in 1919, Bevan won a scholarship to attend the Central Labour College in London. But he found it tedious and joined a breakaway organisation, the Plebs League, founded by a South Wales miner, Noah Ablett, who had complained that the college was not giving enough attention to the ideas of Karl Marx. Bevan was deeply influenced by the League and contributed an article to its journal analysing *The Communist Manifesto*. He became a Marxist in the sense of believing in class conflict as the basic driver of politics. But, unlike some Marxists, he insisted on a commitment to parliamentary democracy. 'In so far as I can be said to have had a political training at

---

7 Michael Foot, *Aneurin Bevan: A Biography: Volume 2, 1945–1960* (Davis-Poynter, 1973), 298.
8 Jennie Lee, *My Life with Nye* (Jonathan Cape, 1980), 147–8.

all,' Bevan was later to reminisce, 'it has been in Marxism [but] quite early in my studies, it seemed to me that classic Marxism consistently understated the role of a political democracy with a fully developed franchise.'[9] The most revolutionary force in the world, Bevan used to insist, is parliamentary democracy.

Bevan's Marxism really amounted to little more than the view that, since the working class constituted the majority, once democracy had been fully achieved Britain would vote for social-ism and build a society in which public ownership rather than private enterprise was the norm. But a socialist society was not, in Bevan's view, to be distinguished from a capitalist one solely in terms of its economic machinery. The transformation of the economy would be a means to the creation of a new kind of society, one quite different from capitalism, a society based on fellowship rather than a competitive struggle for existence. 'Fel-lowship is life,' William Morris had said in his novel *A Dream of John Ball*, 'and lack of fellowship is death.'

Whatever role Marxism played in his political make-up, Bevan never swerved from the conviction that the only possible vehicle for socialism in Britain was the Labour Party. He sometimes flirted with alternatives, but it never occurred to him to join any of the small left-wing parties such as the Communist Party, or splinter movements such as the Independent Labour Party (ILP), which broke off from the Labour Party in 1932. Indeed, he warned his future wife, Jennie Lee, not to flirt with the ILP: 'You will not influence the course of British politics by as much as a hair's breadth. Why don't you get into a nunnery and be done with it? Lock yourself up in a separate cell away from the world and its wickedness.'[10] Bevan of course accepted that the Labour Party had little if any sympathy with Marxism, even that it was

---

9 Aneurin Bevan, *In Place of Fear* (Heinemann, 1952), 17, 19.
10 Foot, *Bevan: Vol. 1*, 124.

barely socialist, despite the fourth clause of its 1918 constitution committing it to the nationalisation of the means of production, distribution, and exchange. 'The Left is very weak,' Bevan told a friendly journalist before the 1959 general election. 'No more than about fifty MPs [around one-fifth of the parliamentary party] are Socialists.' Instead, the party was led by Gaitskell and his 'clique of statisticians'. All the same, he said, 'What other instrument is there? Though I know that, sometimes I didn't know how I could stay in the Labour Party. It isn't really a Socialist Party at all.'[11] The task, however, was to convert the Labour Party to socialism, difficult though that might be.

After two years studying in London, Bevan returned to Wales, where he became a member of his local district and county councils. He might well have remained merely a local leader had it not been for a stroke of luck, the deselection of the Ebbw Vale MP Evan Davies, not on ideological grounds, but because he had neglected his duties. Bevan succeeded in defeating Davies and four other candidates in a secret ballot, winning the nomination. So, in 1929, he became MP for Ebbw Vale, one of the safest Labour seats in the country. He was to remain its MP until his death in 1960, after which he would be succeeded by his biographer, Michael Foot.

In the general election of 1931, the Conservative-dominated National Government coalition won a landslide victory, and only fifty-two Labour MPs were returned. Bevan was one of the fifty-two. Indeed, he was one of just six Labour candidates to be returned unopposed. In opposition, Bevan established a reputation as a radical critic of the National Government, which he accused of insensitivity towards the unemployed, since it imposed the indignity of a means test on those out of work before allowing them unemployment benefit. He demanded an expansion of

---

11 Foot, *Bevan: Vol. 2,* 623.

public spending and control of the location of industry. And, rather foolishly, he attacked the National Government's rearmament policy, consistently opposing its defence estimates.

Still, whatever Bevan did, the National Government had a huge majority in the Commons and seemed impervious to criticism. How on earth could Labour defeat it? Only, so Bevan believed, by combining with other anti-government parties in an electoral pact. Bevan, together with another left-winger, Stafford Cripps, who was to become Labour's chancellor in 1947, argued for a Popular Front of the left, joining with both the Liberals and the Communist Party. But both of these parties were very weak in the 1930s. Neither could have added much strength to Labour, certainly not sufficient to overthrow or even seriously damage the National Government. The Labour establishment did not like the idea that the party could not achieve power on its own. 'The broadcasting of the opinion that we cannot win the next election,' said Hugh Dalton, Labour's foreign affairs spokesman, 'will tend to spread a miasma of defeatism and discouragement all over the country, particularly in constituencies where the fight is difficult.'[12] Bevan and three others were expelled from the party in March 1939. But Bevan was rapidly readmitted later that year, in December, after agreeing 'to refrain from conducting or taking part in campaigns in opposition to the declared policy of the Party'.[13]

During the war, party politics was muffled. The Churchill coalition government, formed in 1940, embraced all three parties, and there was no official opposition in the Commons. Outside Parliament, relations between the parties were governed by an agreement providing that there should be no by-election challenges. Bevan,

---

12 Ben Pimlott (ed.), *The Political Diary of Hugh Dalton, 1918–1940, 1945–1960* (Jonathan Cape, 1986), 256.
13 Foot, *Bevan: Vol. 1*, 269.

however, was not a party to this truce and remained outside the
government on the back benches. He became a radical critic of the
Churchill coalition, arguing in particular for the rapid opening
of a second front to aid beleaguered Soviet Russia. He was one of
Churchill's most effective critics in Parliament.

II

Bevan was one of only a few, even in the Labour Party, who
were not taken aback at the Labour victory in 1945. It certainly
took Labour's leader and deputy leader – Clement Attlee and
Herbert Morrison, respectively – by surprise. Indeed, precisely
because they thought Churchill unbeatable, they had, unlike
Bevan, favoured a temporary continuation of the wartime coalition, rather than a general election. But after the election, Bevan
himself was in for a surprise. He was appointed to a key position
in the new government as minister of health and housing. Bevan
was right to be surprised. At forty-seven, he was the youngest
member of the Cabinet, whose average age was well over sixty. He
was not, of course, young by modern standards. Both Tony Blair
and David Cameron, after all, became prime minister at the age
of forty-four, Liz Truss at forty-seven, and Rishi Sunak at forty-
two. And Bevan was widely thought of as an irresponsible radical.
George VI asked him 'how he liked the responsibility of a Government Department instead of criticising it'.[14] Bevan's appointment
seems to have been very much a personal decision of Attlee's, and
it was widely seen as a risk. One of Churchill's less happy predictions was that Bevan could prove 'as great a curse to his country
in time of peace as he was a squalid nuisance in time of war'.[15]

---

14 John Wheeler Bennett, *George VI: His Life and Reign* (Macmillan, 1958), 652.
15 Hansard, House of Commons, 6 December 1945, vol. 416, col. 2544.

Bevan was to remain at the Ministry of Health for five years and three months – the longest tenure since the ministry had been created by David Lloyd George in 1919. He is no doubt primarily remembered today as a firebrand or rebel – and indeed, for most of his political career, he was in opposition not only to the Conservatives but to the leaders of his own party. But his achievements in government were remarkable. And it is a tragedy for the Labour Party, and perhaps for the country, that of his thirty-one years as a member of the House of Commons, fewer than six were spent in government.

To the surprise of many, Bevan proved himself a most effective minister. The permanent secretary at the department, William Douglas, declared that Bevan was the best minister he had ever served. The principal assistant secretary primarily responsible for the NHS, John Pater, took the same view.[16] Wilson Jameson, chief medical officer, said that Bevan's tenure of office had been 'one of the most successful' in his long civil-service experience and that Bevan had 'won the devotion of the staff'.[17] Bevan showed many skills. He concentrated on essential principles, delegating other matters to his officials, whom he both supported and encouraged. His relations with officials were always congenial, and he never took the view of some on the left that the civil service would obstruct socialist policies. He was also a creative and skilled negotiator, particularly with the British Medical Association (BMA), the body representing the medical profession, which strongly opposed his main proposals.

Minister of health was a crucial position in the Attlee government, since by the end of the war it had been generally agreed that there should be some sort of national health service. This

16 Campbell, *Nye Bevan and the Mirage*, 152–3.
17 Donald Bruce, 'Nye' in Geoffrey Goodman (ed.), *The State of the Nation: The Political Legacy of Aneurin Bevan* (Gollancz, 1997), 134.

service was to be comprehensive in three senses: first, it would be available to all on broadly equal terms; second, it would be free of charge; and third, it would cover all forms of health care, whether from general practitioners (GPs) or from hospitals.

The existing system of health care – if 'system' it can be called – was a patchwork. In virtue of Lloyd George's National Insurance Act of 1911, GP services covered, by 1938, around 43 per cent of the population. Some twenty-one million people made contributions to National Insurance and were, in consequence, entitled to sickness benefit and free treatment from a panel doctor of their choice, though it was alleged that some doctors discriminated between panel and private patients.[18] The National Insurance Act, however, was in no sense comprehensive, for it had been conceived primarily as a social rather than a medical measure. Lloyd George's main aim had been to provide a degree of security for the breadwinner, who at that time was almost always male. The Act was intended to support him by ensuring that his family would not suffer when he was unable to work because of illness. It therefore covered only those in work, but not dependants, with the exception of a small maternity grant. There was no cover for the self-employed, or for wives or children. Insurance, moreover, covered only GP services, not hospital or specialist treatment, except for tuberculosis. Lloyd George in fact regarded the 1911 Act as very much a temporary measure until a full national health service, of the type Bevan was to introduce, could be brought about.

Before the health service, there had been two types of hospitals. There were, first, the voluntary hospitals, of which there were over 1,100 in England and Wales, many of them quite small and so unable to supply a full range of specialist services. Over 500 had fewer than 100 beds; 250 had fewer than 30. Patients

---

18 Webster, *The Health Services: Vol. 1*, 11, 27.

in these hospitals were charged according to means, and most voluntary hospitals had a contributory scheme through which patients could put aside money to provide medical care when the need arose. In 1942, the Beveridge Report concluded that 10 million wage earners were paying an average of 3d per household towards hospital costs.

Secondly, there were over 1,500 local-authority hospitals in England and Wales. Some, such as that run by the London County Council, possibly the largest hospital authority in the world, were generally regarded as excellent, but some others did not reach so high a standard, and many were too small to be effective. Payment at such hospitals was largely on a means-tested basis, although some local authorities offered free treatment to ratepayers. Indeed, by 1942, it was thought that only around 10 per cent of the cost was being recovered by local authorities from patients.[19] The provision by local-authority hospitals was, however, very uneven, and often the geographical areas of greatest need had the least effective local-authority hospitals.

Roy Jenkins has well summed up the pre-war hospital system as 'two-thirds local authority with whiffs of the Poor Law about it, and one-third voluntary with whiffs of Lady Bountiful'.[20]

In 1942 the Beveridge Report had put forward as one of its assumptions for a post-war security system that there be 'a comprehensive health service' which would 'ensure that for every citizen there is available whatever medical treatment he requires, in whatever form he requires it'. But Beveridge did not endorse a national health service of the type to be introduced by Bevan. The main emphasis of the report was on the insurance principle, and Beveridge was open to the possibility of 'hotel charges' for

---

19 Ibid., 6.
20 Roy Jenkins, 'Six Men of Power', *The Times* (10 April 1993).

hospital patients and other charges, such as charges for dental and optical services.

In 1944, the wartime coalition government's health minister, Henry Willink, a Conservative, produced a White Paper (Command Paper 6502) to give effect to the aim of a comprehensive and free health service. The task was, as Bevan was later to put it, 'to take the present bits and pieces of the health services as they have historically emerged and to recast them into a coherent single new service'.[21] But his methods were different from those to be proposed later by Bevan. Willink proposed an evolutionary approach to the health service, based on existing institutions. He proposed that the health service be unified under local authorities and grouped together in larger units, the structure that had been proposed by Beatrice and Sidney Webb in their Minority Report to the Poor Law Commission of 1909. GPs would become, like teachers, salaried employees of local government working with other local-authority health professionals in local health centres. The voluntary hospitals would remain, but local authorities would have a supervisory role over them in return for the assistance they would receive from public funds. Although Willink was a Conservative, his proposals were welcomed in 1944 by the Labour Party conference, the Socialist Medical Association and the Trades Union Congress. Later, after Labour had been elected to government, Herbert Morrison, leader of the Commons and in effect deputy to Attlee, was, like Willink, to argue for a local-authority-based health service, but was to be overruled.

Although they attracted widespread support, Willink's proposals aroused a storm of indignation in the BMA, and he felt compelled to dilute them. In 1945, he prepared a draft bill with

---

21 *Proposals for a National Health Service: Memorandum by the Minister of Health*, National Archives (13 December 1945), CP (45) 339, para. 6.

new proposals providing for a service administered by non-elected, appointed bodies rather than local authorities. This draft bill was, however, overtaken by the general election and the advent of a Labour government.

So, by the time Bevan became health minister, the coalition government had decided that there would be a health service available to all – but it was Bevan who decided what kind of health service it would be. He apparently read Willink's draft bill over a weekend and tore it up, declaring that it was no good, since it was not based on any coherent set of principles. In a memorandum for the Cabinet, he wrote:

> As I see it, the undertaking to provide all people with all kinds of health care using virtually the whole of the medical and other health professions to do it, creates an entirely new situation and calls for something bolder than a mere extension and adaptation of existing services. Here is an opportunity which may not recur for years, for a thorough overhaul and reconstruction of the country's health position.[22]

He broke with the evolutionary approach in the White Paper and decided to base the health service on two interconnected principles which still remain at its heart.

The first was that the hospitals, both local and voluntary, be nationalised. That, according to a Ministry of Information survey in 1942, was in accordance with the wishes of the public.[23] The second was that the service should be financed almost wholly out of taxation, rather than contributions or insurance. These principles were intended to create, in addition to constitutional and political rights, a further right: a fundamental right to health care.

---

22 *Proposals for a National Health Service*, para. 4.
23 Webster, *The Health Services: Vol. 1*, 28.

Bevan's first principle entailed a radical reform of the hospital service. Bevan had a particular animus towards voluntary hospitals forced to rely on weekly contributions from patients and donations. In the second-reading debate on the health service, he declared:

> It is repugnant to a civilised community for hospitals to have to rely upon private charity ... I have always felt a shudder of repulsion when I have seen nurses and sisters who ought to be at their work, and students who ought to be at their work, going about the streets collecting money for the hospitals.[24]

But, in any case, by 1945 the voluntary hospitals – in theory independent charitable organisations reliant on funds derived from voluntary subscriptions, donations or endowments – were already receiving between 70 per cent and 90 per cent of their funds from the public purse. It was simply 'impossible', Bevan believed, to leave bodies so dependent on public funds 'under independent management'.[25]

As for a health service based on local authorities, given that so many were too small to sustain an effective hospital service, this would have to await local-government reorganisation, a process that could take many years, and were the hospitals to be financed by local authorities, there would be a crushing burden on the rates. With a 50 per cent Exchequer grant, there would have been, according to the Guillebaud Report in 1956, an additional rate burden of around 40p in the pound.[26] Nor would Willink's solution of joint boards have been an improvement.

---

24 Hansard, House of Commons, 30 April 1946, vol. 422, col. 47.
25 *National Health Service: The Hospital Services: Memorandum by the Minister of Health*, National Archives (16 October 1945), CP (45) 231, para. 2.
26 *Committee of Inquiry into the Cost of the National Health Service* (HMSO, 1956), Cmd. 9663, para. 128.

These boards would have separated health from other services provided by local government and would not have been directly accountable to voters. But the crucial factor was that the medical profession would not have accepted local-authority control. 'The one thing the medical profession dreaded before 1948,' according to Rowland Hill, representing the BMA, 'and this applies to general practice as well as to hospitals, was the dread that they would find themselves placed under the local authorities.'[27]

Bevan proposed that both the voluntary and the local-authority hospitals in England and Wales be taken over by central government. That, he believed, was essential if the health service was to be genuinely national, with treatment based on need, rather than on the contingency of whether one was fortunate enough to live in a locality where the facilities for treatment happened to be good. The aim must be to 'universalise the best, that we shall promise every citizen in this country the same standard of service'. That could not 'be articulated through a rate-borne institution which means that the poor authority will not be able to carry out the same thing at all'.[28] In poorer parts of the country, where services were most needed, the necessary funds would simply not be available. A local-authority service, Bevan argued, 'must be unequal in its operation. This would be unjust to the public, who will pay equal contributions.'[29] All the same, the National Health Service Act 1946 did provide for local authorities to retain control of some health functions, financed by the rates aided by a 50 per cent Exchequer grant. These were primarily domiciliary and clinical services, such as the school medical service, maternity and child-welfare services, and public health; in addition, there would be local health centres, which would be

27 *Eleventh Report of the House of Commons Select Committee on Estimates* (HMSO, 1951), HC 261, 28.
28 Hansard, House of Commons, 30 April 1946, vol. 422, col. 49.
29 *National Health Service: The Hospital Services: Memorandum*, para 2.

expected to co-ordinate their activities with child-welfare clinics and school clinics – though the health centres never really got off the ground, partly because GPs feared that they would be a step towards salaried employment by local authorities.[30] These local-authority functions were, however, to be centralised by a Conservative health minister, Joseph, in the Heath government of 1970 to 1974, so that the service would become an entirely national one.

The fundamental reason for Bevan's opposition to local responsibility for health was that he believed with others in the Labour government that, as an essential principle of the welfare state – and as Prime Minister Attlee declared in a radio broadcast inaugurating the NHS – its benefits and burdens should depend upon need and not upon geography. If someone were unwell, her access to health care should depend not upon the resources of her local authority, but on the nature of her illness. Bevan wanted to avoid what would now be called a 'postcode lottery', and, although Welsh, he was particularly hostile to a separate Welsh health service. Indeed, he rarely showed interest in specifically Welsh matters. He disliked the innovation of a Welsh Day in the House of Commons in 1944, and it was said that he only joined the group of Welsh Labour MPs in the Commons tearoom when he was in political trouble! During a Welsh Day debate in 1944, he asked sarcastically how sheep in Wales differed from their counterparts in Scotland or Westmorland.[31] Concentration on parochial Welsh matters would, so Bevan believed, serve only to divide the working-class movement. The problems of the Welsh working class were, after all, no different from those of the Scottish or the English working class, to be resolved not by concessions to nationalism or devolution but

---

30 Webster, *The Health Services: Vol. 1*, 381.
31 Hansard, House of Commons, 17 October 1944, vol. 403, col. 2312.

by a strong socialist government in Westminster, where power could and should be concentrated. Bevan would have been as bitterly opposed to devolution as his disciple Neil Kinnock was to be in the 1970s, though Kinnock was to change tack later on.

Bevan's second principle was that the service should be financed almost entirely out of taxation. He believed that it should be comprehensive, universal, and automatically available to all without charge. That meant access to not only GP services, but also specialist hospital services, ophthalmic treatment (including spectacles), dental treatment, and hearing facilities. So it entailed 'something bolder than a mere extension and adaptation of existing services': a 'thorough overhaul and reconstruction of the country's health position'.[32] It meant, in particular, ending an insurance qualification and substituting for it a health service financed by taxation.

In the second reading of the National Health Service bill on 30 April 1946, Bevan declared, 'It is cardinal to a proper health organisation that a person ought not to be financially deterred from seeking medical assistance at the earliest possible stage.' It followed that, as Bevan pointed out, speaking in the Commons on 30 July 1958 in a debate marking the tenth anniversary of the founding of the NHS, 'We really cannot give different types of treatment in respect of a different order of contributions. We cannot perform a second-class operation on a patient if he is not quite paid up.'

Funding the health service almost entirely by taxation had, for Bevan, a further advantage, often overlooked by those analysing the creation of the NHS. It would be a means, so Bevan declared in the same Commons debate in 1958, towards 'the redistribution of national income by a special method of financing the Health Service'. 'What more pleasure,' Bevan asked, 'can a millionaire

---

32 *Proposals for a National Health Service: Memorandum*, para 4.

have than to know that his taxes will help the sick? ... The redistributive aspect of the scheme was one which attracted me almost
as much as the therapeutical.'[33] The NHS would, Bevan hoped,
prove a step on the road to a socialist society.

There had, then, been a consensus on the need for a national
health service. It is, however, an exaggeration to say of the NHS,
as one hospital consultant of Conservative inclinations did in
2015, that 'Bevan was neither its father nor the midwife – he was
at best an obstetrician, arriving when much of the hard work
was done and taking most of the glory.'[34] It is certainly true that
the NHS came about as a result of sustained work by civil servants and politicians from all parties over the four years before the
1946 Act. But it was Bevan who made the key decisions on the
form that the health service was to take. So, while there would
have been a national health service even without Bevan – even
without a Labour government – it would almost certainly have
been a somewhat different sort of health service.

The fact of the wartime consensus on a health service was
to be obscured by the Conservative response to Bevan's proposals. Despite insisting that they favoured a comprehensive health
service, the Conservatives were, somewhat maladroitly, to vote
against the second and third readings of the National Health
Service bill, primarily on the grounds that it undermined the
voluntary hospitals. This enabled Labour to claim that the Conservatives were against a health service on principle, and it has
proved an important propaganda point for Labour spokesmen
ever since.

Attlee, however, in a radio broadcast on 5 May 1948, the day
before the inauguration of the NHS, was pointedly to declare

33 Hansard, House of Commons, 30 July 1958, vol. 592, col. 1389.
34 Hugh Byrne, 'It's time to tear down the cult of Bevan in the NHS', *Conservative Home* (29 March 2015), accessed online.

that 'all parties in the state' had 'borne their part' in creating both the health service and the other new elements of the welfare state, such as National Insurance and National Assistance.[35]

Bevan regarded his scheme as socialist. Yet in some respects it was less socialist than the scheme in the Willink White Paper, which had proposed that GPs become full-time salaried employees of local government rather than independent contractors whose earnings would depend in part upon a capitation fee determined by the number of patients they could attract. In addition, NHS doctors could continue to accept private patients. Of the other compromises with socialist principle, the most important was Bevan's acceptance of a provision by which NHS consultants were allowed to take private patients and admit them to private beds in NHS hospitals. This was essential if the BMA was to be persuaded to accept the NHS. Bevan later declared, 'Ultimately, I had to stuff their mouths with gold.'[36] The purpose of the compromise was to prevent 'the national hospital service driving all private work into a rival nursing home service'.[37] There would then be a dual system of health care – as there was in education, thanks to the existence of public schools – and the NHS might come to be seen as second best. As it was, private patients would henceforth be subsidising the NHS. Nevertheless, this provision went against the socialist principle of equal treatment for all regardless of means. Bevan and other supporters of the NHS hoped that it would provide

---

35 *The Listener* (8 July 1948).
36 Charles Webster, the official historian of the NHS, has shown that this famous, if much misquoted, remark was made at a dinner in the House of Commons to celebrate the publication of the Guillebaud Report on the cost of the health service in 1956 (Webster says 1955, but the report was in fact published in 1956). The report showed that the NHS was not, as some of Bevan's critics had argued, extravagant. Charles Webster (ed.), *Aneurin Bevan on the Health Service* (Oxford University Press: Wellcome Unit for the History of Medicine, 1991), 255.
37 *Proposals for a National Health Service: Memorandum*, Appendix, para. 51.

such an excellent service that demand for private medicine and pay beds would gradually be extinguished – a hope doomed to disappointment.

Bevan was not, as he has sometimes been portrayed, a man of unbending socialist principle, but a man of government, fully prepared to compromise, provided that the core of his proposals was not threatened. The NHS, then, was to be a unified national service under central government, and under a minister responsible to Parliament. Bevan, although, as we have seen, influenced by Marxism in his youth, had a great – some would say excessive – faith in the efficacy of parliamentary institutions to control public services. In an address to hospital almoners in March 1948, he predicted:

> The Minister of Health will be the whipping-boy for the Health Service in Parliament. Every time a maid kicks over a bucket of slops in a ward an agonised wail will go through Whitehall ... What the Health Act will do ... is to put a megaphone in the mouth of every complainant, so that he will be heard all over the country.[38]

Democracy in Britain, Bevan was accustomed to suggest, only really began in 1945 when the working class, now comprising the majority of the electorate, had at last decided to install in power a government which could properly represent them. So, to ensure that the NHS was democratically accountable, all that was needed was to place it under the authority of a minister responsible to Parliament.

In practice, however, neither the NHS nor indeed any other public service would ever become as accountable as Bevan predicted, putting a megaphone into the mouth of every

---

38 *British Medical Journal* report on Bevan speech (1948), 612.

complainant. Instead, the NHS seemed to have put a megaphone in the mouths of those working in it, rather than the patients. The institution has always been in danger of becoming remote, bureaucratic, and over-centralised, unresponsive both to its employees and to those who use it. In 2022, a senior NHS administrator told me that it had become a 'bureaucratic monster'. We have in fact never found a wholly satisfactory method of making large public bodies accountable to Parliament.

If Bevan was an effective man of government in his approach to the health service, he proved an effective man of government in other areas of policy as well. He was minister not only for health, but also for housing. And his record on housing was better than is sometimes thought. During his tenure, some 800,000 local-authority houses were built, despite post-war restrictions and shortages of materials. Bevan hoped, somewhat unrealistically, that all sections of the community would choose to live in local-authority houses, so as to avoid social segregation by class, which he regarded as 'a wholly evil thing ... a monstrous affliction on the essential psychological and biological one-ness of the community'. 'We don't want a country of East Ends and West Ends,' he declared.[39] He wanted mixed council-housing estates in which the social classes mingled. Just as the arrangements for the NHS involved a redistribution of income to the poorer classes, a step on the road to socialism, so housing policy would help in the construction of a socialist society in which all would share.

But, whereas the idea of a national health service which all would use seemed highly plausible, it was unrealistic to suppose that those who could afford to buy their own homes would be content to live in houses rented from their local authority. The Conservatives appreciated this, and the rise in home owner-ship in the 1950s, encouraged by Conservative governments,

---

39 Foot, *Bevan: Vol.* 2, 82.

was undoubtedly a factor in their electoral success, while in the 1980s Margaret Thatcher pioneered the sale of council houses to their tenants. Public-sector housebuilding has now almost entirely ceased. By 2018, just 4,000 houses were being built by local authorities.[40]

Despite favouring mixed council estates, Bevan did not himself live in a local-authority house, but in Cliveden Place in fashionable Belgravia, between Eaton Square and Sloane Square, and he also owned a large farm in Buckinghamshire. Nor, it must be said, did he use an NHS doctor. Just after the NHS was inaugurated, a Labour MP, Woodrow Wyatt, asked Bevan 'who his National Health Service doctor was and his answer was Sir Dan Davies (the physician to the King). Bevan thought in his aristocratic manner that the health service would be all right for ordinary people but he wanted something better for himself.'[41] It perhaps never occurred to him that what he wanted for himself might also be wanted by the people for whom he claimed to speak.

In the Attlee government, Bevan seemed to have made the transition from rebel on the left to a man of government. But, on 4 July 1948, the day before the NHS was inaugurated, he broke with his image as a man of government to make a vitriolic attack on the Conservatives, for which many never forgave him – and which, many believed, was to cost Labour much electoral support in the general elections of 1950 and 1951.

Attlee had intended in a radio broadcast to celebrate the coming into effect of the NHS and to pay tribute to 'the other parties' for what they had done to help create the service. His tactic was to minimise the radicalism of the NHS by creating a

---

40 Paul Johnson, *Follow the Money: How Much Does Britain Cost?* (Abacus Books, 2023), 12.
41 Sarah Curtis (ed.), *The Journals of Woodrow Wyatt, Volume 3* (Macmillan, 2000), 470.

consensus in favour of it, so as to persuade those still not reconciled to what they might have seen as a dangerous socialist
experiment. He therefore hailed the NHS as a national – rather
than a Labour Party or socialist – achievement. Bevan, on the
other hand, was determined to do the opposite, to appropriate
the NHS as a specifically Labour – indeed, specifically socialist
– achievement and to condemn the Conservatives. In a speech
in Manchester on 4 July, he declared that 'successful Toryism
and an intelligent electorate' were 'a contradiction in terms'.
What was Toryism, he asked, 'except organised spivvery?' He
then spoke of his early years, when, as an unemployed youth,
he had been forced to live on his sister's earnings. He had been
advised to emigrate, and cited a friend who had in fact gone to
the dominions. He continued:

> That is why no amount of cajolery, and no attempts at ethical
> or social seduction, can eradicate from my heart a deep
> burning hatred of the Tory Party that inflicted those bitter
> experiences on me. So far as I am concerned they are lower
> than vermin. They condemned millions of first-class people
> to semi-starvation ... I warn you they have not changed; or if
> they have they are slightly worse than they were.[42]

The speech caused an outcry, especially for its use of the word
'vermin', which seemed to echo Nazi language towards the Jews.
Some Young Conservatives reacted by forming 'vermin clubs',
which came to boast a membership of over 100,000. Margaret
Thatcher was apparently an early member.

Bevan received a magisterial rebuke for his 'vermin speech' in
a letter from Attlee on 7 July:

---

42 Foot, *Bevan: Vol. 2*, 238.

My dear Aneurin.

I have received a great deal of criticism of the passage in your speech in which you describe the Conservatives as vermin, including a good deal from your own party.

It was, I think, singularly ill-timed. It had been agreed that we wished to give the new Social Security Scheme as good a send-off as possible and to this end I made a *non*-polemical broadcast. Your speech cut right across this. I have myself done as much as I could to point out the injustice of the attacks made upon you for your handling of the doctors, pointing out the difficulties experienced by your predecessors of various political colours in dealing with the profession. You had won a victory in obtaining their tardy co-operation, but these unfortunate remarks enable the doctors to stage a comeback and have given the general public the impression that there was more in their case than they had supposed.

This is, I think, a great pity because without doing any good it has drawn attention away from the excellent work you have done over the Health Bill. Please be a bit more careful in your own interest.

Yours ever, Clem.

Speaking in Woodford, Churchill, then the leader of the opposition, called Bevan the 'minister of disease', since 'morbid hatred is a form of mental disease'. 'I can think of no better step,' he added, 'to signalise the inauguration of the NHS than that a person who so obviously needs psychiatric attention should be among the first of its patients.'[43]
At the Durham Miners' Gala, Bevan sought to qualify his

---

43 Ibid., 141–2.

remarks. 'When I speak of Tories,' he insisted, 'I mean the small bodies of people who, whenever they have the chance, have manipulated the political influence of the country for the benefit of the privileged few.' But his remarks were not forgotten.[44]

III

Despite his outburst, Bevan had proven himself a man of government not only in the way he had secured support for the health service, but in the statesmanlike manner in which he had supported his Cabinet colleagues on divisive issues of foreign policy, rather than his left-wing allies on the back benches. He insisted in particular on a strong policy against communism. Indeed, in some respects, he went further than some of his Cabinet colleagues. At the time of the Berlin airlift in 1948, when the Soviet Union sought to limit Western access to West Berlin, he argued that tanks should be used forcibly to secure access. He supported the United Nations in its defence of South Korea after it was attacked by the North in 1950, on grounds of collective security. Above all, Bevan supported the Cabinet decision that Britain should become an independent nuclear power. His main reason, the same as that which animated the foreign secretary Ernest Bevin and indeed others in the Cabinet, was not only to better resist the Soviet Union, but to give Britain leverage vis-à-vis the Americans. His ministerial colleague George Strauss reminisced in 1962:

> Nye always held the view that Britain ought to be effectively armed. He always held the view in Government, when we

---

44 Ibid., 237–43.

were discussing the development of the atomic bomb, that Britain should have and must have the atomic bomb. As long as America had it, we must develop it too ... to be effectively independent, because his fear of being subservient to America was always in his mind. He wanted us to have a bomb too, to enable us to play a more useful part in world affairs.[45]

Bevan was determined to show, after the fashion of George Orwell, with whom he had worked on the socialist journal *Tribune*, that one could be a socialist and yet also a patriot. The Labour MP Woodrow Wyatt, who was not a Bevanite, believed that Bevan would have been a good war leader as the head of a coalition. 'Bevan,' he wrote, 'is intensely patriotic, at times almost chauvinistic, and brave.'[46] But in peacetime, as with Churchill, his brilliance and volatility might have kept him from No. 10.

The creation of the NHS had been a massive administrative achievement, even if much of the groundwork had been laid by others. That and his statesmanlike approach in Cabinet should have qualified him for promotion to one of the senior positions in the government. Indeed, Attlee declared on more than one occasion that Bevan was his natural successor as Labour leader, since it was best that the party be led from the left of centre. But when the chancellorship became vacant with the retirement of Stafford Cripps in 1950, and the foreign secretaryship with the resignation of Ernest Bevin in 1951, others were preferred to him for the two posts – Hugh Gaitskell and Herbert Morrison, respectively. It may be that Bevan's vermin speech and similar wild utterances cost him promotion. Whatever the reason, Attlee

---

45 Campbell, *Nye Bevan*, 195.
46 Woodrow Wyatt, *Distinguished for Talent: Some Men of Influence and Enterprise* (Hutchinson, 1978), 176.

handled him badly. Bevan would have apparently been happy to have been offered the Colonial Office, not least because he was coming to believe that the most important problem in world politics was the relationship between the developed and developing countries. But Attlee declared that Bevan was too racially prejudiced for the job – 'pro-black and anti-white'.[47] In the event, he was moved in January 1951 to become minister of labour, a difficult position, since the exigencies of the Korean War and the rearmament drive which it necessitated meant wage restraint, a policy uncongenial to him. And he remained at that ministry for only three months before resigning in protest against the introduction of charges for false teeth and spectacles.

Bevan had never been happy with financial controls on the NHS. The demand for health care was, even then, almost unlimited, and it has become more so with improvements in diagnosis and treatment such as, for example, the development of new methods for treating cancer and heart disease, and with the consequences of an increasingly ageing population. Therefore, so it seemed to Bevan, the NHS should not be pressed by the Treasury to contain spending. Unsurprisingly, the chancellor and other ministers did not agree. The Treasury had to confront the problem of securing budgetary control for a service which was free. Stafford Cripps, chancellor from 1947 to 1950, had sought to resolve this problem by imposing a ceiling on health expenditure, and in 1950 a Cabinet committee was set up to keep health spending under review, something which Bevan saw as a humiliation. After all, if a service is free, it is difficult to see how a ceiling can be imposed on spending on it. Gaitskell, Cripps's successor as chancellor from 1950, went even further than Cripps. In his 1951 budget, he had to finance the rearmament programme necessitated by the Korean War. He proposed charges for false teeth and

---

47 Quoted in Campbell, *Nye Bevan*, 216.

spectacles, arguing that those who needed such appliances were not in fact ill, and so he was not contradicting the principle of a health service free at source. Bevan had been replaced as health secretary in January 1951 by Hilary Marquand who, by contrast with Bevan, was outside the Cabinet and proved more amenable to health charges. Privately, Gaitskell was considering going even further to combat rising health spending by charging for board and lodging in hospitals, something that even Margaret Thatcher would fear to countenance.

Bevan had publicly supported the expanded rearmament programme as a loyal member of the Cabinet, although in private he was sceptical – on grounds of practicality, rather than principle. In his resignation speech to the Commons, he was to declare that the economy could not sustain so rapid an expansion of defence spending, while the large sums being allocated to defence meant retrenchment in the social services. This retrenchment, apart from being undesirable in itself and regressive, was, Bevan believed, unnecessary precisely because it would prove impracticable to spend the full amounts assigned for defence, owing to a shortage of raw materials. Bevan was to be proved correct in this judgement, and the rearmament programme was to be duly scaled down by Churchill's Conservative government in 1952. Bevan made his opposition to the scale of the rearmament programme clear in private Cabinet discussions. But it was not for him a resigning matter, and indeed he was to defend the programme in Parliament. However, the proposal to charge for false teeth and spectacles was for him a matter of principle on which he was prepared to resign.

Bevan argued, in addition, that worries about the costs of health care were exaggerated, since they were levelling out as the backlog of demand was gradually being dealt with – something that proved to be true. In any case, the sum raised by health charges was comparatively insignificant – £13 million in a health budget of £400 million – and it was divisive to introduce such charges when Labour had so small a majority. Its majority of 144 in the general election of 1945 had been reduced to just five in the general election of 1950.

Bevan resigned from the government in April 1951. He was never to hold office again. His creative period in office was over.

IV

Whether Bevan was right or wrong to resign from the government in 1951, he did so in a maladroit and clumsy fashion, making a vitriolic post-resignation speech to a Labour Party meeting, full of venom against Gaitskell and declaiming against any interference with 'my' health service. Benn wrote in his diary that Bevan 'shook with rage and screamed ... The megalomania and neurosis and hatred and jealousy he displayed astounded us all.'[48] The speech reminded more than one of those present of Oswald Mosley, the fascist leader. Bevan's Cabinet colleagues declared that he had behaved in a similarly egotistical way during Cabinet meetings. Bevan had, apparently, frequently threatened resignation before. The view took hold that he was not a team player.

Labour lost the general election of October 1951, six months after Bevan resigned. Attlee had predicted that 'after such a debacle' – the split over health charges – 'the Conservatives might remain in office for a long period'. According to Herbert Morrison, Attlee predicted ten years. If so, Attlee underestimated the period of opposition by three years.[49] Labour did not return to power again until 1964, by which time both Bevan and

---

48 Tony Benn, *Years of Hope: Diaries, Papers and Letters 1940–1962* (Hutchinson, 1994), 152.

49 Webster, *The Health Services: Vol. 1*, 175.

Gaitskell had died, the former in 1960, the latter in 1963. Bevan spent most of his remaining years fighting a long if unsuccessful battle against Labour's right wing for the soul of the party. He suspected, with some justice, that the right of the party was losing its faith in socialism and seeking to downplay the importance of nationalisation. On the right, the argument seemed no longer about the speed and pace at which socialism, defined as a society dominated by public ownership, could be achieved, but about whether it should be achieved at all. For some on the Labour right, such a society seemed not only undesirable in itself, but to have no resonance with the British people. Indeed, leading figures on the Labour right believed that the unpopularity of nationalisation was a prime factor in the party's electoral failure in the 1950s. In 1956, Anthony Crosland, a disciple of Gaitskell's, published a book, *The Future of Socialism*, which argued that nationalisation should no longer be Labour's main domestic aim.

Bevan had considerable support, as Benn in a later generation was to enjoy, amongst Labour constituency parties, but only minority support amongst Labour MPs, many of whom regarded him as vain and egotistical. He also faced the hostility of the trade unions, then led mostly by party loyalists, who, in 1955, just before the general election, nearly secured his expulsion from the party. It is a paradox that support for Bevan, the socialist, lay mostly with middle-class activists in the constituency parties, while the leaders of the organised working class were largely hostile. 'The first thing that must strike any outside observer,' George Orwell had written in 1937, 'is that Socialism in its developed form is a theory confined entirely to the middle class.'[50] But how could one construct a socialist society without the support of the organised working class? The debate

---

[50] George Orwell, *The Road to Wigan Pier* (Gollancz, 1937), 205.

on socialism between left and right increasingly took on the character of a theological dispute, which held little interest for most voters. Labour was coming to lose touch with the aspirations of the British people. In asking how far nationalisation should extend, and what socialism really meant, it was turning in on itself. The debate became as much about symbols – and also, no doubt, power – as it was about substance, of interest only to a small and hardly representative minority. Labour was talking to itself, not to the voters. The quarrels between left and right played an important part in keeping Labour in opposition for thirteen years between 1951 and 1964. And the split between left and right which followed Bevan's resignation gave force to the quarrel, and so helped to make Labour a divided and unelectable party.

In 1955, Attlee retired as Labour leader. At that time, the party leader was chosen solely by MPs. Bevan's enemy Gaitskell was elected with 157 votes. Bevan secured 70 votes, just over a quarter of Labour MPs, while Herbert Morrison, the third candidate, won only 40 votes. Many years later, after all three were dead, Gaitskell's widow told a journalist that 'in retrospect, she felt that Bevan should have been the leader of the Labour Party rather than her own husband. It would have made much more sense politically ... because Bevan was a "natural leader" for a socialist party'.[51] Which, of course, begs the question of whether the Labour Party was in fact a socialist party.

Bevan had never been wholly comfortable as a rebel, and he decided to come to terms with Gaitskell and the leadership, taking the post of shadow foreign secretary in 1956. At the party conference of 1957, he formally broke with the left by signalling his opposition to unilateral nuclear disarmament. The *Daily Telegraph* declared that Bevan had been transformed into Bevin,

---

51 Goodman, *The State of the Nation*, 35.

the hawkish Labour foreign secretary between 1945 and 1951.[52] After Labour's third electoral defeat, in October 1959, Bevan became deputy leader to Gaitskell.

And then suddenly it seemed, after this third defeat, that there might be a chance for Bevan to grasp the leadership after all. At Labour's post-election party conference in November 1959, Gaitskell proposed the abolition of Clause 4 of Labour's constitution, which committed it to nationalisation. Bevan publicly supported Gaitskell, but wrote an article declaring, 'If the Labour Party were to abandon its main thesis of public ownership it would not differ in any important respect from the Tory Party ... The overwhelming majority of the Labour Party will not acquiesce in the jettisoning of the concept of progressive public ownership'.[53] Many trade unions joined with the left in opposing the abolition of Clause 4, partly on sentimental grounds, and Gaitskell was forced to withdraw his proposal. It seemed for a time as if Gaitskell's leadership might be in jeopardy, and his position was to worsen when he was defeated at the 1960 Labour Party conference on the issue of unilateral nuclear disarmament. Had Gaitskell been forced to resign, Bevan might have appeared as the obvious successor. But it was too late, for by then Bevan was dead, struck down by stomach cancer in July 1960.

V

In 1997, Blair wrote that the NHS 'remains ... the most popular and practical living embodiment of British democratic socialism'.[54] Such a view appeared more plausible then than it

---

52 Clare Beckett and Frances Beckett, *Bevan* (Haus Publishing, 2004), 126.
53 Foot, *Bevan: Vol. 2*, 651.
54 Goodman, *The State of the Nation*, 11.

does today, when health outcomes seem worse in Britain than in many countries on the Continent.

How viable is Bevan's vision of democratic socialism in relation to the health service? Bevan's hope was that capitalist market incentives could be replaced by the idea of duty towards others, the moral obligation that the better off owed to the less fortunate. In a Fabian Society lecture in 1950, he spoke of the 'authority of moral purpose' which would be 'freely undertaken'.[55] That view might have seemed plausible in the immediate post-war years, when there was a spirit of social solidarity and few members of the working class paid income tax. In 1949, a married man with two children would have had to achieve just over the average earnings before paying any income tax, and almost twice that figure before paying at the standard rate.[56] Bevan's idealism came to be much less realistic with the growth of affluence and a more individualistic society, in which voters, whatever they may have said to opinion pollsters, became resistant to paying more tax. His model of the health service may have been suitable for the immediate post-war years of austerity, but it became less and less so as living standards rose. 'Bevan's understanding of human nature,' two sympathetic critics have noted, 'was rooted in pre-war working-class solidarity and a little Welsh village. His dream reflected this, but the mood of the times did not'.[57] Post-war social solidarity was based not only – or even primarily – on civic feeling, as Bevan and other socialists tended to believe, but on the insecurity and fear generated by war and poverty. This in turn engendered a faith in benevolent government. That faith gradually weakened during the post-war years, as fear of war disappeared and poverty came to be alleviated. Many of those

---

55 Mark Hayhurst, 'Duty Bound', *Guardian* (28 May 2005).
56 I owe this point to John Barnes.
57 Beckett and Beckett, *Bevan*, 135.

who were to rejoice in the new individualism of the affluent society were to find community ties constraining, rather than uplifting.

Before the 1992 general election, Labour was to propose the introduction of a new top rate of income tax of 50 per cent for those earning over £40,000 a year. The Conservatives won the election, albeit with a much-reduced majority. Although the new rate would have applied only to the wealthy, analysts concluded that it had lost votes for Labour, since many of its potential voters hoped that they or their children might themselves eventually enter the ranks of the very well paid. Since 1992, both major parties have been chary of promising extra funding for the NHS to be paid for by increased taxation. But Bevan's principle has meant that alternative sources of revenue for the NHS – such as private capital, insurance or charges – have been neglected. There is, however, no reason in principle why alternative sources of finance should not be used to increase health-service spending. In the Netherlands, just 10 per cent of health finance is raised from taxation, and in Germany just 14 per cent, but in Britain only around 15 per cent of spending on health does *not* come from public funds.

Bevan's second principle, nationalisation of the hospitals, implied that the health secretary would be answerable in detail to Parliament for all NHS spending. By contrast, where charges are made for a public service, the minister is responsible only for capital and for deficit financing.

Making spending by central government accountable is very different from making spending by local government accountable. In the case of the latter, local councillors are answerable to their local electorates, but the health secretary has no equivalent direct relationship with the public that he serves. In local government, moreover, some councillors at least appreciate that extra spending will mean a higher council tax. But to those working in the health service, central-government revenue seems to be unlimited – or, rather, the only limit seems to be that imposed by 'political' decisions made by the government, decisions which are easy to characterise as unreasonable or arbitrary. Health professionals could always argue, as they did in the disputes over pay for nurses and junior doctors in 2022–23, that more could be spent on the NHS if only the government of the day were not so miserly. Indeed, the pay disputes of 2022–23 offer a graphic illustration of the difficulties a government faces in controlling NHS spending. In the private sector, pay is determined by the market. In the public sector, by contrast, someone must decide how much nurses and other health services professionals are to be paid. Who should that someone be? If it is to be the minister, he will be faced with making an impossible judgement, one bound to be in a sense arbitrary and 'political'. In 1983, the Nurses' Pay Review Body was established to take the decision 'out of politics'. But in 2023, the nurses' union, The Royal College of Nursing, asked the government to overrule the recommendation of the Nurses' Pay Review Body. The health secretary could always do this if he could persuade his colleagues to provide more money, either through higher taxation, more borrowing, or a reduction in spending for other services such as education or defence. But the health secretary, as a Cabinet minister, has to weigh the consequences for other services of overruling the review body, and he must also weigh the consequences for the economy as a whole. These considerations inevitably weigh less heavily with nurses and other health-service professionals suffering from the cost-of-living crisis. This problem is inherent in determining just rewards in a nationalised service, which introduces a necessarily adversarial relationship between the government and those working in it.

Furthermore, since the only limit on health spending seems to be the unwillingness of government to spend more, it follows that the efforts of those working in the NHS must be directed to overcoming that unwillingness. This can best be done by pointing to serious deficiencies in the service. Those working in the NHS, therefore, have, in a sense, a vested interest in pointing out its deficiencies due to a lack of funds. Anyone who fails to do this will be letting the side down, for the government will then happily divert resources to other services – for example, education or defence. So, those working in the NHS are in a sense permanently embattled against the government; indeed, from its earliest days there were complaints that it was underfunded. The NHS, like other nationalised bodies, puts a premium upon denigration and grumbling. The emphasis must always be on deficiencies in the service, so that central government can be persuaded to provide more resources. To trumpet success is to suggest that the NHS does not really need extra funding. Such a psychology must have a demoralising effect on those working in the service. An organisation which can never be seen to be successful and must always point out its own deficiencies, so that it is awarded extra funds, is hardly likely to stimulate the pride in performance which so often produces improvements in service. The NHS has institutionalised a culture of complaint. There is, yet again, a contrast with services run by local government, where local councillors can point with pride to the improvements they have made despite being strapped for cash. There is a sense of ownership and local pride – the service is *our* service – which contrasts starkly with attitudes towards a service run from the centre.

While it is undeniable that the various municipal and voluntary hospitals were both insufficient and inadequate in the 1940s, a return to localism and voluntarism might now be beneficial. In a decentralised system of government, each local or voluntary hospital would strive to ensure that its performance were better than that of its competitors. The emphasis would be on local pride and achievement, on what has been achieved in 'our' hospitals, rather than upon deficiencies in the service.

A further consequence of Bevan's nationalisation of the hospitals was that the health service came to be divided from the preventative services – such as housing and education – so closely associated with health care, services which remained with local government. Poor housing was obviously an important cause of poor health, while the schools had a role in teaching rules of hygiene and other health matters. In addition, health was separated from social care, which remained in the hands of local authorities and subject to means-tested payments rather than being free at source. The separation between curative and preventive services was inevitable once the decision was made to nationalise the hospitals. It may be that this is now in the process of being remedied through devolution in England to combined authorities. In the Greater Manchester combined authority, there has been devolution of certain health functions so that they can be linked to social care and other public services. It is too early to tell whether this is to be a model for the future and, if it is, how effective it is likely to be. But the policy of devolution does seek to remedy yet another flaw in Bevan's conception of the health service, which yielded an over-centralised and top-heavy monolith unresponsive to the public and with insufficient incentives to provide high-quality services.

If a service is free of charge to the users, demand will always exceed supply. Rationing will be achieved through waiting lists, and demand in the health service will be reduced by patients not wanting to 'bother the doctor', often at some cost to their health.

Suppose a National Food Service had been established after the war on the same lines as the National Health Service, with food – as essential, after all, as health – provided free and paid for out of taxation. The food would be of poorer quality, and there would be shortages in the catering trade – whose wages would be determined by the government – together with food shortages and queues. After all, when the supply of telephones was a national monopoly under British Telecom, it took around six months to have a phone installed.

The particular structure chosen for the NHS by Bevan might have been unavoidable in the 1940s. But successive governments can be criticised for not reforming it to meet changing social and economic conditions. By the time of the seventy-fifth anniversary of the NHS in 2023, far from being thought of as, in Blair's words, 'popular' and 'practical', the NHS was on its knees. In 2023, the chief executives of the Health Foundation, Nuffield Trust, and King's Fund wrote to the leaders of the three largest parties, declaring that the NHS was 'in critical condition', with public satisfaction at its lowest since survey evidence first began to track it in 1983. Even so, public support for it remained 'rock solid', they said, and it still topped many surveys on what made people most proud to be British. The public were, apparently, 'unwavering' in 'their support for the founding principles'. The reason was that – as Nigel Lawson, chancellor of the Exchequer from 1983 to 1989, declared in his memoirs – Bevan's NHS 'is the closest thing the English have to a religion'.[58] While other welfare services created by the coalition and post-war Labour governments – such as schools provision, National Assistance, and the provision of council houses – have changed beyond all recognition, the NHS alone retains almost exactly the same principles as when it was established. Bevan, in trying to make people feel, succeeded all too well. Too many believe in the NHS without considering whether there might not be better alternatives. It is time that this religion were subjected to rational evaluation. Bevan hoped that the NHS would be a model for

---

58 Nigel Lawson, *The View from No. 11: Memoirs of a Tory Radical* (Corgi, 1993), 613.

other countries, emphasising his view that democratic socialism in Britain was setting an example for the world. But, far
from being an example, by 2023 the NHS had become a warning
of what is to be avoided. Currently Britain spends around 11.3
per cent of its GDP on health care, around the same as Austria,
Switzerland, the Netherlands, and Belgium, and above the EU
and Organisation for Economic Co-operation and Development
(OECD) average. The private sector also plays a much smaller
part in the hospital sector than in many other countries – around
10 per cent in Britain compared to 30 per cent in Austria, 38 per
cent in France, 60 per cent in Germany, 72 per cent in Belgium,
and 100 per cent in Norway and the Netherlands.[59] Our crum-
bling health service is a consequence not of failing to build on
Bevan's legacy but of refusing to repudiate it.

Significantly, few advanced societies have copied the British
model. Many countries, and in particular most of those in
Europe, prefer a social-insurance model.

The very fact that Bevan himself used private medical care
raises a question: why should not all users of the NHS, whether
or not they have the financial resources, be able to avail themselves of the same privilege? As taxpayers they fund the NHS, but
they have much less control over it than Bevan hoped through the
parliamentary system. Perhaps users of the health system would
do better if they were to be given more power to purchase their
own health care, as Bevan did? Social-insurance systems, prevalent on the Continent, give patients that power. Those who need
health care become not passive clients, but consumers. Systems
of social insurance need not discriminate against the poor and
vulnerable, for the disadvantaged, the elderly, and the chronically
sick can be specifically provided for. In Germany, for example,

---

59 Kristian Niemietz, 'As the NHS keeps failing, the cult around it intensifies',
Institute of Economic Affairs (1 September 2023), accessed online.

there is special provision for the low paid and the chronically sick. Low-income families are exempt from charges exceeding 2 per cent of their gross household income, while for the chronically sick the cap is 1 per cent. A system of the German type gives to a much wider public the same rights and the same amount of choice that the better off now enjoy – access to high-quality health care. It is only under Bevan's NHS that the worse off and the inarticulate have to put up with poor-quality services.

Jeremy Hunt, chancellor of the Exchequer under Liz Truss and Rishi Sunak, and a former health secretary, has argued against systems such as the German, on the grounds that 'they allow wealthier people to pay top-ups for better insurance schemes'. The NHS, he claims, is fairer in providing equity of access.[60] But in Britain the better off can buy better provision, as Bevan did, through using a private doctor and other private health-care facilities. They are increasingly doing so, as pressures on the health service have made it more difficult to access both primary care and hospital care. It is in fact impossible to prevent the better off from purchasing better provision, except by banning private practice and private medical care, something repugnant to liberal-minded people and impossible to achieve except in an authoritarian society.

VI

Bevan wanted to be remembered not just for the NHS, but for his advocacy of socialism. Between 1945 and 1960, it has been said, Bevan was 'the man who did more than any other of his age to

---

60 Jeremy Hunt, *Zero: Eliminating unnecessary deaths in a post-pandemic NHS* (Swift Press, 2022), 73.

keep alive the idea of democratic socialism'.[61] In his hagiographical biography, Michael Foot, Bevan's disciple, paints Bevan as a romantic rebel, heir to the Levellers and the Chartists. But that, as we have seen, is misleading. Bevan had little in common with those ineffectual rebels. As a man of government, he sought the power to change society. After 1951 he hoped to be a teacher, to lead the people into the promised land of democratic socialism. That, he believed, would not be too difficult, for as a democratic Marxist he understood that the working class was now a majority in Britain and would surely see that socialism was in its interest as a class. It would therefore vote for it, once the blinkers had been removed. The Labour victory in 1945 was seen as but the first stage in that process. All that was needed was to mobilise the working class so that it would come to appreciate its true interest. Socialism would come about almost automatically with the development of democratic institutions. Socialists, therefore, were working with the tides of history. 'We are the masters at the moment,' the attorney general Hartley Shawcross had told the Commons in 1946, 'and not only for the moment, but for a very long time to come.'[62]

But during the 1950s, the tides of history seemed to be flowing against socialism; in retrospect, the 1951 general election now appears as the end of an era, an era in which the future had seemed to lie with the left. The Attlee government appears in the light of history not as the first stage in Labour's long march, but rather as a culmination of socialist achievement, an ending rather than a beginning. By 1951, many fewer than in 1945 believed in socialism in the form of a complete transformation of society. Today, hardly anyone does.

During the 1950s, the Conservatives won three elections – in

---

61 Beckett and Beckett, *Bevan*, 148.
62 Hansard, House of Commons, 2 April 1946, vol. 421, col. 1213.

1951, 1955, and 1959 – with increased majorities. The working-class solidarity on which Bevan relied was coming to be eroded by the growth of affluence and the search for individual prosperity to which it was giving rise. Indeed, the working class itself was fragmenting and declining in size. Far from being strengthened, class feeling was weakening. By 1959, Labour's class image appeared old-fashioned and this was, no doubt, one of the causes of its election defeat. Bevan hoped that the working class would undermine capitalism. Instead, the opposite was happening. Capitalism and rising living standards were undermining the working class, which was becoming a declining constituency. By 1971, Benn was to rail against an Austrian Social Democrat who thought that 'socialism means everybody being allowed to have a Rolls Royce'. This, so Benn believed, was 'the individual escape from class into prosperity, which is the cancer eating into the Western European Social Democratic parties'.[63] During the 1950s, Bevan was a critic of this 'escape from class into prosperity', which he saw as rewarding instant gratification at the expense of the investment which Britain so badly needed. In his last speech to a Labour Party conference in 1959, Bevan inveighed against the affluent society, calling it a 'vulgar' society of which no one could be proud. He shared the view of the influential American economist J. K. Galbraith that the affluent society was one in which private affluence was accompanied by public squalor, so that vital public services such as health and education came to be underfunded. Affluence, Bevan thought, was unsoundly based, and the working class had been seduced by it thanks to commercial advertising and the mass media. But such a critique served only to distance Bevan further from the voting public, many of whom were only too grateful for the chance to 'escape from class into prosperity' and enjoy consumer goods

---

63 Tony Benn, *Office Without Power: Diaries 1968–72* (Hutchinson, 1988), 356.

of which their parents could only dream – washing machines, refrigerators, cars, television sets, and holidays abroad. Voters sought not to identify with the working class, but to escape from it. When Bevan died, one journalist wrote in the *Evening Standard*, 'In the coalfields from which he came, Marx and Engels have been supplanted by Marks and Spencer, and the sound of class war is being drowned by the hum of the spin-dryer.' He concluded, 'There will be no more Aneurin Bevans.'[64] In 1887, William Harcourt, a leader of the Liberal Party, speaking on a bill introduced by a Conservative government providing for the compulsory acquisition of land for allotments, had declared, 'We are all socialists now.'[65] By 1997, Blair could secure a large majority for Labour only by assuring voters, in effect, that none of them were socialists now. Keir Starmer has been following the same trajectory. At the beginning of the twentieth century, socialism had seemed the wave of the future. By the end of the century, however, the very term 'socialism' had gone out of fashion. The removal of Clause 4 of the Labour Party constitution in 1995, with its commitment to nationalisation, could be held to mark explicit recognition that Labour was no longer, if it ever had been, a socialist party.

By the end of the 1950s, Bevan was coming to appreciate that he was working against the tide of history. The British working class had failed to take its chance of keeping Britain on the path planned for it by the 1945 Labour government. In 1951, Labour had secured more votes than the Conservatives, but by a quirk of the electoral system, the Conservatives had been returned to power with a majority of seventeen. Had Labour won that election, it might well have remained in power during the long boom of the 1950s. Then, just possibly, Britain might have become a

64 Campbell, *Nye Bevan*, 372.
65 Hansard, House of Commons, 11 August 1887, vol. 319, col. 140.

more egalitarian socialist society, along the lines of Norway or Sweden. But it was not to be. 'History,' Bevan concluded in 1959, 'gave [the British working class] the chance – and they didn't take it. Now it is probably too late. The great changes in the world will take place in spite of them.' This, of course, begs the question of whether the British working class really wanted to take the 'chance' that Bevan was offering them.[66]

Bevan had sought to be a teacher of the left. But what did he teach? It seemed that he was offering little more than reassurance. The laws of history, discovered by Marx and his disciples, showed that socialism lay in the logic of history. There was no need for the Labour Party to adapt or modernise itself. Was he a teacher who failed to listen to those he sought to teach? Was there an element of wilful self-blindness in his make-up? After all, a party of the left, if it is to be successful, needs above all a willingness to rethink and, if necessary, to jettison traditional ideas in the face of changing realities – an easy lesson to formulate, no doubt, though not so easy to put into practice. By the end of his life, indeed, Bevan's socialism seemed to have become a conservative philosophy dedicated to preserving the gains of the 1945 government, rather than adapting to social change. The paradox was that, by 1959, Jenkins wrote, 'He was a hero who was also an anachronism.'[67] Had he stopped thinking?

In his book *In Place of Fear*, published in 1952, Bevan did appear to have accepted the need for revision. He wrote:

Democratic Socialism is a child of modern society and so of relativist philosophy. It seeks the truth in any given situation, knowing all the time that if this be pushed too far it falls into error. It struggles against the evils that flow from private

66 Foot, *Bevan: Vol. 2*, 626.
67 Jenkins, 'Six Men of Power'.

property, yet realizes that all forms of private property are not necessarily evil.

He also wrote:

> Democratic socialism is essentially cool in temper ... Because it knows that all political action must be a choice between a number of possible alternatives it eschews all absolute prescriptions and final decisions.[68]

Perhaps at the end of his life he was groping towards conclusions reached by the revisionists in the Labour Party, men such as Gaitskell and Crosland, who took the view that capitalism had been fundamentally transformed by the reforms of the 1945 Labour government and that Labour had to adapt accordingly. Might Bevan, if he had lived, have tired of the stale formulas of the left, which seemed to condemn the party to eternal opposition? Realising that nothing could be achieved without power, might he have come to terms with the social changes which he so abhorred? Is it just possible that Bevan might have been the great leader that the Labour Party and indeed the country so badly needed after Attlee's retirement in 1955, but was unable to find? We shall never know.

VII

It has been rightly said that Bevan's imprint on British history, primarily because of the NHS, 'is greater than that of any but two or three twentieth-century politicians. Few of them can claim that their work changed fundamentally the way their

---

68 Bevan, *In Place of Fear*, 170, 169.

countrymen live.'[69] Bevan's principles – that the NHS should be based primarily upon taxation, not upon insurance contributions, and that the hospitals should be centralised so as to provide a universal national service that is comprehensive and automatically available to all – remain at the core of the health service. And, although his socialist ideas now seem very much of the past, he remains, in the words of one Labour historian, 'perhaps the most attractive figure the British socialist movement has yet produced'.[70] He was also fundamentally a good man. Yet, as the philosopher Isaiah Berlin once reminded me, the task in life of the wise is to undo the damage done by the good.

---

69 Beckett and Beckett, *Bevan*, 143.
70 Kenneth O. Morgan, 'Nye Comes in from the Cold', *Guardian* (27 March 1987).

2

Enoch Powell and the Sovereignty of Parliament

I

Enoch Powell (1912–1998) was for a time in the late 1960s and early 1970s the most popular politician in Britain. If Britain were ruled by a directly elected president rather than a Cabinet and Parliament, he might well have become leader of the country.

Unlike Bevan and Jenkins, Powell had no major legislative or governmental achievements to his credit. Indeed, he was in government only for a very short time. He was a member of the Cabinet for just fifteen months and held junior posts for a further four years, a shorter time than any of the politicians considered in this book apart from Farage.

One reason why Powell was in government for such a short time is that he was not an easy colleague. He found it difficult to get on terms with a succession of Conservative leaders, in particular Macmillan and Heath. I remember being shocked when I met Powell as a graduate student after a seminar at Oxford, and he declared of Macmillan, 'I couldn't stand the sight of him.' I was shocked by such directness, something quite unusual for a major political figure. Usually when politicians are asked about a colleague whom they dislike, they reply, 'Of course he has many great qualities, but ...' However, seeing how shocked I was, Powell added with a smile, 'I am sure that he felt exactly the same way about me.' That, I have no doubt, was true. Indeed, it is said that Macmillan put Powell to the side of him at the Cabinet table so that he did not have to look at those staring, obsessive eyes.

Powell, then, was not a comfortable colleague. In 1958, he resigned from Macmillan's government – in which he was financial secretary to the Treasury, an influential but non-Cabinet post – since he thought Macmillan and his close colleagues insufficiently committed to the battle against inflation. He was brought back to the government in 1960, and then in 1962 was promoted to Cabinet as minister of health. But a year later, he refused to serve Macmillan's successor, Douglas-Home, whom he believed had been selected by a 'magic circle' against the wishes of Conservative ministers and MPs. After entering into opposition in 1964, however, Douglas-Home brought Powell back to the Shadow Cabinet, and he was retained there by Heath, Douglas-Home's successor in 1965, becoming shadow defence secretary. In that position, he regularly challenged his Shadow Cabinet colleagues and in 1968 he was to be sacked by Heath after making his controversial and, in the view of many, racist, 'rivers of blood' speech on immigration. After being sacked by Heath, the two never spoke to each other again. Powell was never to hold office after that, although the early part of his period in the political wilderness coincided with a period of great popularity in the country. Distrusted by his colleagues, who believed that he was exploiting popular prejudices to advance his political career, he was enthusiastically cheered by many outside Parliament who believed that he was speaking for 'the people' against the establishment.

One reason why Powell failed to maintain cordial relations with successive Conservative leaders was that his approach to the great questions of the day was somewhat different from theirs. The Conservative Party, at least until the time of Margaret Thatcher, prided itself on its pragmatism, approaching issues on their merits rather than arguing from first principles, which it tended to regard as characteristic of ideological parties of the left. Instead of pushing principles to their doctrinal limits, they sought to reconcile, to secure the best of all worlds. Powell, however, was quite different. He would argue with a disturbing intensity from first principles to inflexible conclusions. He was a man of causes – controlling immigration, keeping Britain out of the EC – as the EU then was – and defeating devolution. In some ways, Margaret Thatcher also sought to argue from first principles, and it is no coincidence that she was the only Conservative leader with whom Powell found some genuine affinity, even if, by the time she became leader in 1975, he was no longer a member of the party. He had advocated voting for Labour in the two general elections of that year and was, in the second of the two general elections of 1974, chosen as an Ulster Unionist for the constituency of South Down in Northern Ireland, where he was duly elected.

Some regard Powell as an early Thatcherite, but although Margaret Thatcher sought to recover what she regarded as the first principles of Conservatism, she was in practice cautious, sometimes adopting indirect and circuitous methods to secure her aims. Powell's methods, however, were direct and confrontational. By contrast with Margaret Thatcher's, they were the methods of a political outsider. His base indeed lay outside the Cabinet and Parliament, in Conservative constituency parties and amongst the people, particularly working-class voters. But compromise seemed alien to him, and so he was ill-suited to a system of Cabinet government, which requires a sense of collegiality and a willingness to discover formulae to paper over differences of opinion. Powell was not in the least collegial. He was an individualist who sought to bend others to his will, and if he could not do so, he would resign. He was like the young cricketer who, if he could not get his way, would take his bat back to the pavilion.

Since Powell's achievements in government and Parliament were negligible, his significance lies, as with Benn and Joseph, in what he stood for, in what he taught. He argued indeed, as no doubt Benn and Joseph would have done, that the task of the politician was to articulate the thoughts of the people, to provide them with words and ideas which would help them make sense of their situation.

He altered, for better or worse, the nature of the political debate on four issues. They are:

1. The free market, which he believed essential for a free society.
2. Immigration, the rigorous control of which he believed essential if the British nation were to be preserved.
3. The EC, which he believed would extinguish British nationhood.
4. Devolution, which he believed would lead to the break-up of the United Kingdom.

These are, of course, issues which remain at the forefront of current political debate. It would be difficult, therefore, to deny Powell's contemporary relevance. His supporters argue that he was prescient, that he predicted, with uncanny accuracy, the future of British politics. His opponents counter that he aroused irrational fears, appealing to the worst instincts of the voters, which he both intensified and magnified.

II

Powell was christened John Enoch Powell, but his mother did not like his first names, and he was generally known in childhood as Jack. He was born in June 1912 in Stechford, Birmingham, which ironically was to become the constituency of one of his most determined opponents, Jenkins, in 1950. Symbolically, a violent thunderstorm accompanied his birth. Powell was an only child. Both of his parents were teachers, and Powell said that it would have been against nature had he not become a teacher too – which he did, not only as an academic but also perhaps as a politician. His father was to become headteacher of a primary school, but his mother was required to give up her teaching post upon marriage. She compensated for this by teaching her son, who was to be her star pupil. Powell was a precocious learner, learning to read at the age of three. Indeed, he was already reading books at that age, and would lecture others on subjects that interested him, gaining the nickname 'The Professor'. His natural conservatism came out early in life. Visiting Caernarfon Castle with his parents, he removed his cap on entering one of the rooms. When asked why, he said it was in that room that the Prince of Wales, later Edward II, had been born.

Powell's mother had taught herself Greek from the New Testament, and when Enoch was aged twelve, she taught him the language too. He was to prove an outstanding classical scholar, winning all the classical prizes at his school, King Edward VII in Birmingham. But he found to his horror that one of the commentators on the Greek historian, Thucydides, on whom he wanted to write, was called John U. Powell. Thereafter, he began to call himself J. Enoch Powell, and finally Enoch Powell, the name by which he is now known.

In December 1929, Powell went to Cambridge to take the scholarship examination in classics at Trinity College. The examination consisted of a number of three-hour papers, but Powell walked out of each one after one and a half hours. He later said that in his Greek prose-composition paper, he had provided two versions of the required composition – one in the style of Thucydides and one in the style of Herodotus. In his translation paper, he offered two translations – one in the style of Plato and one in the style of Herodotus. In addition, he annotated the translations. Not surprisingly, he won the scholarship. At Cambridge, he did nothing but work. He played no part whatever in politics. Later in life, he said of himself:

> I saw my life when I went up to Cambridge far too much, I realise in retrospect, as a simple condition of the prize/scholarship-winning, knowledge-eating process of the working side of my school life. I literally worked from half-past five in the morning until half-past nine at night, behind a sported oak, except when I went out to lectures. This was not because I disliked my fellows ... It was that I didn't know there was anything else to do.[1]

When a school friend called on him to ask him out for tea, Powell declined, saying, 'Thank you very much, but I came here to work.'[2] He also declined an invitation from the master of the college to a freshman's dinner, pleading pressure of work. As an undergraduate, he contributed an article to a learned classical journal. Not surprisingly, he won all the university's classics prizes, achieved a double first, and was immediately offered a fellowship by his college. But that was not enough. Determined to become the youngest professor in the Commonwealth, he was appointed to a chair of Greek at the University of Sydney in 1937, at the age of twenty-five. In 1939, he was appointed professor of Greek and classical literature at the University of Durham, a post which he was due to take up in January 1940. But then war intervened. Powell indeed had believed that war

---

1 Quoted in Rex Collings (ed.), *Reflections of a Statesman: The Writings and Speeches of Enoch Powell* (Bellew Publishing, 1991), 8.
2 Simon Heffer, *Like the Roman: The Life of Enoch Powell* (Weidenfeld and Nicolson, 1998), 14.

was inevitable from the time of Hitler's blood purge in 1934, in which the Führer had eliminated various enemies of the regime. Powell had been a bitter opponent of the Munich Agreement, by which Britain and France agreed to surrender the German-speaking Sudeten areas of Czechoslovakia to Hitler's Germany. Appeasement, while it might bring Britain a few more months of peace, would do so only, he believed, through the permission of her German slave-masters. Feeling as he did, Powell had no hesitation in joining the army when war broke out. But shortly before the war, he had published *A Lexicon to Herodotus*, a vast index to every single word in the works of that historian of ancient Greece. This was a book which he believed would secure him immortality, since it would have to be read by anyone studying Greek; it would preserve his name even if, as he expected, he was to be killed in the war. He also wrote poetry – including a poem describing his feelings when war broke out:

> I wrote a poem in which I described people joining up at the outbreak of the war, like bridegrooms going to meet their bride. That's how it was to me. The thing expected for so many years. The thing which one had feared wouldn't happen but would, instead, be replaced by disgrace and humiliation. It had happened. The chance had come at last. As I once described it, I felt I could hear the German divisions marching across Europe and I could hear this drumming coming through the earth and it was coming up again in Australia where no one else could hear it.[3]

Powell came to adore the army:

> I took to it like a duck to water. ... It seemed to me such a

---

3 Quoted in Collings, *Reflections of a Statesman*, 9.

congenial environment, but the whole institution of the army, the framework of discipline, the exactitude of rank, the precision of duty, was something almost restful and attractive to me and I took great pride in smartness at drill. One always remembers I suppose ... some absurd compliments ... One of them that I remember, I shall remember all my days, was my Platoon Sergeant saying to the company commander that I was the smartest soldier in the company. I take that as a very, very great compliment.[4]

Powell's career in the army was as successful as his academic career had been, even though, to his regret, he never saw active service. Beginning the war as a private, he ended it as one of the youngest brigadiers in the army, the only soldier to have made this progression. At the end of his life, he chose to be buried in his brigadier's uniform.

During his army service, he was stationed in India and fell 'hopelessly and helplessly in love' with the country, although perhaps the India that he fell in love with was imperial India, then in its last days, not the burgeoning independent India of Jawaharlal Nehru and Mahatma Gandhi.[5] Nevertheless, it was India that aroused his political interests. He came to believe that India was of fundamental importance to Britain if the empire was to be preserved. One day late in the war, when the monsoon broke in Delhi in June 1944, he described how he felt:

I suddenly said to myself: You're going to survive. There'll be a time when you won't be in uniform; painful though it may be, you've got to face it ... There will be a lifetime for you, and a lifetime not as a soldier ... This was the opening of the door

4 Ibid., 9.
5 *The Times* (7 May 1983).

from one mental room to another. And there was the answer,
of course – you'll go into politics, in England.[6]

He went into politics to preserve the Indian empire, joining the
Conservative Research Department to pursue that aim.

It is perhaps a sign of Powell's political naïveté that he believed,
first, that preservation of the Indian empire was a serious propo-
sition, and second, that the Conservative Party would spend its
political capital on such an obviously lost cause. It was hardly
surprising that the Conservatives were to disappoint him. But,
in any case, Labour was in power and committed to Indian independence. This was a bitter blow to Powell. He remembered
spending 'one evening, I think, in 1947, after separation of India
had become a political fact, walking about the streets all night
trying to digest it'.[7] He made his views clear to those in power in
the Conservative Party, apparently even including Churchill, the
leader of the party. Some early biographies of Powell claim that
Churchill had 'rung up the research department to ask, "Who
was that young madman who has been telling me how many
divisions I will need to reconquer India?"', but Powell has said
that this story is apocryphal.[8]

The independence of India had a profound effect on Powell.
He never believed in the rhetoric of Commonwealth, regarding
it as a sham. A relationship between different states based solely
on sentiment was not, he believed, something that could be
relied upon. India had, in his view, cut itself adrift from Britain.
There was, therefore, no point in retaining bases on the route
to India, such as that in the Suez Canal, nor a presence east of
Suez, since both India and Australia would now go their own

---

6 Quoted in Collings, *Reflections of a Statesman*, 10.
7 Andrew Roth, *Enoch Powell: Tory Tribune* (Macdonald, 1970), 51.
8 T. E. Utley, *Enoch Powell: The Man and his Thinking* (William Kimber, 1968), 60.

way, unencumbered by links with Britain. As early as 1954, he told his Wolverhampton constituents that 'territories and positions that had a value as part of a worldwide system may in isolation have no value or less than no value'. The agreement by which Britain evacuated the Suez Canal base in 1954 'showed decisively that Britain was no longer able or willing – there is no real difference – to maintain that world system at one of its vital points, if that meant the exertion of force'.[9] Powell's thoughts, therefore, turned back to Britain. At first, he thought that Britain's future lay with Europe. But, so he claimed, when he came to appreciate the constitutional and political consequences of the EC, he concluded that it meant extinguishing Britain as an independent state, and turned violently against it.

Yet, despite Powell's absolutist way of thinking, so different from that of traditional Conservatives, and despite his other eccentricities and his background – one quite unusual at a time when most Conservative MPs still came from the landed classes – Powell was adopted as a parliamentary candidate, first for the safe Labour seat of Normanton in a by-election of 1947, and then for the new constituency of Wolverhampton South West, which he won in 1950, remaining as its MP until February 1974. After 1950, whenever he drove into Wolverhampton with his wife, he would sing, 'Wonderful, wonderful Wolverhampton,' to the tune of 'Wonderful Copenhagen' from the Danny Kaye film *Hans Christian Andersen*. But, before the selection process began, the chairman of the selectors had felt the need to warn his colleagues, 'Don't be put off by appearances.'[10]

In the Commons, Powell rapidly established himself as a devotee of the free market, which put him against the 'middle

---

9 Paul Corthorn, 'Enoch Powell, Julian Amery and debates over Britain's world role after 1945' in Olivier Esteves and Stephanie Porion (eds.), *The Lives and Afterlives of Enoch Powell: The Undying Political Animal* (Routledge, 2019), 117.
10 Heffer, *Like the Roman*, 125.

way' statist instincts of the Churchill/Macmillan Conservative
Party of the 1950s. Nevertheless, he was given junior office by
Anthony Eden, prime minister between 1955 and 1957, while
Eden's successor, Macmillan, appointed Powell a junior Treasury
minister – financial secretary of the Treasury under the chancellor of the Exchequer Peter Thorneycroft. Yet only a year after his
appointment, in January 1958, Powell resigned, together with the
chancellor and the other Treasury minister, against the refusal of
the Cabinet to agree to contain government expenditure to the
same level as the previous financial year.

It was perhaps 'Harold Macmillan's joke' that Powell returned
to government in 1960 as minister of health in what was – and
is – a very high-spending department.[11] But Powell proved a
remarkably effective minister, showing particular concern for the
neglected areas of the health service such as tubercular patients,
long-stay young patients and, above all, mental-health patients
– in a speech commemorating the centenary of the psychiatric
hospital Broadmoor in June 1963, he declared, 'Nothing but the
best would do for Broadmoor.'[12] But he resisted pay claims by
nurses; according to Heath, Powell argued that the government
could afford to stand up to them, and said, 'I can bring in all
the nurses we need from the West Indies.' 'I was in the Cabinet
Room at the time,' Heath remembered, 'and I heard him say it.'[13]
This was to prove ironic in the light of Powell's later complaints
about the extent of Commonwealth immigration.

In October 1963, Powell resigned again, refusing to serve
under Macmillan's successor, Douglas-Home. He had supported Rab Butler for the leadership, but Butler had agreed to

11 Iain McLean, *Rational Choice and British Politics: An Analysis of Rhetoric and
Manipulation from Peel to Blair* (Oxford University Press, 2001), 139.
12 Lunch at Broadmoor to commemorate its centenary, 2 June 1963, Enoch Powell
Speech Archive.
13 Edward Heath, *The Course of My Life* (Hodder and Stoughton, 1998), 292.

join the government. Powell declared that he could not himself serve, because he had previously declared that he would not serve under Douglas-Home and would therefore appear a hypocrite if he changed his mind simply to secure office.

In July 1965, in opposition, Powell himself stood for the leadership after Douglas-Home resigned, intending to lay down a marker for his free-market views. He secured a derisory number of votes, just 15, as compared to 133 for Reginald Maudling and 150 for the winner, Edward Heath. Powell's votes included that of a future chancellor, Geoffrey Howe, on free-market grounds, though Howe was later to be alienated by Powell's views on immigration.

III

Heath appointed Powell to his Shadow Cabinet as shadow defence secretary. From almost the beginning of his tenure in this position, Powell appeared to challenge official party policy by questioning the wisdom of preserving British bases east of Suez and expressing scepticism as to whether the US could achieve victory in Vietnam. On both issues, it is fair to say, his doubts were to be justified by events. In 1968, following the devaluation of the pound, the Labour government decided to withdraw from east of Suez, and Heath, although promising to reverse this policy, failed to do so when he gained office in 1970. In 1975, the US in effect accepted defeat in Vietnam. Regardless of these vindications for Powell, to be in advance of one's time is rarely a recipe for winning the support of one's close colleagues, who may be slower to appreciate the realities.

It was on immigration that Powell was to make his greatest impact, an impact culminating in perhaps the most explosive political speech of the post-war period in Britain, made in

Birmingham on 20 April 1968, a speech which came to be known, albeit inaccurately, as the 'rivers of blood' speech. This speech made him, for the first time, a highly visible and popular figure in the country, but its racist overtones made it highly unlikely that he could ever hold a leadership position.

It is at first sight odd that a man who promoted the free market was against the free market in labour across borders. He was, he told the political scientist David Butler in 1964, 'in the peculiar position of being a high Tory who believes in liberal economics'.[14] Free movement of labour was desirable only within communities, not across them. When the two principles conflicted, the needs of the nation, as Powell saw them, would always take precedence. For the same reason, he defended the NHS, opposing those economic liberals who argued for an insurance service. A health service was something which the nation owed to its members, he felt. Democracy, in his view, could only work effectively in a homogeneous nation, with every voter seeing herself as part of the whole. That, in his view, could never occur in the EC, nor in a country riven with ethnic and religious differences in which the danger was communalism – political allegiances being determined by ethnic or religious identities – of the sort that he had seen in India. However, such differences could be mitigated by free-market policies, since the market was colour-blind, dictating that goods be bought as cheaply as possible whoever produced them, and sold for the best possible price whatever the identity of the buyer. From this point of view, there was no contradiction between the two central tenets of Powellism – the ideal of the nation and the free market.

The problem of immigration was one that was inherited from Britain's colonial past. During the heyday of empire, the self-governing member states and the colonies had enjoyed a

---

14 David Butler Election Archive, 22 January 1964.

common citizenship based on allegiance to the Crown. In consequence, the empire was one unit from the point of view of immigration. All were British subjects. 'It is the practice of the United Kingdom,' the British government declared in 1937, 'not to make any distinction between different races in British colonies as regards civil and political rights, or the right of entry into and residence in the United Kingdom.'[15] But the independent members of the Commonwealth had since 1918 enjoyed the power to restrict entry into their territories. The logical consequence was that these states should enact their own nationality laws. Canada was the first to do so, in 1946. In addition, the concept of citizenship based on allegiance to the Crown was no longer tenable when India decided, on achieving independence in 1947, to become a republic.

Westminster's response to these developments was to enact the British Nationality Act in 1948, which proposed, in place of common allegiance, two different means by which people could become British subjects. The first was by being a citizen of an independent Commonwealth member state. The second was by being a citizen of the UK or its colonies or dependent territories. All would enjoy the new status of 'Citizen of the UK and Colonies'. Those in both categories would be British subjects and, as such, would continue to enjoy the right of free entry. In theory, the government could have taken a different route, introducing a merely local British citizenship, which would have excluded other Commonwealth states and the colonies. But there was hardly any support for such an option, since it would effectively discriminate on grounds of colour and therefore, in the view of government and opposition alike, go against the concept of

---

15 Quoted in Nicholas Deakin, 'The British Nationality Act of 1948: A Brief Study in the Political Mythology of Race Relations', *Race*, 11/1 (1969), 78. This article provides a clear and valuable discussion of the 1948 Act.

a multiracial Commonwealth, exemplified by India's decision to remain in the Commonwealth as a republic. 'Some people,' the home secretary James Chuter Ede declared in a Commons debate on the British Nationality Bill, 'feel that it would be a bad thing to give the coloured races of the Empire the idea that in some way or other, they are the equals of people in this country. The Government do not subscribe to this view.' An anonymous MP is recorded as having responded to this statement by asking, 'Who does?' In the same debate, David Maxwell Fyfe, Conservative front-bench spokesman, declared that he and Chuter Ede were 'at one on this', continuing, 'We were proud in this country that we imposed no colour bar restrictions, making it difficult for [colonial subjects] when they came here.'[16] In the Lords, meanwhile, William Jowitt, the lord chancellor, declared that, although it would be possible to 'say that people who come from one part of the British Empire shall not be allowed in and people from another part shall be allowed in ... in this great metropolitan centre of the Empire I hope we never shall say such a thing'. John Simon, the former Conservative lord chancellor, then declared that it was 'one of the finest things in the whole of our British Commonwealth, that anybody who is a British citizen knows that, without challenge or question, he will be admitted here, and that we reserve for aliens our powers of exclusion'.[17] Citizenship, then, was defined in imperial terms, even though the empire itself was in the process of dissolution.

Powell was at that time a member of the Conservative Parliamentary Secretariat and then the Conservative Research Department, whose duties included advising Conservative shadow ministers. He argued strongly against the British Nationality Bill – not, as he was later to claim, because it would

---

16 Hansard, House of Commons, 7 July 1948, vol. 453, cols. 394, 403.
17 Hansard, House of Lords, 21 June 1948, vol. 156, cols. 1006, 1013.

make immigration control more difficult, but because it ended the notion of citizenship based on allegiance, and it did so in response to a decision by a member state, India, which had explicitly renounced its allegiance to the Crown by becoming a republic. But both Labour and the Conservatives were committed to a Commonwealth which could accommodate republics as well as monarchies; otherwise, hardly any of the African and Asian ex-colonies would have agreed to remain in the Commonwealth, and it seemed incompatible with that concept to discriminate between monarchies and republics in the Commonwealth by denying the right of free entry to the latter. 'We believe wholeheartedly,' Chuter Ede declared, 'that the common citizenship of the United Kingdom and Colonies is an essential part of the development of the relationship between this Mother Country and the Colonies.'[18]

The 1948 Act reinforced the existing principle of free entry; it did not create it. But the Act would make it easier for Parliament than it had been in the past, when rights had been indivisible and based on common allegiance, to make distinctions between different citizens of the UK and Colonies, as was to become the case from 1962. Powell opposed the bill, but had his opposition succeeded, it would ironically have perpetuated the right of free entry. Indeed, some Conservative spokesmen opposed the bill on precisely these grounds: that it would make it easier in the future to discriminate. So the 1948 Act did not 'introduce a new privilege', but rather avoided 'jeopardising a right whose existence was taken for granted by politicians of every shade of opinion'.[19]

There was, however, an obvious objection to the Act, or at least an objection that became obvious in hindsight. It was that it sought to enact a common citizenship for a very heterogeneous

---

18 Hansard, House of Commons, 7 July 1948, vol. 453, col. 411.
19 Deakin, 'The British Nationality Act', 82.

group of territories. To what extent could citizens of Commonwealth states and colonies really be regarded as British subjects?
In the words of one back-bench peer, the Act was not 'a recognition of reality, but a departure into complete and utter unreality'.
That was 'because the peoples of the Colonial Empire are not
united with each other by the ties of which true national citizenship is made'.[20] This also became Powell's view. He declared in
Wolverhampton in May 1965:

> It was [an] absurd anachronism in the law of this country
> whereby the myriad inhabitants of African, Asian and Ameri-
> can territories which were once under British rule could not
> be distinguished for any purpose from the citizens of Birming-
> ham or Wolverhampton and possessed an identical right to
> enter this country at will.[21]

The 1948 Act was, of course, enacted in the days before mass air
transit. But, already in the 1950s, there were some concerns, both
at a popular level and in the government, at the scale of non-white
immigration from the West Indies and the Indian subcontinent.
In 1954, Churchill told his Cabinet, 'The rapid improvement in
communications was likely to lead to the continuing increase
in the number of coloured people coming to the country, and
their presence here would sooner or later come to be resented by
large sections of the British people.'[22] Shortly before the end of
Churchill's peacetime government, in January 1955, a bill was
drafted to control West Indian immigration. The aged Churchill,
according to Macmillan, apparently believed that 'Keep England

---

20 Hansard, House of Lords, 11 May 1948, vol. 155, cols. 784, 788.
21 Speech to Conservative Women's Coffee Morning, Wolverhampton, 21 May
1965, Enoch Powell Speech Archive.
22 Quoted in Andrew Roberts, *Eminent Churchillians* (Weidenfeld and Nicolson,
1994), 221–2.

White' would prove 'a good slogan'.[23] Indeed, throughout the 1950s, Conservative ministers toyed with the idea of legislating on this issue, but nothing was done. The ethos of the Commonwealth still held sway. As Henry Hopkinson, the colonial secretary, declared in 1954, 'We still take pride in the fact that a man can say *Civis Britannicus sum* whatever his colour may be, and we take pride in the fact that he wants and can come to the Mother Country.'[24]

However, in 1962 the Conservative government enacted the Commonwealth Immigrants Act, which ended the concept that the British Commonwealth and Empire comprised one single territory and that all those living in it were free to enter Britain. Subsequently, only those who had been born in Britain or were holders of passports issued in Britain, as opposed to British passports issued by colonial authorities, would retain the right of free entry. All others living in the Commonwealth would be liable for immigration control, based on whether they had professional qualifications or were likely to be able to secure employment. They would no longer have the right of free entry.

Nevertheless, worries about immigration persisted, especially in the West Midlands. In the 1964 general election, some Conservative candidates in that area clearly believed that votes were to be won by championing anti-immigrant feeling. The most notorious example occurred in the Smethwick constituency, where the Conservative candidate, Peter Griffiths, a primary-school headteacher, defeated Labour's shadow foreign secretary, Patrick Gordon Walker, with a 7 per cent swing to the Conservatives, despite the general election resulting in a national swing to Labour of 3 per cent. Griffiths achieved this result by mobilising

---

23 Peter Catterall (ed.), *The Macmillan Diaries: The Cabinet Years 1950–1957* (Pan Books, 2004), 382.
24 Hansard, House of Commons, 5 November 1954, vol. 532, col. 827.

hostility to Caribbean immigrants. At his adoption meeting, Griffiths had declared that Britain was in danger of becoming 'a dumping ground for criminals, the chronic sick and those who have no intention of working'. Some in the constituency used the slogan 'If you want a n—— for a neighbour, vote Labour'; Griffiths did not use this slogan, but he refused to condemn those who did, saying that it was 'a manifestation of popular feeling'. It was alleged that Powell had refused to speak for Griffiths in Smethwick, but Powell later claimed that this was only because of a confusion of dates. When Griffith entered Parliament, the new prime minister, Wilson, referred to him as a 'parliamentary leper', though the moral force of his protest was somewhat undermined when it was discovered that the Smethwick Labour Club operated a colour bar.[25] Griffith was to be defeated in the 1966 general election; he re-emerged to became MP for Portsmouth North from 1979 to 1997, but made little further impact. Even though election analysts did not discover any general effect of immigration in the 1964 election, which was won by Labour, the swing to Labour in the West Midlands was the lowest in the country.

The Labour Party under Gaitskell had opposed the Commonwealth Immigrants Act 1962, arguing for the retention of free entry. But when Labour was elected in 1964 under Wilson, Gaitskell's successor, it retained the controls in the 1962 Act, and in a White Paper in 1965 it actually strengthened them. It did so by drastically reducing the number of immigrant employment vouchers from 20,000 a year to 8,500; in future, the majority of vouchers would be issued for those with special qualifications or skills, such as doctors, with just a few left over for those without such qualifications but with a specific job to come to. It was

---

25 A. W. Singham, 'Immigration and the Election' in D. E. Butler and Anthony King, *The British General Election of 1964* (Macmillan, 1965), 364, 365.

hoped that, in consequence, few would wish to go to the more deprived areas of the country, where racial tensions were likely to be greatest. But already tacit approval was being given to the idea that non-white immigrants were not particularly welcome.

By the time of the 1966 election, tensions over immigration seemed to have lessened. There was an above-average swing to Labour in the Midlands, and Peter Griffiths lost his seat. 'Immigration,' wrote the authors of the Nuffield British Election Study for that year, 'seems to have affected pre-election commentators much more than voters'.[26] By 1967, Powell believed that the situation appeared to be stabilising. 'I have the impression,' he wrote in the *Daily Telegraph*, 'that ... the sudden impact of Commonwealth immigration is over.'[27]

But in late 1967, Powell visited the US – a country for which he had little sympathy – for the first time, and was appalled by the racial antagonisms and riots that he found there, fearing that these problems would be imported into Britain as a result of mass immigration. This led to him to be sceptical of the possibilities of integration. After his visit, he told a journalist that 'integration of races of totally disparate origins and culture is one of the great myths of our time'.[28] In his April 1968 'rivers of blood' speech, he was to say that the 'tragic and intractable phenomenon which we watch with horror on the other side of the Atlantic ... is coming upon us here by our own volition and our own neglect'.[29]

His anxieties were increased by the sudden inflow in 1968 of

---

26 Butler and King, *The British General Election of 1964*, 342; Michael Steed, 'The Results Analysed' in Butler and King, *The British General Election of 1964*, 354; and Michael Steed, 'The Results Analysed' in D. E. Butler and Anthony King, *The British General Election of 1966* (Macmillan, 1966), 283, 289.

27 Enoch Powell, 'Facing Up to Britain's Race Problem', *Daily Telegraph* (16 February 1967).

28 Robert Shepherd, *Enoch Powell: A Biography* (Hutchinson, 1996), 338.

29 Utley, *Enoch Powell*, 190.

Asians from Kenya. The Asian minority in Kenya and Uganda, who formed a large part of the professional, commercial, and administrative elite there, feared that they would no longer be safe once those countries became independent, and under majority rule. In consequence, many sought refuge in Britain. The problem arose first in Kenya. When Kenya had become independent in 1963, those of non-African origin were given two years to apply for Kenyan citizenship. Those who did not do so could retain their jobs only for as long as no Kenyan national could replace them. Most members of the Asian community of around 200,000, fearing the Africanisation policies of the Kenyan government, did not wish to apply for Kenyan citizenship.

The British government had anticipated this situation and, when preparing for the independence of the East African states, had allowed those who wished to do so to retain the status of Citizen of the UK and Colonies, with passports issued on the authority of London, rather than by a colonial governor, so that they would be excluded from the immigration-control provisions of the 1962 Act. Most Kenyan Asians took advantage of this provision. Those with such passports would remain exempt from immigration control; they would enjoy the same right of free entry as anyone else whose passport was issued in London. At the time, it may have been white settlers that the British government had in mind, rather than the Asian community. Nevertheless, since Kenya did not allow dual citizenship, anyone who opted for Kenyan citizenship would lose their British citizenship and their British passport. Not surprisingly, few Asians took that option.

In 1967, the Kenyan government passed legislation restricting the right of those who were not Kenyan citizens to conduct business, and towards the end of the year it was established that those without Kenyan citizenship would in future have to apply for 'entry certificates', even if they had been born there. At this stage, Asians decided to make use of their British passports.

There was in consequence a sudden influx from Kenya into Britain – by 1 March, around 80,000 immigrants had arrived.

On 9 February 1968, Powell, in a speech in Walsall, said he had detected 'a sense of hopelessness and helplessness' on the part of the indigenous inhabitants of the West Midlands, predicting that there would be a million more immigrants in Britain in twenty years' time without stringent new controls. He called for restrictions on the right of entry of Asians into Britain and for the 'virtual termination of work vouchers and the end of unconditional right of entry for dependants'.[30]

This speech no doubt contributed to the atmosphere in which the Labour government, fearing the scale of Asian immigration and the consequences for race relations, rapidly introduced a new Commonwealth Immigrants Act in 1968, retrospectively imposing controls on those with British passports issued in London unless they or one of their parents or grandparents were born, adopted, naturalised, or registered as citizens in Britain itself. Others with British passports lost their right of free entry. For those now subject to immigration controls, there was now an annual quota of just 1,500 heads of households and dependants a year. Most would be expected to be skilled professionals who were unlikely to immigrate to the inner cities, where tensions were greatest.

This in effect created a distinction between predominantly white citizens of Commonwealth countries, whose ancestry was British, and non-white citizens, most of whom did not have British ancestry. The bill, supported by the Conservatives in opposition, went through all of its stages in Parliament in just seven days. The effect was that those with British passports and recent British ancestry, almost all of whom were white, remained

---

30 Speech to Walsall South Conservative Association, 9 February 1968, Enoch Powell Speech Archive.

free from controls, while those from British colonies without such ancestry, who were mainly Asian or black, would become subject to controls. In consequence, those Asians who had not registered as Kenyan citizens became in effect stateless, without right of abode in any country at all. In 1973, the European Commission of Human Rights found that three separate articles of the European Convention on Human Rights had been breached by this legislation and that 'the racial discrimination to which the applicants have been publicly subjected by the application of the [1968] immigration legislation ... amounted to "degrading treatment"'.[31] It was perhaps some compensation that, in 1972, Heath's Conservative government had accepted the admission of Asians who had been expelled by the government of Idi Amin in Uganda, while in 2004, the Labour home secretary, David Blunkett, was to end what he called a 'historic wrong' by giving the 35,000 Asians left stateless as a result of the 1968 Act the right to take up full British citizenship.[32]

Following the restrictions in the 1968 Act, the Labour government sought to enact the second element of its immigration policy, the improvement of race relations, proposing a new Race Relations Bill to outlaw discrimination in housing and employment. This was the context in which Powell made his explosive 'rivers of blood' speech in Birmingham on 20 April, three days before the second reading in the Commons of the Race Relations Bill.

The Conservative Shadow Cabinet had to decide its attitude to the Race Relations Bill. The party had opposed the 1965 Race Relations Bill, on the grounds that good race relations depended on alterations in attitudes which could not be secured by law. In

---

31 Mark Lattimer, 'When Labour Played the Racist Card', *New Statesman* (22 January 1999).

32 Alan Travis, 'Blunkett ends passports injustice, 34 years on', *Guardian* (3 July 2002); Hansard, House of Lords, 4 July 2002, vol. 637, col. 52WA.

1968, the Shadow Cabinet had to find a compromise between liberals who wished to support the bill and those who wished to oppose it. A compromise was reached. The Conservatives would offer a reasoned amendment to the bill, supporting its objectives but declaring that the bill would not achieve them. Powell was on the sub-committee which drafted the reasoned amendment. The Shadow Cabinet seems also to have accepted that its approach should not be understood as one that encouraged racial discrimination. Therefore, so as not to inflame race relations or encourage racists, Conservatives should carefully measure their words when speaking on the bill. Powell apparently made no objections in the Shadow Cabinet to the compromise reached.

It was shortly after the decision of the Shadow Cabinet that Powell made his speech. It was not distributed through the Central Office machinery, so that shadow ministers had no opportunity to scrutinise it in advance. In the past, when Powell was about to make a controversial speech, Heath had sent his chief whip, William Whitelaw, to dissuade him. But there was no opportunity to dissuade Powell before this particular speech. The text was, however, distributed in advance to the media, so that television cameras were able to film part of the speech. Powell seemed well aware that the speech would cause a furore, telling a friend beforehand, 'You know how a rocket goes up into the air, breaks up and explodes into lots of stars and then falls down to the ground. Well, this speech is going to go up like a rocket, and when it gets to the top, the stars are going to stay up.'[33]

Powell began his speech by quoting a conversation with a constituent, 'a middle aged, quite ordinary working man employed

33 Quoted in Nicholas Jones, 'Powell and the media: an insider's account' in Esteves and Porion, *The Lives and Afterlives*, 53. Nicholas Jones's father, to whom the comment was made, was the editor of the *Wolverhampton Express and Star* and a close friend of Powell's until the 1968 Birmingham speech, which ended their friendship.

in one of our nationalised industries', who told him, 'If I had the money to go, I wouldn't stay in this country.' Powell replied in jocular fashion that even the current awful Labour government would not last forever. But the constituent responded, 'In this country in fifteen or twenty years' time the black man will have the whip hand over the white man.' Powell continued, 'What he is saying, thousands and hundreds of thousands are saying and thinking ... in the areas that are already undergoing the total transformation to which there is no parallel in a thousand years of English history.' In fifteen or twenty years, Powell declared, according to figures by the Registrar General, there would be 3.5 million Commonwealth immigrants and their descendants in Britain. By the year 2000, he said, there could be between five and seven million Commonwealth immigrants and their descendants in Britain, near to the population of Greater London. These immigrants and their descendants would constitute 'an alien element'. This could only be combatted by 'stopping, or virtually stopping, further inflow, and by promoting the maximum outflow. Both answers,' Powell declared, 'are part of the official policy of the Conservative Party.' This, however, was disingenuous. Promoting 'the maximum outflow' was not 'part' of official Conservative policy, though it admittedly sought voluntary repatriation.[34]

Immigration control did not extend to dependants of those already in Britain, and the notion of who was to be counted as a dependant was at this time loosely interpreted. This caused an explosion of rhetoric from Powell, beginning with a quotation from the Greek poet Euripides. 'Those whom the gods wish to destroy, they first make mad. We must be mad, literally mad, as a nation to be permitting the annual inflow of some 50,000 dependants, who are for the most part the material of the future

34 Speech to the West Midlands Conservative Political Centre in Birmingham, 20 April 1968, Enoch Powell Speech Archive.

growth of the immigrant-descended population. It is like watching a nation busily engaged in heaping up its own funeral pyre.' It was no doubt right that families should be reunited, Powell said, but this could best be done, he suggested, by reuniting them not in Britain but in their countries of origin. That was certainly not part of official Conservative policy.[35]

Powell had so far discussed two elements of Conservative immigration policy, drastic restriction and encouragement of repatriation. But the third element of the policy was that all British citizens should be equal before the law without discrimination. Powell insisted that the Race Relations Bill, far from achieving this aim, would put immigrants and descendants 'into a privileged or special class'. He went on:

> The discrimination and the deprivation, the sense of alarm and of resentment, lies not with the immigrant population but with those among whom they have come and are still coming. This is why to enact legislation of the kind before Parliament at this moment is to risk throwing a match on to gunpowder ... The existing [British] population ... for reasons which they could not comprehend, and in pursuance of a decision by default, on which they were never consulted ... found themselves made strangers in their own country ... The sense of being a persecuted minority which is growing among ordinary English people in the areas of the country which are affected is something that those without direct experience can hardly imagine ... They now learn that a one-way privilege is to be established by act of parliament.

He then told a distasteful anecdote recounted to him by a correspondent from Northumberland about an elderly widow in

---

35 Ibid.

his constituency who was the only white woman living in her 'respectable street'. She had refused to let rooms to Caribbeans, and was being harassed in consequence, with 'excreta pushed through her letter box'. When she went to the shops, she was harassed by children, 'charming, wide-grinning piccaninnies. They cannot speak English, but one word they know. "Racialist," they chant. When the new Race Relations Bill is passed, this woman is convinced she will go to prison. And is she so wrong? I begin to wonder.'[36]

Integration was, he said, 'a dangerous delusion', since most immigrants did not wish to integrate. He foresaw the danger of communalism as he had seen in India, with politics being based on communal allegiance rather than political viewpoints. He then used a quotation from Virgil's *Aeneid*, which gave the speech its title. 'Like the Roman,' he said, 'I seem to see "the River Tiber foaming with much blood".'[37] The historian Simon Heffer was to title his magisterial biography of Powell *Like the Roman*. The speech, however, became inaccurately known as the 'rivers of blood' speech.[38]

However, remarkably for a classical scholar, the quotation was entirely inappropriate. It was not a 'Roman' who had seen the Tiber flowing with blood, but a soothsayer, the Sibyl from Cumae, a Greek colony; she was almost certainly of Greek origin. In any case, the 'Roman' hero of the Aeneid, Aeneas, was an immigrant from Troy who had fled with his family following defeat in war with the Greeks and sought intermarriage with his Roman hosts!

---

36 Ibid.
37 The words in Latin are '*Bella, horrida bella, et Thybrim multo spumantum sanguine cerno*' – 'I see wars, horrible wars, and the Tiber foaming with much blood'.
38 Speech to West Midlands Conservative Association, 20 April 1968, Enoch Powell Speech Archive.

The speech caused a furore. In form, it did not perhaps differ in any striking way from official Conservative policy. Indeed, in the party's 1970 election manifesto, it promised that there would be 'no further large-scale immigration'.[39] But Powell placed far more emphasis on repatriation than the Shadow Cabinet, which felt that very few Commonwealth immigrants would wish to return to their countries of origin, where living standards and opportunities were far lower than in Britain. In January 1970, Powell was to declare that repatriation must be the first priority for areas of high immigration concentration. Heath replied that such a policy was 'unchristian' and an example of 'man's unhumanity to man'.[40] Besides, the encouragement of repatriation was a breach of the principle that all should be treated equally, and it amounted to discrimination on the grounds of colour. In addition, it was clear that Powell opposed the Race Relations Bill in principle, rather than seeking to improve it through the Shadow Cabinet's reasoned amendment. And the Shadow Cabinet did not share Powell's view that most immigrants did not wish to integrate. Therefore, it put far less weight on repatriation than Powell.

The main reason why the speech caused a furore, however, was not so much its specific proposals but its highly inflammatory tone. Heath was to declare in the *Daily Express*, two days after the speech, 'The reason I dismissed him from the Shadow Cabinet post was not for stating these policies. It was because of the way he did it.'[41] The *Sunday Times*, on the day after the speech, called it 'bloodcurdling mob oratory' and 'crudely inflammatory'.[42] The next day, *The Times* called it 'an evil

---

39 Conservative Party 1970 manifesto, 'A Better Tomorrow'.
40 Douglas Schoen, *Enoch Powell and the Powellites* (Macmillan, 1977), 47–48, 49.
41 Quoted in Nicholas Hillman, 'A "chorus of execration"? Enoch Powell's "Rivers of Blood" Forty Years on', *Patterns of Prejudice*, 1 (2008), 93–4.
42 *The Sunday Times* (21 April 1968).

speech' and declared, 'This is the first time that a serious British politician has appealed to racial hatred in this direct way in our post-war history.'[43] Powell could protest that much of the offensive language – including the statement that in twenty years' time the black man would have the whip hand over the white man, the story of the old lady, and use of the word 'piccaninnies' – were not his own but were quoted from his constituent and the letter he received from his Northumberland correspondent. But this too was disingenuous, for he said that he was 'going to allow just one of those hundreds of people [who had written to him on immigration] to *speak for me*' (italics my own). By relating the constituent's comment and the letter, he appeared to be giving them implicit endorsement. Powell was accused of encouraging hostility towards people of colour and promoting an atmosphere of harassment, so that Commonwealth immigrants and their descendants would be pressed to leave. At this point, the distinction between voluntary and compulsory repatriation might be a difficult one to draw. Indeed, Heath believed that the argument which Powell was to 'consistently put forward must lead inexorably to the mass expulsion of all coloured people from the United Kingdom'. Geoffrey Rippon, a Shadow Cabinet minister, told Heath that Powell did indeed favour this option, though he never publicly espoused it.[44]

Many were to compare Powell to Oswald Mosley, the British Fascist leader of the 1930s who had made inflammatory anti-Semitic speeches and had provocatively led marches of uniformed men into areas inhabited by Jews. On most occasions, Powell denied that he was a racist, though in July 1968 he told the *Daily Mail* that 'every person in every country in the world is a racialist', and in 1995, he asked the television interviewer Michael

43 *The Times* (22 April 1968).
44 Heath, *The Course of My Life*, 293–4.

Cockerell, 'What's wrong with racism? Racism is the basis of nationality.'[45] But he said different things at different times. In May 1968, he regarded 'many of the peoples in India as being superior in many respects – intellectually, for example, and in other respects – to Europeans'.[46] In December, he declared that he had 'no sense of superiority because of a white skin, either to an Indian or to a West Indian. I'm aware of a difference'.[47] He had, as we have seen, fallen in love with India.

In the 1930s, Powell had helped a Jewish professor escape Nazi Germany, and while in India had refused to stay in a club which admitted only white people.[48] Having learnt Urdu while in India, he was able to talk to his Indian constituents in Wolverhampton in that language. There is no evidence that he ever discriminated against non-white people.

Nevertheless, Powell's Birmingham speech undoubtedly inflamed racial tensions. On 24 April, four days after the speech, Josephat Karanja, high commissioner of Kenya, wrote to *The Times*, 'When I drove to Parliament yesterday to hear the debate on the Race Relations Bill, I was shocked and surprised to be shouted at and booed by the assembled throng of dockers. My driver, who is Kenyan, was also shouted at and told to go back to Jamaica!' Twelve days after the speech, *The Times* reported that fourteen white youths chanting 'Powell' and 'Why don't you go back to your own country?' attacked those attending a West Indian christening party in Powell's Wolverhampton. One of the victims was so badly injured that he needed eight stitches over

---

45 Michael Cockerell, 'Odd Man Out: A Film Portrayal of Enoch Powell' [TV documentary], BBC (11 November 1995).

46 Hillman, 'A "chorus of execration"?', 88.

47 'Christianity and Immigration: Enoch Powell Talking to Douglas Brown', *The Listener* (26 December 1968).

48 See the reminiscence by his widow in Lord Howard of Rising (ed.), *Enoch at 100: A Re-evaluation of the life, politics and philosophy of Enoch Powell* (Biteback Publishing, 2012), 309–10.

his left eye. Non-white children, amongst them the young Paul Boateng, later to become a Labour Cabinet minister, reported being harassed at school and being told to 'go home'. Lenny Henry, the comedian, who had been born in Britain to Jamaican parents, later mocked the National Front's offer to Commonwealth immigrants of £1,000 to 'go home', declaring that this would be more than enough to cover his fare home to Dudley. Many years later, in 1996, secret video evidence of the youths who were cleared of the murder of Stephen Lawrence exposed their extreme racist views and desire to kill all immigrants of colour in Britain, with one of the youths declaring, 'I wanna write him a letter saying Enoch Powell mate: you are the greatest ... Get back into Parliament mate and show these [redacted] what it's all about.'[49] So, despite Powell's declaration of equality between different ethnicities, his speech gave rise to much racism.

There was much discussion concerning the identity of the elderly widow who had been harassed. Similar stories had apparently been told about elderly widows in other parts of the country, such as Southall, where there had been a concentration of Commonwealth immigrants. Powell refused to disclose the widow's name, in order to protect the identity of his constituent. This led many to believe that she was an apocryphal figure. However, in 2004, the BBC discovered that the elderly widow had in fact existed – her name was Druscilla Cotterill, and her husband had been killed on active service in the war – though the excreta were placed in another person's letter box, and because of a family feud rather than any racial motive. Indeed, her former West Indian neighbours said that their relations with Cotterill were good. She babysat for them, and they had sent flowers to her funeral. But, in any case, it was of course an appalling mistake in logic to imply that bad behaviour by one group of non-white

---

49 Quoted in McLean, *Rational Choice and British Politics*, 131.

immigrants was somehow typical, any more than bad behaviour by a particular group of white people was in any way typical. There was no reason to believe that one group was more prone to bad behaviour than the other. And it was highly implausible that the 'piccaninnies', if from the Caribbean, were unable to speak English. Powell had lent his authority to quite untypical anecdotes. In a later speech in Eastbourne, Powell went even further by insisting that the experiences of the elderly widow were 'not something rare, not something abnormal, but something which is part of the daily life and experience of fellow countrymen of ours'. But such 'evidence' as he adduced was quite insufficient to justify his sweeping conclusions and would be likely to incite prejudice and intolerance. If that happened, it would make integration less, not more, likely.

It was also absurd to believe that the Race Relations Bill would give 'the black man' the 'whip hand' over white people. Many previous studies, notably one by the think tank Political and Economic Planning in 1967, had discovered widespread discrimination against the non-white population, much of which those discriminated against were unaware of.[50] Indeed, this study, commissioned by Jenkins, formed the rationale for the 1968 Race Relations Bill. This bill made discrimination a civil wrong, but not a criminal offence, and the emphasis was to be on conciliation, not legal proceedings. Only if there were incitement to racial hatred would a criminal offence have been committed – so the elderly widow was in no danger of being imprisoned as a result of the Race Relations Bill. And the bill was in no way discriminatory, since it could be invoked by white people alleging discrimination as well as by non-white people. The fact that it was not so invoked was because it was overwhelmingly non-white people who suffered from discrimination.

---

50 W. W. Daniel, *Racial Discrimination in England* (Penguin, 1968).

Most important of all, perhaps, Powell's predictions that Britain was in danger of communalism, and that the immigrant population would prove a hostile and even violent element, have proved mainly false, although in 2022 there were communalist riots in Leicester – which had hitherto been regarded as a symbol of successful integration – between Hindus and Muslims, and clashes in Camberwell between Ethiopians and Eritreans. Nevertheless, the vast majority of immigrants and their descendants have made vital contributions to British life and, while there have been many blemishes in race relations, integration has on the whole been successful, just as it has been with historical waves of immigration by groups such as Huguenots or Jews. In Britain, after all, allegiance has always been based on territory and a willingness to be represented in the House of Commons rather than on blood, religion, or ethnicity. There is little sign in Britain of the voting habits of ethnic minorities being determined by their ethnicity rather than by their views on national policies. It was absurd to believe that immigrants of colour would vote as a bloc. Remarkably, in the Conservative leadership election contest in 2023, the candidates would include a man with Kenyan and Tanzanian roots, an Iraqi Kurd who had fled Saddam Hussein and was unable to speak English when he arrived in Britain, a Buddhist of Indian origin, and a white man with a Chinese wife and mixed-race children. In contrast, in Germany, Angela Merkel's last Cabinet in 2017 was 100 per cent white! And later, in 2022, Britain was able to celebrate its first Asian prime minister, Rishi Sunak, descended from Kenyan Asians. At the time of writing, two of the four most senior members of the government are people of colour, and both the mayor of London, Sadiq Khan, and the first minister of Scotland, Humza Yousaf, are Muslims. Indeed, Powell's own constituency, Wolverhampton South West, came to be represented by a Sikh Conservative, Paul Uppal, from 2010 to 2015, and then from 2017 to 2019 by a

Labour MP, Eleanor Smith, whose mother had come to Britain from Barbados to work as a nurse.

A number of members of the Shadow Cabinet were outraged by Powell's Birmingham speech and declared that they could never trust him again. Geoffrey Rippon, the only member of the Shadow Cabinet to belong to the right-wing Monday Club, told me some years later that he would never be able to sit in a Cabinet or Shadow Cabinet with Powell again. Some members threatened in 1968 to resign from the Shadow Cabinet were Powell to remain. 'Had I not sacked him,' the party leader, Heath, later wrote, 'the party would not have had a Shadow Cabinet left.' When the protesting shadow ministers saw Heath, they found him, if anything, even more outraged than they were. Heath duly sacked Powell, because he regarded the Birmingham speech as 'racist in tone and liable to exacerbate racial tensions'.[51]

It is not clear whether Powell expected or wanted to be sacked. In his autobiography, Heath quotes a comment which Powell had made before the Birmingham speech, to the effect of 'I deliberately include at least one startling assertion in every speech in order to attract enough attention to give me a power base within the Conservative Party. Provided I keep this going, Ted Heath can never sack me from the Shadow Cabinet.'[52] On this occasion, he miscalculated. After Powell's death, his widow declared that he was 'very surprised ... and he thought what a bloody fool Ted Heath had been'.[53]

It soon became clear that Powell had considerable support in the country, much of it from those who had hitherto supported the Labour Party. Opinion polls taken shortly after the speech showed that between 60 per cent and 75 per cent agreed with him

---

51 Heath, *The Course of My Life*, 293.
52 Ibid., 291.
53 Lord Howard of Rising, *Enoch at 100*, 307.

and disapproved of him being sacked by Heath.[54] Dockers from the East End and porters from Smithfield Market marched in support, astonished and gratified, perhaps, to discover a person of culture and refinement prepared to echo their baser thoughts. Powell received a total of around 450,000 letters from members of the public, the vast majority agreeing with him. Opinion polls showed that he had become the most popular politician in the country, far more popular than Heath, and that a large majority deplored Heath's sacking of him: 'No other insurgent politician in the history of polling in the UK has achieved the popularity scores that Powell did between 1968 and 1974.'[55]

In 1968, an early and unscientific analysis of Powell's postbag showed that few letters were explicitly racist in the sense that they believed non-white people to be inherently inferior; many accepted that those who had already settled in Britain had the same rights as others.[56] Nor was there much support for discrimination. The majority of those who agreed with Powell stressed fears for British culture, while some feared the strain on the social services. There was hardly any support for compulsory repatriation, though some wished to pay immigrants to leave. Many, however, equated Britishness with being white.[57] The letters came from every social class and every part of the country; they did not seem restricted to working-class voters. But many came from the 'unsophisticated'. They confirmed the view of one historian, who wrote in 1968:

... that it was 'a mistake to regard this hostility to the

54 Schoen, *Enoch Powell and the Powellites*, 37.

55 McLean, *Rational Choice and British Politics*, 140.

56 Diana Spearman, 'Enoch Powell's Postbag', *New Society* (9 May 1968), 667 ff; and 'The Anti-Enoch Letters', *New Society* (27 June 1968), 945 ff.

57 Amy Whipple, 'Revisiting the "Rivers of Blood" Controversy: Letters to Enoch Powell', *Journal of British Studies*, 48/3 (July 2009), 719. This article contains a more scientific study of Powell's postbag than the *New Society* articles by Diana Spearman.

immigrant as necessarily "racial" in character, any more than the nineteenth-century anti-Irish feeling was "religious", as it was thought to be at the time. The fact is that heavy immigration is, in the most literal sense, a disturbing phenomenon: and if those who are disturbed are socially very conservative they are likely to react strongly against it.[58]

The most striking theme in the correspondence was a sense of alienation from politics. Many felt that the political system was not working for them. Typical were statements such as 'At last, a man who puts country before party'. Diana Spearman, the Conservative sympathiser who examined the correspondence, concluded, 'The letters reflect the feeling that *they* by their actions have produced problems for *us*, which do not in any way affect *them* and which they are not doing anything to help *us* solve. *Their* idea is to tell us what *we* must and must not do.'[59] These correspondents believed that a multiracial society was being constructed by an elite disconnected from the people, who had never consented to this change and were forced to confront the strains that it involved. Powell's speech, therefore, was the first to raise the issue – later raised in quite different forms by Jenkins, Benn, Joseph, and Farage – of whether the political system was still able to represent popular views or whether it tended to screen out views which did not conform to the current consensus. An American historian declared that many people believed Powell 'was the first British politician who was actually listening to them'.[60]

---

58 Henry Pelling, *Popular Politics and Society in Late Victorian and Edwardian Britain* (Macmillan, 1968), 178.
59 Spearman, 'Enoch Powell's Postbag'.
60 George L. Bernstein, *The Myth of Decline: The Rise of Britain Since 1945* (Pimlico, 2004), 274. The same conclusion is reached in David Butler and Donald Stokes, *Political Change in Britain*, 2nd edn. (Macmillan, 1975), 290–2, 306–8.

By contrast, the comparatively small minority of those opposed to Powell claimed, plausibly, that although he might not have intended the speech to be racist, his inflammatory language would encourage racism. But many of those opposing Powell did not oppose the actual proposals that he put forward. They opposed forced repatriation, but he had not explicitly advocated that. Spearman's conclusion was:

> If the extremists on both wings are excluded, support and opposition are not really so far apart. The supporters, as a whole, do not blame or attack the immigrants; many of the opponents would agree with the policy in the Powell speech, cessation of immigration, promotion of re-emigration and complete integration of immigrants already here.

This comment, however, misses the point that Powell had insisted that such integration, at least with the numbers now coming into Britain, was in fact impossible.[61]

The wider context of the 'rivers of blood' speech was the unpopularity of both major parties and their political leaders. By 1968, Wilson's Labour government seemed to have failed in its bid to regenerate the economy. Many of those who had voted for it in 1964 and 1966 had become disillusioned, a disillusion that had increased with the devaluation of the pound in November 1967, widely seen as an acknowledgement of defeat. The new chancellor, Jenkins, warned the public to be prepared for 'two years of hard slog', and in early 1968 he told the British people that they would be worse off at the end of the year. In May 1968, a Gallup poll found that just 27 per cent approved of Wilson's leadership. But, although the Conservatives were far ahead in the opinion polls – a record 28 per cent ahead,

---

61 Spearman, 'Enoch Powell's Postbag'; and Spearman, 'The Anti-Enoch Letters'.

according to a Gallup poll published in the *Daily Telegraph* in May 1968 – there was little positive enthusiasm for them. The Conservative leader, Heath, was particularly unpopular, being perceived as remote, wooden, and lacking a popular touch. Just 31 per cent approved of him, according to Gallup. British self-confidence appeared to have been undermined, and it seemed natural to seek scapegoats. In Scotland and Wales, there were the first stirrings of support for nationalism – a nationalism which blamed the English. In England, the natural scapegoat was the Commonwealth immigrant.

Powell was more popular than either Wilson or Heath, not only because he had understood popular feeling about immigration, but also because he was not associated in the public mind with an out-of-touch political elite. He was the first post-war exponent of something that we have now become very familiar with – some would say too familiar: populism.

A populist believes that the traditional governing parties of moderate left and moderate right, which claim to oppose each other, in reality embody a consensus, agreeing on the basics. The real debate for the populist is not between left and right, but between the people and the 'elite', the political class which, so populists argue, has its own interests in common, interests which are not those of the people. 'A deep and dangerous gulf in the nation' had opened up, Powell declared in Eastbourne in November 1968, 'the gulf between the overwhelming majority of people throughout the country on the one side, and on the other side a tiny minority, with almost a monopoly hold upon the channels of communication'.[62] The mood engendered by populism has a particular appeal to those who feel ignored, looked down upon, threatened, or humiliated, which explains Powell's appeal

---

62 Speech to the Annual Conference of the Rotary Club, Eastbourne, 16 November 1968, Enoch Powell Speech Archive.

to the working class. Populism also appeals to those who feel unsettled by modern cultural developments, in particular mass immigration and multiculturalism. It appeals to those who feel their identity threatened by the clamour of minorities. Whereas liberals would see members of ethnic minorities as discriminated against, Powell argued that it was the white working class which was discriminated against and whose status was in decline. That, Powell believed, was unfair, since they were the very patriots who had built up the country.

Many of those who wrote to Powell were disturbed by other political developments which they linked to immigration. They were concerned that Britain was less powerful than she had been, that she had lost the empire, that she was unable to stand up for herself by resisting those who made demands on her. They also worried that permissiveness had taken hold of British society, a permissiveness which some linked with the supposedly lower moral standards of immigrants – though Indians from the subcontinent and Asians from East Africa were more likely to adhere to religion than the indigenous British population, and parents from those communities tended to be shocked, rather than attracted, by the supposed permissiveness in British society. Nevertheless, it seemed from the letters that 'immigration was as much a symptom as a cause of social ills and national weakness'.[63] Such correspondents seemed unaware that Powell did not share their diagnosis. He had renounced imperialism many years before and had supported such 'permissive' legislation as the abolition of capital punishment and the reform of laws relating to homosexuality and abortion.

After his sacking by Heath, Powell became even more of an irritant to the Conservative establishment. During the 1970 general election, he embarrassed both parties by emphasising the issue of

---

63 Whipple, 'Revisiting the "Rivers of Blood"', 720.

immigration, at a time when both party leaderships had sought to avoid inflaming opinion by using moderate language and, as far as possible, keeping off the subject. The consensus, however, was first broken not by Powell, but on the left, by Benn. On 2 June 1970, less than three weeks before polling day, Benn spoke of 'the filthy obscene racialist propaganda still being issued under the imprint of Conservative Central Office', and declared that 'Enoch Powell has emerged as the real leader of the Conservative Party'. He went on to say that 'the flag hoisted at Wolverhampton is beginning to look like the one that fluttered over Dachau and Belsen'.[64] Powell's reply was dignified and to the point: 'In 1939, I voluntarily returned from Australia to this country to serve as a private soldier in the war against Germany and Nazism. I am that same man today.'[65] It was, of course, unfair to associate Powell with Nazism, and even Heath had to declare that, although he had 'differences of view' with Powell, the latter's 'patriotism cannot be doubted'.[66] Benn's comment was almost certainly a tactical mistake, since Benn's attack was bound to highlight the fact that Powell was a popular figure, and that hostility to immigration might prove a vote-winner for the Conservatives.

IV

For much of the 1966–70 parliament, the Conservative opposition were ahead in the opinion polls, and from 1968 Powell undoubtedly helped them maintain their lead over Labour. Yet, by 1970, the UK's Balance of Payments was at last in balance, and the economic situation seemed to have improved. Labour began

64 Quoted in David Butler and Michael Pinto-Duschinsky, *The British General Election of 1970* (Macmillan, 1970), 160.
65 Quoted in Butler and Pinto-Duschinsky, *Election of 1970*, 160.
66 Heffer, *Like the Roman*, 557.

to move ahead in the polls, and Wilson called an election for June 1970. At one stage in the campaign, the Conservatives were behind in the polls by as much as 12 per cent. The general expectation was that Labour would be returned to power. Powell's widow admitted in an interview in 2012 that she and he 'most definitely wanted' Heath to lose the election and that would have meant the end of Heath's leadership.[67] However, Powell did not wish to be blamed for defeat, so he had to dispel the feeling that he did not want the Conservatives to win. On 16 June, speaking to his constituents just two days before the election, he appealed to them to 'vote, and vote Tory'. In doing so, he insisted, he had the 'accidental advantage' that Heath had made it clear that Powell would not be included in a Conservative Cabinet. But the election, he went on, was not about himself, nor even was it one between 'a man with a pipe' (Harold Wilson) and 'a man with a boat' (Edward Heath). It was instead 'between two futures for Britain, futures irrevocably, irreversibly different', between a socialist Britain based on state ownership, and one based on free enterprise. 'On Thursday,' he concluded apocalyptically, 'your vote decides whether that freedom survives or not. You dare not entrust it to any government but a Conservative government.'[68]

On 13 June – five days before the election – the cover of *The Economist* had a picture of Wilson and his chancellor, Jenkins, under the title 'Harold Wilson's Britain'. It assumed that Wilson's Labour would be returned to Downing Street. In fact, the Conservatives won with a majority of thirty seats. Most analysts of opinion polls have concluded that there was a late swing against Labour. One explanation for this might be Heath's dogged attack on Labour's assertion that the economy was set fair. This was buttressed by the release of adverse balance-of-payments

---

67 Lord Howard of Rising, *Enoch at 100*, 311.
68 Collings, *Reflections of a Statesman*, 450–453.

figures shortly before election day. The higher-than-average swing to the Conservatives in the Powellite stronghold of the West Midlands was not in itself sufficient to have swung more than just one or two seats to the Conservatives. It was countered by lower-than-average swings to the Conservatives in seats with high immigration concentration, where the assumption must be that most non-white immigrants would have voted Labour. And there is no evidence that Conservative candidates with Powellite views did any better than Conservative candidates who did not share those views.

But there is contrary evidence – though in the nature of things, it cannot be conclusive – that Powell's last-minute intervention may have been decisive in securing the Conservative victory. The issue is not the size of the swing in the West Midlands, nor the relative success of Powellite as opposed to non-Powellite candidates, but whether Powellism – or hostility to immigration – was a strong nationwide issue, swinging votes to the Conservatives across the whole country. There is some evidence that this was indeed the case. In a National Opinion Poll survey held in June and July 1970, shortly after the general election, 60 per cent declared that Powell had influenced the way they voted. Amongst those who had voted or intended to vote Conservative, 47 per cent said that Powell had made them more likely to vote Conservative – less than 10 per cent were negatively influenced. Amongst those who had voted or intended to vote Labour, around 20 per cent said that Powell had made them more likely to vote Conservative. Amongst those who had not voted, 57 per cent declared that Powell had been an influence on their abstention. The political analyst Douglas Schoen concluded, 'The inference is very plain that such non-voters were heavily made up of normally Labour voters cross-pressured into abstention by Powell.'[69] In fact, as

---

69 Schoen, *Enoch Powell and the Powellites*, 57. The National Opinion Poll table is

three psephologists have pointed out, 1970 was 'an exceptional election', since 'cross-class voting ... in the working-class was undoubtedly higher than in the 1960s', and 32 per cent of working-class voters opted for the Conservatives, a record high.[70] It is plausible to assume that a majority of these working-class voters supported the Conservatives because of Powell.

Powell confessed to David Butler shortly after the election that he had been 'very surprised' by the Conservative victory.[71] Whether or not he helped swing the election, the outcome left him seriously wounded, since it 'sealed his exile'.[72] In reality, his chances of leadership were probably never as high as he and his supporters assumed. Even if the Conservatives had been defeated in 1970, he would probably not have won the leadership. He would still have been blamed for dividing the party, and his support in the Commons amounted to little more than a scattering of individual MPs. He totally lacked the organised support of a Bevan, a Benn, a Jenkins – or a Joseph Chamberlain.

It was not long before Powell was quarrelling with the Heath government. That was in large part due to the fact that, in 1972, following the first miners' strike, Heath executed what was to be called a U-turn, in which he abandoned the non-interventionist policies of the 1970 manifesto, moving instead to a policy of industrial intervention and a statutory incomes policy, both of which were anathema to Powell.

---

analysed by Schoen, whose book offers the best psephological analysis of the Powell effect.

70 Anthony Heath, Roger Jowell, and John Curtice, *How Britain Votes* (Pergamon Press, 1985), 34.

71 David Butler Election Archive, 28 July 1970.

72 Cockerell, 'Odd Man Out'.

V

The main policy on which Powell took issue with the Heath government was Europe, which, like immigration, seemed to be an issue polarising 'the people' against the elite. Heath, the most Europhile prime minister Britain has ever had, was determined to ensure Britain's entry into the EC; Powell had become equally determined to prevent it. He was, as Farage was later to put it, 'the first British Eurosceptic'.[73]

Yet Powell's conversion to Euroscepticism had come later than is usually thought. He had admittedly been one of just six Conservative MPs who in 1950 abstained on a motion opposing the Labour government's decision not to join the European Coal and Steel Community, telling his constituency association that he was opposed to 'any pooling of sovereignty with the European countries which would automatically result in severing her from the non-European countries of the Empire'.[74] But he had supported the two failed applications to enter by Macmillan and Wilson in 1961 and 1967, respectively. Indeed, he appears to have been quite an enthusiastic supporter of the Common Market, as the EC was then widely known. In 1965, speaking as shadow defence secretary, he declared, 'Britain is a European power.' In that same year, the One Nation Group, of which Powell was a member, had published a pamphlet entitled *One Europe*, mainly written by Nicholas Ridley, another future Eurosceptic, arguing that 'the party must declare that its policy is to join Europe, by whatever means is best, on returning to power'. As a Shadow Cabinet member, Powell could not himself sign the pamphlet, but he did nothing to indicate that he disagreed with it, and *The*

73 Jason Cowley, 'Nigel Farage: the arsonist in exile', *New Statesman* (8 December 2017).
74 Paul Corthorn, 'Enoch Powell, Julian Amery and debates', 120.

Times believed that he supported it.[75] In April 1965, he gave a radio talk in which he declared, 'The instinctive resistance of the British to anything which would limit their treasured independence and national sovereignty has been much softened. They have become accustomed to the notion that the decisions of international bodies on which Britain is represented but which she does not control might be accepted without abandoning their pride that "Britons never shall be slaves".'[76] In March 1966, on the BBC radio programme *Any Questions*, he was asked about the pros and cons of membership. He replied, 'There aren't any cons provided we can get ourselves into the Common Market.' This would give Britain 'access to a very much greater market than we could otherwise enjoy,' he said.[77] In July 1966, he went even further, telling listeners to the BBC Overseas Service, 'Economically, Britain seems destined to be absorbed into the life of the adjacent mainland, and the very increasing advantages of this may be expected to break down political obstacles on both sides ... There will always be enough that is unique in the situation and characteristics of Britain to ensure that the national identity we so prize is not submerged. Economic integration does not, in itself, imply political integration; but I would expect that continuous collaboration in both the military and economic spheres is bound to be reflected in permanent political institutions.'[78] In November of the same year, he warned the Young Conservatives in Llandudno against reducing British forces in Europe, since that might make it more difficult to secure continental acquiescence to British membership of the EC.[79] I remember a conversation

---

75 '"Join Europe", Line Urged on Tories', *The Times* (8 April 1965); and Heffer, *Like the Roman*, 517.
76 Paul Corthorn, *Enoch Powell* (Oxford University Press, 2019), 106.
77 Heffer, *Like the Roman*, 517.
78 Quoted in David Clarke Shiels, *Enoch Powell and the 'crisis' of the British Nation, c. 1939–71* [PhD thesis] (University of Cambridge, 2022), 148.
79 Heffer, *Like the Roman*, 419.

with Powell in the summer of 1967 at a dinner to which I had been invited, after a debate at the Oxford Union. He told me that it was a sign of the unrealism of the Labour Party that just when the empire had come to be transformed into the Commonwealth – in his view, a meaningless and powerless institution – Labour, having once been anti-imperialist, was now starry-eyed about it. By contrast, it was a sign of the superior realism of the Conservatives, he said, that they appreciated that Britain's future lay with Europe. By the late 1960s, indeed, there was a consensus shared by all three parties that Britain should enter the EC, even though a large number of voters – and perhaps a majority – were opposed to entry. This made Euroscepticism a natural choice for a populist politician seeking to polarise 'the people' against 'the elite'.

The first indication that Powell was adopting a Eurosceptic position came in a speech he made to a Conservative Women's Rally in Clacton in March 1969. In this speech, he reviewed a series of humiliations that Britain had suffered in recent years, beginning with Suez and continuing with the end of her global role, symbolised by withdrawal from Africa and Asia; regular balance-of-payments deficits which had rendered Britain 'persistent borrowers'; and the fact that we were being 'surpassed in wealth and production by our neighbours and rivals'. As might have been expected, he added to the list the high level of Commonwealth immigration, which underlined the fact that Britain, thanks to her imperial past, had no satisfactory definition of British nationality.[80]

It was time now, he continued, to 'stand back, as it were, and take a fresh look at 'Europe and all that' without prejudice or passion, but also with 'no holds barred'. He admitted that he had

---

80 Speech to Conservative Women's Rally, Clacton, 21 March 1969, Enoch Powell Speech Archive.

been 'what is called "a European"', and that he had supported Macmillan's application to join the EC in 1961. As regarded the second application in 1967, he had been 'less sure'. But he 'did not see how Edward Heath and the Tory Party could creditably do other than wish him success'. Now, however, after de Gaulle's second veto, 'the slate is clean: we have carte blanche'. Leaving the application on the table, Wilson's stance after the second veto was 'fast becoming an absurdity and a humiliation'. Powell therefore argued that the application should now be withdrawn.[81]

Britain, Powell went on, had no need 'to be tied up with anybody ... we are not a drowning man clutching at a rope or screaming for someone to throw him a lifebelt'. Britain's main need was for free trade. But the EC was explicitly protectionist, with its common external tariff. Further, the EC was composed of 'a series of complex, bureaucratic institutions not easy to reconcile with our own very different system of administration under parliamentary control'. That bureaucracy, Powell believed – as Margaret Thatcher would come to believe – would make it more difficult to secure free-market policies. There was, it seemed, a contradiction between Europe and the free market. Benn was later to believe that there was a contradiction between Europe and socialism![82]

What Britain really wanted, Powell believed, was a Europe of Nations, as did de Gaulle:

A Europe of Nations, of sovereign nations, is the only Europe to which Britain, so long as she herself remains a nation, could belong; and the instinctive sense that this is so, underlay[s], in my opinion, the hesitations, doubts and opposition which accompanied our first, and only serious, attempt to join the EEC.

---

81 Ibid.
82 Ibid.

He added:

> If by "unity" and "union" [the EC meant] the same as in
> "United Kingdom or 'United States", then such a thing is a
> chimera, which the people of Britain find not so much undesir-
> able as inconceivable.[83]

Powell objected both to the economic and the political implications of membership. Economically, he believed, Britain
would benefit from global free trade and would be harmed by
the EC's common external tariff. But perhaps his most fundamental objection was to the implications for sovereignty. Powell
appreciated, while many others – including senior ministers and
legal academics – did not, that the EC was not just an international organisation based on intergovernmentalism, such as, for
example, the General Agreement on Tariffs and Trade (GATT)
or even the North Atlantic Treaty Organization (NATO), but a
new legal order which would take precedence over British law,
with the British government and British courts being under a
duty to enforce it.[84]

Powell claimed that when he had supported previous applications, he had concentrated upon the economic consequences and
ignored the political implications. But the EC was more than
just a trade organisation, and its economic and political aims
could not be separated. The new French president, elected in
June 1969, Georges Pompidou, was on record as being in favour
of 'a union which ... will be able to have its own policy, its own
independence, its own role in the world'. This would mean that
Britain would be 'giving up for all time the freedom in future to

---

83 Ibid.
84 See Ian Loveland, 'Britain and Europe' in Vernon Bogdanor (ed.), *The British
Constitution in the Twentieth Century* (Oxford University Press, 2003).

take a decision', as Scotland had done when she merged with Great Britain in 1707.[85] In the Commons, Powell insisted:

> The fundamental question which we have to put to ourselves is: can we conceive the people of this country, and, if we can, do we wish to do so, forming an element – a small minority element – in the electorate which would sustain the government and the institutions of this new political entity?

Clearly not.

> In respect of our nationhood, then, I say that we are not a part of the continent of Europe. The whole development and nature of our national identity and consciousness has been not merely separate from that of the countries of the Continent of Europe but actually antithetical; and, with the centuries, so far from growing together, our institutions and outlook have rather grown apart from those of our neighbours on the continent ... We are a people rather oceanic than continental, a people profoundly separated from the continent of Europe in what we are nationally and politically.[86]

In another speech to the Commons, in February 1972, Powell detected four potential consequences of entry into the EC. The first was that 'this House and Parliament will lose their legislative supremacy. It will no longer be true that law in this country is made only by or with the authority of Parliament ... The legislative omni-competence of this House, its legislative sovereignty, has to be given up.'

Secondly, the Commons would lose 'its exclusive control

---

85 Hansard, House of Commons, 21 January 1971, vol. 809, cols. 1370–1372.
86 Ibid. vol. 809, cols. 1375–7.

– upon which its power and authority has been built over the centuries – over taxation and expenditure.' Powell explained:

> In future ... moneys received in taxation from the citizens of this country will be spent otherwise than upon a vote of this House and without the opportunity, necessarily preceding such a vote, to debate grievance and to call for an account of the way in which those moneys are to be spent. For the first time for centuries it will be true to say that the people of this country are not taxed only upon the authority of the House of Commons.

Third, he said, 'the judicial independence of this country' would have to be 'given up':

> In future, if we join the Community, the citizens of this country will not only be subject to laws made elsewhere but the applicability of those law as to them will be adjudicated upon elsewhere; and the law made elsewhere and the adjudication elsewhere will override the law which is made here and the decisions of the courts of this realm.

The fourth consequence Powell detected was 'not manifest' but 'inherent and implicit': 'the progressive strengthening of the Executive as compared with this House, or, to put it the other way, the continuing diminution of the power of this House to influence and control the Executive'.[87] At the time, the only significant common EC policies were the common external tariff, customs union, competition policy, and the common agricultural policy. But clearly future common policies were in train, as the EC had already committed itself to economic and monetary

---

87 Hansard, House of Commons, 17 February 1972, vol. 831, cols. 699–700.

union. As the powers of the EC expanded, so, correspondingly, the powers of Parliament would be diminished.

Moreover, Powell claimed, the people had never consented to entry. The people had not been consulted, and in the 1970 election all three major parties had supported entry, so there had been no way in which a voter opposed to entry could have indicated that opinion through her vote. The second reading of the European Communities Bill in the Commons was carried on the day Powell was speaking, by a majority of just eight. In none of the original six member states of the EC could such major constitutional changes be made by a narrow majority in the legislature. Nevertheless, in January 1973, Britain entered the EC.

In June of that year, however, Powell, in a speech in Shipley, declared that the principle of self-government was more important than party allegiance, and in an interview shortly afterwards, he insisted that he would be prepared to face Labour rule for the rest of his life so long as that party were willing to preserve parliamentary sovereignty.

It did indeed seem for a time that Labour might be relied upon to preserve parliamentary sovereignty. After the 1970 election, Labour, now in opposition, rowed back on its commitment to Europe. Indeed, at one point it seemed as though it were moving towards a position of outright opposition to EC membership, something which would have caused a split in the party. Wilson was only able to prevent this happening by proposing a renegotiation of the entry terms secured by the Heath government. He pledged to put these renegotiated terms to voters, either in an election or in a referendum. Voting Labour at the next general election would therefore give those opposed to membership, such as Powell, a chance – perhaps their only chance for the foreseeable future – to reverse the decision to enter the EC.

The general election, when it came, in February 1974, was brought about not by Europe, but on the issue of the Conservative government's statutory incomes policy. The National Union of Mineworkers had called a strike after the government had rejected its wage demand, which went beyond what was allowed under the statutory incomes policy. Heath went to the country on the cry 'Who Governs?'

Except for the period when Powell was in government from 1960 to 1963 – when Powell was required, if he was to observe the principle of collective responsibility, to implement a statutory incomes policy against the nurses – he had opposed such policies. Powell could also justifiably complain that a statutory incomes policy was directly contrary to a statement in the 1970 Conservative manifesto: 'We utterly reject the philosophy of compulsory wage control.'[88] A government could not, he believed, maintain its authority if it had explicitly repudiated the principles on which it had been elected. At that time, he declared that he did not intend to leave the Conservative Party. He, after all, was standing by the principles in the 1970 Conservative manifesto. It was the leadership that had abandoned them.

In addition, Powell believed that the 'Who Governs?' issue was bogus. The quadrupling of the oil price following the 1973 Yom Kippur War in the Middle East had made coal relatively more valuable than oil, and whoever was returned in the election would have to pay the miners more. Indeed, the Heath government was, before the election, considering how it might increase miners' pay without formally breaking the incomes policy. Powell insisted, on 7 February 1974, in a letter to his constituency chairman just twenty-one days before polling day, that it was 'an act of gross irresponsibility that this general election has been called in the face of the current and impending situation.'[89] He claimed, 'The election will in any case be fraudulent, for the object of

---

88 Conservative Party 1970 manifesto, 'A Better Tomorrow'.
89 BBC: On This Day 7 February 1974, accessed online.

those who called it is to secure the electorate's approval for a position which the Government itself knows to be untenable in order to make it easier to abandon that position subsequently. It is unworthy of British politics and Government to try to steal success by telling the public one thing during an election and doing the opposite afterwards'.[90] Powell therefore indicated that he had decided not to stand as a Conservative candidate. Some suggested that he stand instead as an independent, but he said that made no sense in a parliamentary system of which party was the essence. What, then, was he to do? Which party would he recommend that the voters support?

As we have seen, for Powell, the European issue had become for him fundamental because it would undermine the sovereignty of Parliament. As with home rule in the late nineteenth century, rejection of British membership of the EC was a cause which, for him, transcended party. In the second half of 1973, Powell had warned his election agent that he could not stand again as a Conservative unless the party changed its position on Europe. Then, when the election was called, he said, 'The trigger was pulled and I was there.'[91] On 25 February, just three days before the election, he spoke for the Keep Out movement, declaring that a vote for Labour was the only way to ensure that Britain left the EC. He did not explicitly advise his supporters to vote Labour, although two days later, on the day before the election, he was to declare that he had cast a postal vote for the Labour candidate in his old constituency of Wolverhampton South West. But what he told the Keep Out movement was:

Here is a man who promised his electors in 1970 that he would do everything in his power to prevent British membership;

---

90 *Daily Telegraph* (16 January 1974).
91 David Butler Election Archive, 4 April 1974.

who voted against it in every division, minor or major, which took place in the ensuing Parliament; who did so even when success would have precipitated a dissolution; who allied himself openly on the subject with his political opponents; who made no secret of his belief that its importance over-rode that of all others; and who warned that this was one of those issues on which men will put country before party.

When someone at this meeting shouted out 'Judas', he retorted, 'Judas was paid. I made a sacrifice.'[92]

The February 1974 general election resulted in a Labour minority government. Labour won four more seats than the Conservatives, even though the Conservatives had won more votes. In such a narrow election, any one of a host of factors could have determined the result, and there can be little doubt that Powell's intervention was one such factor. Whereas the average swing to Labour was 1.3 per cent, there was a very large swing of 7.5 per cent to Labour in the West Midlands; in the six constituencies surrounding Wolverhampton, the swing was 10 per cent, and in Powell's former constituency, it was 17 per cent. In most other urban areas, the swing was between 2 per cent and 3 per cent. According to a MORI survey conducted immediately after Powell had announced that he would not be standing as a Conservative candidate, 14 per cent declared that they would be more likely to vote Conservative as a result, while 28 per cent said that they would be less likely to vote Conservative. Of Labour supporters, 28 per cent said that Powell's decision had made them more likely to support Labour, while 13 per cent said that it had made them less likely to do so. Conversely, just 9 per cent of Conservative supporters said that Powell's withdrawal had made them more likely to vote Conservative, while 25 per

---

92 'Here is a Man' speech, Shipley, 25 February 1974, Enoch Powell Speech Archive.

cent said that it had made them less likely.[93] It is very plausible that, had Powell not declared the election to be fraudulent and had he not declared that the European issue overrode all others, and that it dictated a Labour vote as the only chance for Britain to leave the EC, the Conservatives might have won the election. There is therefore some support for the statement that Powell was to make in 1995 about his great enemy, Heath: 'I put him in [in 1970] and I took him out [in February 1974].'[94]

At a second election, in October 1974, Labour was returned with a narrow majority of three. Powell again recommended a vote for Labour, since the alternative, a Conservative government, would deny voters the chance of a referendum on Europe. At the October election, he was returned not as a Conservative, but as an Ulster Unionist MP for the Northern Ireland constituency of South Down, a seat which he was to hold until 1987. Ian Paisley, the fundamentalist preacher and Democratic Unionist Party MP for North Antrim, mischievously characterised Powell as the Wolverhampton Wanderer. He was 'the only Cabinet-ranking politician in the era of the Troubles who became directly involved in the local politics of the province'.[95] He argued against devolution and against any accommodation with the Irish Republic, even though devolution in Northern Ireland, by contrast with Scotland or Wales, was sought not on separatist grounds but on precisely the opposite – to express the unionism of the majority. Northern Ireland, Powell insisted, should be ruled directly from Westminster, just like any other part of the UK.[96] However, as a member of a small minority

93 Schoen, *Enoch Powell and the Powellites*, 152. Schoen provides much further evidence of the Powell effect in February 1974.

94 Cockerell, 'Odd Man Out'.

95 Henry McDonald, 'Ian Paisley: from Northern Ireland Ayatollah to Chuckle Brother', *Guardian* (12 September 2014).

96 David Clarke Shiels, 'Enoch Powell, British nationality and the Irish question, 1968–1987' in Esteves and Porion, *The Lives and Afterlives*, 97.

party in Northern Ireland, he became an increasingly isolated and lonely figure at Westminster.

Powell's hope that Britain would leave the EC was to be unfulfilled during his lifetime. Labour did indeed renegotiate the terms of British entry, but the renegotiation was of a cosmetic kind and far less fundamental than Eurosceptics had hoped. When the outcome of the renegotiation was put to voters in Britain's first national referendum in 1975, continued membership of the EC was endorsed by a two-to-one majority. The general view was that the debate about membership had now ended. But Powell presciently pointed out that what he accepted as a 'provisional' result could always be reopened, for a sovereign parliament could always choose to regain its sovereignty – as indeed it was to do after the Brexit referendum in 2016.[97] Indeed, in a speech in February 1975, he declared that the only purpose of the referendum to be held later that year would be to decide whether Britain would leave the European Community now or later![98] 'The Referendum, therefore', he added, 'was not a "verdict" after which the prisoner is hanged forthwith'.[99]

VI

Opposed to devolution for Northern Ireland, Powell believed that Northern Ireland should be fully integrated into the UK. And he widened his hostility to devolution by opposing Labour's proposals in the 1974–9 Parliament for devolution in Scotland and Wales. This opposition to devolution was, like his hostility to the EC, based on his view that it would undermine parliamentary

---

97 *Daily Telegraph* (9 June 1975).
98 Martin Walker, 'Oracle Enoch said it all in his greatest speech', *Guardian* (31 May 1975).
99 *Daily Telegraph* (9 June 1975).

sovereignty. Formally, of course, devolution, by contrast with federalism, would not undermine sovereignty. Westminster would
remain supreme. It could at any time still legislate for Scotland
and Wales, even over matters within the purview of the devolved
bodies, as it was to do after Brexit in 2016, when it passed the
Internal Market Act 2020, withdrawing parts of agriculture and
other devolved services from the purview of the devolved parliaments. Westminster also retained the legal power to abolish a
devolved body by a simple Act of Parliament, as it had done with
the unionist-dominated Northern Ireland Parliament in 1972. In
practice, however, so Powell insisted, Westminster's rule over
Scotland and Wales would no longer correspond to real political
authority. So, the sovereignty of Parliament would bear a different meaning in relation to Scotland and Wales from its meaning
in relation to England. Indeed, Westminster would become a
quasi-federal Parliament for Scotland and Wales.

Powell insisted, however, that such a solution would prove
unstable, indeed that there was no middle way between the
unitary state and separation, apart from federalism – which
was, he believed, unsuited to British conditions, since in England
there were no provinces and little regional feeling. Devolution
would not conciliate nationalists, who sought independence,
while, being asymmetrical, it would alienate England, since it
would give rise to what came to be called the West Lothian question. This was named after Tam Dalyell, a Scottish Labour MP
hostile to devolution, who from 1962 to 1983 represented the
constituency of West Lothian. But, in fact, the question owed
more to Powell than it did to Dalyell.

The West Lothian question asks whether it is right that an MP
representing a Scottish constituency, such as West Lothian, should
be able to vote at Westminster on English domestic legislation,
such as, for example, education and health, after education and
health had been devolved to Scotland – while an MP representing

an English constituency, such as West Bromwich, would not be able to vote on Scottish legislation on education and health. After devolution, Westminster bills on such matters as education and health would be in effect English bills, yet Scottish MPs would still be entitled to vote upon them. The question would be asked with considerable insistence when, as in 1964 or 1974, the government – Labour in both cases – were to be dependent upon MPs from Scottish constituencies. The strains caused by the anomaly to which the West Lothian question drew attention would, in Powell's view, prove a constant cause of instability, which would lead eventually to separation. Indeed, the nationalist parties in Scotland and Wales supported devolution precisely because they hoped and believed that it would in fact lead to separation.

Although Powell did not succeed in preventing Labour's devolution proposals from reaching the statute book, devolution did not come into effect in the 1970s. It was rejected in Wales in a referendum by four to one; in Scotland, although it secured a narrow majority in a referendum, this fell far short of the threshold set by Parliament of 40 per cent of the electorate voting for it. Powell's arguments, however, had considerable influence on Margaret Thatcher, confirming her view that devolution would be a mistake. During their long period in government under Margaret Thatcher and John Major, from 1979 to 1997, the Conservatives remained resolutely hostile to it. But in 1997, Blair's Labour Party, which was committed to devolution, was returned to power. When he heard the result, Powell said to his wife, 'They have voted to break up the United Kingdom.'[100] The Blair government duly enacted devolution legislation for Scotland, Wales, and Northern Ireland, after pre-legislative referendums in Scotland and Wales and a post-legislative referendum in Northern Ireland confirmed that it now had popular support.

---

100 Heffer, *Like the Roman*, 950.

Labour had favoured devolution to contain nationalism and, in particular, to prevent Scotland becoming independent, as Ireland had done in 1922. In 1995, Labour's shadow secretary of state for Scotland, George Robertson, predicted that devolution would 'kill nationalism stone dead'.[101] The 1997 Labour Party manifesto declared that, with devolution, 'The Union will be strengthened and the threat of separatism removed'.[102] In Scotland, that has certainly not happened. Since 2007, the Scottish National Party (SNP) has been the largest party in the Scottish Parliament, and, despite proportional representation, it was able to win an overall majority in the 2011 Holyrood election. In consequence, the prime minister at the time, David Cameron, felt impelled to offer a referendum on independence. This was duly held in 2014, and independence was defeated by 55 per cent to 45 per cent. But Brexit, which Scotland voted against, has led to pressure for a second referendum – which, so far, British governments have been able to resist. So, on the question of whether devolution will or will not lead to separation, the jury is still out.

VII

Powell did not live to see the establishment of the devolved bodies when Blair became prime minister. He had for some years been suffering from Parkinson's disease, and he died in 1998. Nor, of course, did he live to see the Brexit referendum of 2016 and the fulfilment of his prophecy that the British people would not permanently agree to surrender their legislative and tax-raising powers to Europe.

---

101 Quoted, for example, in Gianfranco Baldini, 'Devolution and Scottish Politics Ten Years On', *Government and Opposition*, 48/1 (2013), 128.
102 Labour 1997 manifesto, 'New Labour Because Britain Deserves Better'.

The unifying thread to Powell's political career lay in his conception of nationhood. The title of one of his books of speeches, *A Nation or No Nation?*, summed up his central concern. He believed that Britain's nationhood was threatened by large-scale immigration, by devolution, by the weakening of the Union with Northern Ireland, and, above all, by membership of the EC.

He believed that Britons' understanding of their nationhood was distorted by the experience of empire, which, so he believed, had been but a moment in British history – a significant moment, no doubt, but one that was now over. The memory of empire, and the assumption that it could be replaced by a multiracial Commonwealth comprising numerous republics, stood in the way of a realistic appraisal of the real policy options open to Britain, which was in the process of becoming a nation like any other, with its own particular history, traditions, and ideas – most notably the sovereignty of Parliament. That dynamic had profound consequences, not only for the constitution but also for immigration. In 1981, Margaret Thatcher's government recognised reality by enacting a new British Nationality Act, which finally broke the legal links between Britain and her former colonies, creating, as Powell had always wanted, a specifically British citizenship. But his views on Commonwealth immigration have continued to embarrass Conservative leaders even into the current century. In 2007, for example, Nigel Hastilow, the Conservative candidate for Halesowen and Rowley Regis, was forced to stand down after declaring, 'When you ask most people in the Black Country what the single biggest problem facing the country is, most say immigration. Many insist: "Enoch Powell was right".'[103] Powell has remained a disturbing figure even from beyond the grave. Ironically, the main

---

103 David Hencke, 'Tory candidate quits after race row', *Guardian* (4 November 2007).

effect of Powell's inflammatory speeches on immigration has been to inhibit liberals from having a more rational discussion of immigration without being accused of racism. It has also prevented discussion of the problems which might have arisen from the religious and cultural differences of immigrants, for fear of giving credence to Powell. It also, so the journalist and former Conservative minister William Deedes wrote in 2001, 'created a phobia in influential quarters about establishing facts on race, lest the facts be exploited by Powell's supporters'. Powell's legacy, Deedes wrote, 'made it impossible for us to tackle the immigration problem.'[104] A contemporary commentator, David Goodhart, agrees: 'Just when a discussion should have been starting about integration, racial justice, and distinguishing the reasonable from the racist complaints of the white people whose communities were being transformed, he polarised the argument and closed it down.' In consequence, Powell's rhetoric 'put back by more than a generation a robust debate about the successes and failures of immigration'.[105] In 2016, Trevor Phillips, founding chair of the Equality and Human Rights Commission and a former politician of Caribbean ancestry, spoke of 'liberal self-delusion' on matters of race, and a failure to recognise 'the dark side of the diverse society'. He accused 'many Muslims' of being 'resistant to the traditional process of integration'.[106]

A main cause of Brexit, however, was indeed resentment at the high rate of immigration, although in this case it was directed at white European immigrants, not people of colour migrating from the Commonwealth. Powell, nevertheless, can claim to have exerted a deep influence on the debate on Europe.

Were it not for Europe, however, Powell might be dismissed as

---

104 William Deedes, 'The real trouble with Enoch', *The Spectator* (18 August 2001).
105 David Goodhart, *The British Dream: Successes and Failures of Post-War Immigration* (Atlantic Books, 2013), 144.
106 Trevor Phillips, *Race and Faith: The Deafening Silence* (Civitas, 2016).

a clever man who achieved little. He lacked the first quality of a constructive politician: the ability to win the support of colleagues. His insistence on arguing from first principles repelled many of his colleagues, so that, despite his extraordinary gifts, he achieved less than other politicians with far fewer gifts than he, and he alienated politicians whose habits of thought were slower, splitting his party in the process. In consequence, his political career is relatively barren of achievement, and there is no major legislation which lies to his credit.

Powell, however, argued that the role of the politician was to articulate the otherwise inarticulate feelings and attitudes of the wider population. For a time between 1968 and 1974, he succeeded in doing that, creating a wide coalition of opinion which cut across class, mobilising his supporters in two general elections, though in opposite directions – to the Conservatives' advantage in 1970, and to Labour's in February 1974.

Powell's support of the free market helped to legitimise what had hitherto been unpopular policies. After his death, Margaret Thatcher confirmed that the 'contents' of the economic policies which she and Joseph had advocated 'owed so much to Enoch's own thankless advocacy in earlier years'. 'Powellism,' she continued, 'lived on in the Conservative Party,' even after he abandoned it in 1974, 'and, with a number of subtractions and additions, helped generate Thatcherism.'[107] Powell was, with Benn, the first politician to comprehend the rising popular disillusionment and alienation of the 1960s. But, unlike Benn, he believed that this alienation was pushing voters to the right, not the left, and towards greater national rather than class cohesion.

Powell is often thought of as a great parliamentarian. But many of his major speeches after 1964 were made outside Parliament,

---

107 Margaret Thatcher, 'When Powell was right', *Daily Telegraph* (23 November 1998).

to friendly Conservative audiences, in contexts where he could not be heckled or criticised and where he would not be followed by other MPs sceptical of his arguments and conclusions. He was, in fact, much less popular in Parliament than in the country. His colleagues neither liked nor trusted him – first, because of his intellect, which he deployed aggressively and forcefully, rather than with a gentle touch; and second, because they did not wish to follow what seemed his obsessive logic, which led to positions they did not wish to advocate. Most of his colleagues in the Conservative Shadow Cabinet, meanwhile, felt that he had deceived them in 1968. It was indeed the very speeches that made him a celebrity in the country which made him disliked and distrusted by his parliamentary colleagues.

Powell made no attempt to build up an organised body of supporters, either inside or outside Parliament, and there was never to be a real Powellite faction as there had been Bevanites, Jenkinsites, and Bennites. His natural constituency on the Conservative right sat uneasily with some of his other policy views – he was, for example, a supporter of homosexual-law reform and against capital punishment; he was hostile to the presence of British forces east of Suez; and he was far less sympathetic to the US and the NATO alliance than most other Conservatives. In addition, the Conservative Party, unlike Labour, was not then a party of factions, but of individualists. There was no real Conservative right-wing faction. The free-market right by no means coincided with the pro-capital-punishment right, the authoritarian right, or the right which believed Britain should remain east of Suez.

Powell was often compared to Joseph Chamberlain, whose biography he was to publish in 1977. Chamberlain, however, had, with the exception of home rule, concentrated on social and economic issues. His prime concern was with improving the condition of the deprived, and rescuing Britain from economic decline. He was essentially a bread-and-butter man. Powell, on the other hand, was preoccupied mainly with constitutional issues. Unlike Powell, Chamberlain proved to have a genius for organisation, both as mayor of Birmingham, as a Liberal Union-ist, and as a Tariff Reformer; he had built up a powerful basis of support – not only in the country – which acted as a battering ram, both on MPs and also on the party leadership, which came to be converted to his views on tariff reform.

Like the other politicians discussed in this book, Powell sought to break a consensus. He succeeded in doing so on the issue of Europe, setting up the key arguments later used by the Euro-sceptics – that Britain's interests lay in free trade, not a customs union; that membership of the EC would mean uncontrolled immigration; that the bureaucratic institutions of the EC did not fit with the British system of government; and, above all, that the loss of parliamentary sovereignty meant the loss of control – in short, that Britain was a different sort of country from those of the continent. From this point of view, he altered Britain. On immigration, however, his impact was perverse. He made it more difficult, not less, for immigration to be controlled, since pro-posals for control would be marked by the taint of racism. In consequence, governments were slow and ineffectual in dealing with what was a genuine problem.

Powell's speeches on immigration, however, helped to facili-tate the dissolution of class ties, already beginning to dissolve in the Britain of the 1960s, but at a glacially slow pace. Immigration was an issue which made the glacier melt more rapidly. There is, as we have seen, good reason to believe that the general election of 1970 turned as much on immigration and other issues empha-sised by Powell as on traditional class issues. Later, Europe was to dissolve class ties even further since the Eurosceptic and Brexit cause was to attract many working-class voters to the Conserva-tive Party. In the 1980s, the SDP hoped to 'break the mould' of

British politics.[108] But the mould had already been broken, not by the SDP, but by Powell, later by Keith Joseph and Margaret Thatcher. The dissolution of class ties which had sustained tribal voting is one of Enoch Powell's legacies in British politics.

But although Powell transformed British politics, it did not help him secure power. His strength lay in the country, not in Parliament, so his only chance of power would have been to use that strength as a battering ram and impose himself on government and Parliament. That, however, is a very difficult thing to do in a parliamentary system, a system which reflects, perhaps, the stolid habits of the British people. 'You have taken upon yourself,' Benjamin Disraeli, one of Powell's heroes, had told one of the early socialists, 'a very – heavy work – indeed ... It is a very difficult country to move ... a very difficult country indeed, and one in which there is more disappointment to be looked for than success.'[109] Powell was to find the same.

108 'The new party's programme includes a demand for electoral reform and a commitment to "breaking the mould"'. *Guardian* (27 March 1981).
109 H. M. Hyndman, *The Record of an Adventurous Life* (Macmillan, 1911), 224.

3

Roy Jenkins and Social Democracy

I

Roy Jenkins (1920–2003) was on the right of the Labour Party, Bevan on the left – yet their backgrounds were curiously similar. Both were the sons of Welsh miners, although Bevan came from a large family, whilst Jenkins was an only child. Like Bevan, Jenkins was born in the valleys, in Abersychan, just 20 km from Tredegar, where Bevan was born. Later in life, however, many did not realise that Jenkins hailed from Wales, since all traces of Welshness had gone from his accent, which seemed to some just a little affected and assumed for the purposes of social as well as political advancement. When at university he was asked where he came from, it is said that he replied, 'The Marches.'[1] He also developed what seemed to some a slightly affected drawl, accentuated by his being unable to pronounce his Rs properly. He entirely lost any Welsh accent that he might once have possessed. In the 1950s, someone suggested to Bevan that Jenkins was not really very ambitions. 'Not ambitious?' Bevan replied. 'Anyone who comes from South Wales and learns to speak like that must be very ambitious.'[2]

---

1 Alan Watkins, 'Backbencher' in Andrew Adonis and Keith Thomas (eds.), *Roy Jenkins: A Retrospective* (Oxford University Press, 2004), 35.
2 Patrick Maguire, 'The history boy: can Nick Thomas-Symonds reunite Labour and nation?', *New Statesman* (1 May 2020).

Jenkins was born in 1920. His father, like Bevan's father and indeed Bevan himself, had gone down the mines immediately on leaving school. But Arthur Jenkins's career was to prove very different from that of Bevan's father. He was to become a salaried trade-union official in the South Wales Miners' Federation, eventually reaching the position of vice president. In 1908 he won a scholarship to Ruskin College, Oxford, and from there he went on to the Central Labour College in London. He then spent some time at the Sorbonne in further study. Returning to South Wales, he rose steadily in his union and became, like Bevan, a councillor – in 1918 a district councillor, and a year later a county councillor. He was eventually to become an alderman and chair of the council, and as early as 1925 a member of Labour's National Executive Committee as a trade-union representative. But the most striking episode of Arthur's life came during the General Strike of 1926, during which he acted as a picket in support of the miners' strike. While he was picketing, there was an affray. He was convicted of illicit assembly and sentenced to nine months' imprisonment, although in the event he served just three months.

A left-winger in the Labour Party would have made much of such a pedigree. One Labour MP told a journalist, 'If my father had been a Welsh miner who'd gone to prison, you wouldn't have heard the end of it.'[3] But neither Arthur nor Roy Jenkins ever spoke of it. In Roy's case, that was partly out of fastidiousness. He would have hated the idea of using his origins for purposes of political advancement. But there was another, far more important, reason: far from being proud of his arrest, Arthur was ashamed of it. An old-fashioned trade unionist on the moderate wing of the Labour Party, he was, like the founders of the party, deeply law-abiding, insisting that trade unionists, like everyone

---

3 Alan Watkins, *Brief Lives* (Hamish Hamilton, 1982), 91.

else, must be subject to the law. Indeed, Arthur's ambition was to become a justice of the peace – as both he and his wife eventually did. Arthur's wife, Roy's mother, was if anything even more respectable, and she told her son that his father had been absent inspecting German coal mines. Besides, Arthur insisted that he was quite innocent. Although he had been organising a picket, he had sought to pacify the men, not to incite them, in accordance with his law-abiding nature. So, while those on the left might have praised him for organising a riot and confronting the police, Arthur would have found such behaviour abhorrent. He claimed that he had been set up by the police, and it is now generally accepted that the police fabricated evidence against him.[4]

The paradoxical effect of Arthur's arrest was to make him even more respectable and establishment-minded than he had been before – indeed, he was, if anything, to the right of his son. The effect on Roy was to instil in him a scepticism of criminal convictions based entirely on police evidence, a scepticism that remained with him when he became home secretary, at a time when the idea that not all police officers were models of probity was thought to be somewhat heretical. 'But such scepticism,' Roy insisted, 'is in my view no bad thing for a home secretary.'[5]

Meanwhile, Arthur's career was advancing. In 1935, he was elected as a Labour MP for the safe seat of Pontypool, and in 1937 he became parliamentary private secretary to Attlee, the party leader, receiving minor ministerial posts in the wartime coalition and the post-war Labour government. He would probably have achieved Cabinet rank, had ill health not forced his retirement in October 1945. He died shortly after, in April 1946. He was, therefore, a member of Labour's establishment, and his

---

4 Roy Jenkins, *A Life at the* Centre (Macmillan, 1991), 18.
5 Ibid.

close links with Attlee proved helpful to Roy when he came to write his first book, an 'interim biography' of Attlee, published in 1948. So, despite a superficial similarity to Bevan, Jenkins came from a quite different background. He was an insider in the Labour movement, Bevan an outsider.

Arthur Jenkins was also rather better off than Nye Bevan's father. Indeed, the Jenkins family owned a car and lived in a detached house with a live-in maid. Unlike Bevan, Roy did not leave school at thirteen, and Arthur Jenkins, unlike Bevan's father, was able to pay for his son to go to university. After Roy completed a year at the College of South Wales and Monmouth-shire, Arthur paid for him to go to Balliol College, Oxford, at that time intellectually the most prestigious college in the university. At Oxford, Roy first displayed characteristics which he was to display all his life – in particular his ability to work hard and so organise his life that he was also able to enjoy social activities. He secured a first-class degree in philosophy, politics and economics at a time when this success was more difficult to achieve than it is today. He claims in his autobiography that his first made no difference to his life, but it must surely have strengthened his self-confidence. He also played an active role in the Oxford Union, though he twice failed to secure the presidency, and in the Oxford University Labour Club, dominated at the time by the left wing and led by Denis Healey – later his Cabinet colleague and leadership rival – and the novelist Iris Murdoch. The club followed the Communist Party line in opposing the British declaration of war in 1939, regarding it as an imperialist conflict. Jenkins's response, with another later Cabinet colleague, leadership rival, and close friend, Anthony Crosland, was to form a breakaway Democratic Socialist Club, in a premonition perhaps of the Social Democratic Party (SDP) breakaway in 1981 under Jenkins's leadership.

In a 1948 by-election, Jenkins became the youngest MP in

the Commons when he won Southwark Central, a constituency due to disappear in boundary changes before the next general election. But in 1950 he secured the safe seat of Birmingham Stechford, which he represented until 1976, even though his feelings for Birmingham fell well short of idolatry. He once asked an acquaintance as the train drew out from Birmingham to London, 'Don't you always feel an enormous sense of relief at this point?'[6]

Once in the Commons, Jenkins showed himself to be an incisive and powerful debater, rapidly establishing his reputation as a parliamentarian. He began as a radical, advocating 'a large-scale capital levy', the abolition of public schools, and workers' control in the nationalised industries, as well as tax rates on higher incomes of 95 per cent.[7] But, after a brief flirtation with the left, he aligned himself firmly with the Labour right, in particular with Gaitskell, who became a close friend. This friendship was to endure even though they were later to find themselves on opposite sides in the debate on Britain's relationship with the EC. In his autobiography, Jenkins declares, 'I admired and indeed loved him more than anyone else with whom I have ever worked in politics.' When unexpectedly asked on *Desert Island Discs* who was his political hero, Jenkins unhesitatingly answered, 'Hugh Gaitskell.'[8]

After the defeat of the Labour government in the 1951 election, Gaitskell, who had been chancellor of the Exchequer, was coming to the view that further nationalisation should no longer be at the centre of Labour's programme, a view which was to receive theoretical endorsement in Crosland's book *The Future of Socialism*, published in 1956, the year after Labour's second electoral defeat in 1955. Instead of nationalisation, so Crosland

---

6 Watkins, 'Backbencher', 41.
7 Campbell, *Nye Bevan*, 124, 127.
8 Jenkins, *A Life at the Centre*, 109.

believed, Labour's central aim should be the pursuit of equality, to be achieved largely by fiscal means – through redistributive taxation – and by educational reform, in particular the establishment of comprehensive schools. Jenkins agreed with this assessment, and in a contribution to the 1952 essay collection *New Fabian Essays* entitled 'Equality', he argued the egalitarian case. But by 1967 he had come to believe that redistribution had its limits. Indeed, he said:

> Its effects could not possibly be large enough either to make a real impact on the position of the lower paid or to finance a big advance in the social services. The haul ... just would not be big enough ... Savage increases in direct taxation would be ... a blind alley.[9]

He was already beginning to move away even from the moderate and revisionist socialism of Gaitskell and Crosland.

But Jenkins's liberalism was to be permanent. He first showed his commitment by sponsoring, and steering into law in 1959, a private members' bill, the Obscene Publications Bill, which provided for a defence of 'the public good' if a work could be shown to be 'in the interests of science, literature, art or learning, or of other objects of general concern'. This meant, in particular, a defence of literary merit could be weighed against any alleged obscenity. It was to be used successfully by the defence in 1960 when a jury allowed the publication of the unexpurgated version of D. H. Lawrence's last novel, *Lady Chatterley's Lover*. At the same time, Jenkins continued with his work as a writer, following up his biography of Attlee with a book on the House of Lords crisis of 1909–11 entitled *Mr Balfour's Poodle*. The title refers to a quip by Lloyd George, chancellor of the Exchequer at the time.

---

9 Quoted in Roy Jenkins, *Essays and Speeches* (Collins, 1967), 285–6.

The House of Lords, he had said, was not the watchdog of the constitution, but Mr Balfour's poodle, Arthur Balfour being the leader of the Conservative Party at the time. However, several booksellers misunderstood the allusion and shelved the book in the section on pets![10] Jenkins also published two biographies, one on the Liberal politician Charles Dilke, published in 1959, the other on the Liberal prime minister H. H. Asquith, published in 1964 at the end of the long period of Conservative rule. Working on the latter biography brought Jenkins in touch with the descendants of Asquith, who had remained Liberals, and this perhaps led him gradually to believe that the replacement of the Liberals by Labour as the main party of the left had not been an unmixed blessing. He was later to hanker after a new progressive alliance of the type that had existed before 1914, when the Liberals and Labour cooperated, in consequence securing a hegemony of the left. In contrast, the years after 1918, when the progressive alliance had been sundered and Labour and the Liberals had opposed each other, had been years of Conservative dominance.

Gaitskell, Jenkins's friend and hero, became leader of the Labour Party after its second electoral defeat in 1955, and Jenkins could assume that he would be given high office in a Gaitskell administration. But Labour was to lose the 1959 election, and in 1960 Jenkins asked not to be reappointed to Labour's front bench so that he could campaign for British membership of the Common Market, as the EU was then known. When Gaitskell came out in opposition to British entry at the Labour Party conference of 1962, their friendship was temporarily strained, but it survived. However, just three months after the conference, in January 1963, Gaitskell died prematurely, aged just fifty-six. His successor, Wilson, had been an opponent of Gaitskell's, standing against him for the leadership in 1960. With Gaitskell gone,

---

10 Watkins, 'Backbencher', 44.

Jenkins toyed briefly with the idea of leaving politics and becoming editor of *The Economist*. But he decided to plough on and was rewarded by becoming minister of aviation, albeit outside the Cabinet, when Wilson became prime minister in 1964. It is perhaps a paradox that Jenkins had split from his hero, Gaitskell, on a major political issue in the last months of Gaitskell's life, and that it was Wilson, with whom 'there was neither friendship nor trust', who gave Jenkins his opportunity.[11] Wilson was in fact remarkably forgiving of those who had been on the other side to him in the Labour Party's internecine disputes – one reason, perhaps, why he was able to retain the leadership for so long – and Jenkins soon joined the Cabinet in 1965 as home secretary – the youngest, at forty-four, since Churchill in 1910. Jenkins was to prove the most successful home secretary of the twentieth century. Then, in 1967, he became chancellor of the Exchequer, with the task of saving Wilson's government after the trauma of the 1967 devaluation of sterling.

II

In 1959, shortly before the general election, Jenkins had written a short book entitled *The Labour Case,* in which he set out Labour's stall. In it, he declared that Britain was suffering from imperial overstretch and that its sterling-area commitments should be phased out – something which, as chancellor, he would succeed in achieving. But empire should not be replaced with isolation, he argued. Instead, Britain should commit herself to the new development on the Continent, the EC.

In the last chapter of the book, entitled 'Is Britain civilised?', he discussed subjects 'which are normally regarded as outside

---

11 Jenkins, *A Life at the Centre*, 149.

the scope of party politics', but which were, in his view, 'at least as important as many of the matters which are regularly chewed over by party propagandists'. He set out what he called an 'unauthorised programme' – since it was not at the time official Labour Party policy – of Home Office reform, arguing that the state should do 'less to restrict personal freedom'. Socialism, he argued, should be about increasing individual choice as well as reducing inequalities.[12]

Here were the two themes of a liberalised social democracy, which Jenkins was the first leading politician to appreciate – a Britain in which individuals could regulate their personal lives without interference from the state, and a Britain which exerted influence in the world by committing herself to Europe.

Jenkins's long Home Office agenda in *The Labour Case* began with the abolition of capital punishment, 'the ghastly apparatus of the gallows', but this had already been achieved by the time Jenkins arrived at the Home Office.[13] His predecessor, Frank Soskice, was the first home secretary not to preside over any hangings.[14] Jenkins followed the abolition of capital punishment with further wide-ranging penal reforms in the Criminal Justice Act in 1967, which ended corporal punishment in prisons. He sought to reduce the numbers given custodial sentences, calling for a greater use of bail and more suspended sentences. He also introduced majority verdicts for juries.

The other reforms on Jenkins's list in *The Labour Case* included the legalisation of homosexuality, the abolition of the lord chamberlain's power to censor plays, reform of licensing and betting laws, and reform of 'harsh and archaic abortion laws'.[15] The major reforms which Jenkins advocated were introduced

---

12 Roy Jenkins, *The Labour Case* (Penguin, 1959), 134.

13 Ibid., 136.

14 Jenkins, *A Life at the Centre*, 180.

15 Ibid., 181.

through private members' bills rather than government-sponsored legislation. The government was in theory neutral on these initiatives, treating them as matters of conscience, for division of opinion on the reforms cut across party lines, and the Cabinet was itself divided. In particular, working-class opinion in the Labour Party appeared more sceptical of reform than its middle-class counterpart. Nevertheless, the government ensured that time was made available to pass the legislation, so that it avoided the normal fate of private members' bills, which were – and are – generally consigned to oblivion. It was also agreed that while there would be a free vote in the Cabinet on the reforms, Jenkins would be allowed to speak in favour of them from the government front bench, giving them all the authority of a home secretary. This proactive attitude was largely the result of pressure from Jenkins, since Prime Minister Wilson took a more conservative view and was sceptical of, if not downright indifferent to, some of the reforms. Indeed, in 1961 he had warned that legalising homosexuality and prostitution would cost Labour six million votes.[16]

'The law relating to homosexuality remains in the brutal and unfair state in which the House of Commons almost accidentally placed it in 1885,' Jenkins had declared in *The Labour Case*.[17] The law applied only to gay men; lesbians were not specifically targeted. It used to be held that this was because, when legislation criminalising homosexuality was passed in 1885, Queen Victoria refused to believe that women were capable of homosexual activity, but that appears to be a myth. In 1957, the Wolfenden Committee had advocated reform, but no action had

---

16 Andrew Holden, *Makers and Manners: Politics and Morality in Postwar Britain* (Politico's, 2004), 118. Richard Crossman, *The Diaries of a Cabinet Minister, Volume 3: Secretary of State for Social Services, 1968–70* (Hamish Hamilton and Jonathan Cape, 1970), 57.
17 Jenkins, *The Labour Case*, 136.

been taken. In July 1966, however, a Labour back-bench MP, Leo Abse, introduced a bill removing the taint of criminality from homosexual activities between adults undertaken in private. The bill was introduced under the 'ten-minute rule' allowing back-benchers to introduce a bill provided that in making the case, they took no longer than ten minutes. Such bills normally proceed no further, but in this case the government agreed to provide time to debate the bill.[18] Later, it seemed stuck at report stage due to the length of speeches given by determined opponents of the reform. But the government agreed to provide extra time. According to the political writer Peter G. Richards, 'had the home secretary, Roy Jenkins, not been strongly favourable to reform, the Bill would probably have failed at this point'.[19] As it was, the bill received royal assent in July 1967.[20] Typically, Jenkins celebrated by 'recuperating at a pre-luncheon American Embassy Independence Day party followed by an afternoon at Wimbledon'.[21]

Reform of abortion law came about through a private members' bill introduced in 1966 by David Steel, then a young back-bench Liberal MP aged just twenty-eight, and later to become leader of his party. Jenkins, although declaring that the government had a neutral attitude towards reform, offered drafting assistance for the bill. As with the reform of the law on homosexuality, Jenkins ensured that the bill secured sufficient time in the Commons, and, despite numerous attempts at filibustering, it became law in October 1967. It legalised abortion up to twenty-eight weeks after conception with the approval of

18 Peter G. Richards, *Parliament and Conscience* (George Allen and Unwin, 1970), 77–8.
19 Ibid., 79.
20 The legislation did not, however, apply to Scotland or Northern Ireland, which did not reform their laws until 1980 and 1982, respectively.
21 Jenkins, *A Life at the Centre*, 209.

two doctors under fairly strict conditions. The time limit was to be reduced to twenty-four weeks in 1990, and in practice the strict conditions have been relaxed, so that abortion is in effect available on demand, although that was not by any means the intention of all those who favoured reform. Abortion law was not reformed in Northern Ireland until 2019.

The third reform in Jenkins's 'unauthorised programme', designed to increase personal freedoms, was that of theatre censorship. At that time, the decision whether or not to permit a play to be performed lay, under the terms of the Theatres Act of 1843, with the lord chamberlain, a court official, whose decisions were made under the royal prerogative and could not therefore be challenged in Parliament. Such decisions were inevitably arbitrary and often ludicrous, for most lord chamberlains knew little more about the theatre than any other moderately well-educated playgoer. In any case, wealthy or well-connected theatre fans could get around the lord chamberlain's decisions, since banned plays could be performed in private clubs. In 1949, the licence for a play, *Pick-Up Girl*, was made conditional on alterations to the script. The producer refused, and so the play was performed in a theatre club with an unchanged script. Queen Mary, mother of George VI, was amongst the audience. In 1957, the lord chamberlain objected to a line in John Osborne's play *The Entertainer*, 'those playing fields of Eton have really got us beaten', and objected also in 1959 to the line in Osborne's play, *The World of Paul Slickey*, 'They'll make it much too hot for us to tackle any crumpet'.[22] In 1957, Samuel Beckett's play *Endgame* was licensed for performance in French, but banned in 1958 for performance in English on grounds of blasphemy. It appeared that either the lord chamberlain did not understand French, or

---

22 John Heilpern, 'It's me, isn't it?', *Guardian* (6 March 2007); Hansard, House of Lords, 17 February 1977, vol. 724, col. 1217.

those who did understand French were already so corrupted as to be beyond redemption.[23] In 1960, Harold Pinter's play *The Caretaker*, which contained the words 'piss off', was refused a licence. Finally, in 1965, in a case of reductio ad absurdum, the lord chamberlain refused to license two plays being produced at the Royal Court Theatre: *Saved* by Edward Bond, and *A Patriot for Me* by John Osborne. The theatre immediately turned itself into a private club, rapidly attracting 3,000 new 'members'. Nevertheless, the producers of *Saved* were prosecuted and found guilty.

Restraints on what could be produced in the theatre were not accompanied by restraints in any other area of artistic endeavour, such as books. The fact that a play refused a licence by the lord chamberlain could be presented in a private theatre club, and could also be published without censorship, made the system appear even more ludicrous and capricious.

In 1958, a Theatre Censorship Reform Committee was formed, and Jenkins became a member. In 1966, he persuaded a Labour peer and academic, Noel Annan, to move a motion to establish a joint committee of both Houses of Parliament to consider the issue. The committee reported unanimously in favour of reform. In 1968, a private members' bill was introduced by a Labour back-bencher in the Commons, and in 1968 the Theatres Bill, abolishing stage censorship in the theatre, was enacted. It may be, however, that a play could still be banned on grounds of obscenity or gross indecency. In 1970, the prosecuting authorities considered banning an erotic revue, *Oh! Calcutta*, on grounds of obscenity, but decided not to do so, while in 1982, the campaigner Mary Whitehouse launched an unsuccessful private prosecution against a play featuring homosexual rape, *The Romans in Britain*, on grounds of gross indecency.

---

23 Richards, *Parliament and Conscience*, 119–21.

There had, however, been no opposition in principle to the 1968 Theatres Act, and the royal household was probably glad to be relieved of an increasingly embarrassing responsibility. Jenkins's part in this reform, although largely confined to the back room, had been considerable, for although his 'part in public discussions was negligible, in private his influence was great'.[24]

After Jenkins left the Home Office, a further instalment of the 'unauthorised programme' was to be enacted: divorce-law reform. The Divorce Reform Act of 1969 took away the requirement to prove fault from those seeking a divorce, replacing it with the concept of the marriage having irretrievably broken down. A couple could divorce, if both wished it, after two years' separation, or after five years' separation if one person wished it.

Jenkins was the most liberal home secretary since the Second World War – perhaps the only really liberal home secretary there has ever been. Labour home secretaries before and since – Chuter Ede, James Callaghan, Jack Straw, David Blunkett – have not been noted for their liberalism. Attlee had led a government notable for social reform, but on Home Office matters it had been somewhat authoritarian, mirroring perhaps the attitudes of its working-class supporters, a section of the community more likely to be victims of crime than the better off, and perhaps less tolerant of deviations from conventional morality.

These reforms, which Jenkins characterised as establishing a 'civilised society', were in the 1980s to be criticised – some would say caricatured – by social conservatives as having created a permissive society. Many of the critics had forgotten – or were perhaps never aware – that Margaret Thatcher herself, like Powell, had voted for reform of the laws on homosexuality and abortion. The Conservatives, in power for eighteen years from

---

24 Ibid., 129.

1979 to 1997, made no moves to repeal or substantially amend the legislation. Indeed, the 'civilised society' reforms remain almost all that have survived of the Wilson government of the 1960s. Hardly anyone today would propose to criminalise homosexuality or restore theatre censorship. There are some, admittedly, who would seek to criminalise abortion, but they are, in large part, members of religious minorities. For the majority, abortion is now regarded as a step in female emancipation and as increasing the rights of women.

In *The Labour Case*, Jenkins concluded his final chapter with a peroration:

> Let us be on the side of those who want people to be free to live their own lives, to make their own mistakes, and to decide, in an adult way, and provided they do not infringe the rights of others, the code by which they wish to live ... In the long run these things will be more important than even the most perfect of economic policies.[25]

Through his 'civilised society' reforms, Jenkins has perhaps done more good to more people in relieving unhappiness than any other politician in the post-war era. The reforms remain as his permanent memorial. Philip Allen, permanent under-secretary at the Home Office from 1966 to 1972, has said of abortion-law reform and homosexuality-law reform that 'they would never have become law without him'.[26]

---

25 Jenkins, *The Labour Case*, 146.
26 Philip Allen, 'A Young Home Secretary' in Adonis and Thomas, *Roy Jenkins*, 65.

III

At the end of 1967, Jenkins moved from the Home Office to become chancellor of the Exchequer. He entered No. 11 Downing Street at a difficult time for the Labour government. Having resisted the devaluation of the pound for over three years, the government was forced to surrender in 1967. The chancellor who had sought to hold the line, James Callaghan, left the Exchequer for the Home Office, swapping posts with Jenkins, who was now in a politically dominant position, for Wilson and the Labour government were dependent on his success in rescuing the economy; having lost one chancellor, Wilson could hardly afford to lose another.

If Jenkins's political position was strong, the economic difficulties that he faced were formidable. For devaluation to work effectively, resources would have to be released from home production to the export trade, to reduce the balance-of-payments deficit. That meant restrictions on domestic consumption as well as cuts in public expenditure. Many Labour flagship policies had to be postponed. Prescription charges, abolished in 1964, were reintroduced. The raising of the school-leaving age from fifteen to sixteen was postponed for four years. There were cuts in the housing budget and a reduction in expenditure on roads. There were also cuts in defence spending. The government, moreover, was forced to accept withdrawal from bases east of Suez, marking the effective end of Britain's role as a global power. For devaluation to work, there had to be what Jenkins called 'two years of hard slog'.[27] Jenkins summed up the differences between the Home Office and the Exchequer in a characteristic metaphor: 'At the Home Office sudden storms blew up out of a clear sky and vanished almost as suddenly as they arose; by

---

27 Hansard, House of Commons, 17 January 1968, vol. 756, col. 1805.

contrast the Treasury was a long Arctic winter slowly lightening into spring.'[28]

During the years of 'hard slog', there were to be three heavily deflationary budgets, all of which involved significant increases in taxation. The 1968 budget increased indirect taxes – purchase tax, the predecessor of VAT; vehicle-licensing fees; betting taxes; petrol duties; duties on tobacco, wine, and spirits; and taxation on investment income. Taxation in total was increased by £923 million, over twice as much as any previous budget, including those in wartime. A cartoon by Osbert Lancaster in the *Daily Express* on 20 March 1968 had its protagonist saying, 'Were I a non-smoking teetotaller, with a brand new car, mad on collecting savings certificates and living in an underdeveloped country, I'd say Mr Jenkins has done a splendid job!'[29] Oddly enough, Jenkins won great applause for his tough budget. His political reputation came to be immensely strengthened, and the budget speech itself was rated 'a masterpiece. Never has pain been inflicted with greater elegance. There has been no finer Budget speech since the war. Politically it was a triumph.'[30] The 1968 budget was followed by two more deflationary budgets, increasing taxation by a further £600 million, raising interest rates, and tightening credit restrictions.

Jenkins also had to persuade holders of sterling balances in London not to withdraw their deposits. He did so by guaranteeing holders the value of their balances in dollars and paying them high interest rates. By the end of Jenkins's period at the Exchequer, the balances had been strengthened.

Economic confidence eventually returned, though it was a

---

28 Dick Taverne, 'Chancellor of the Exchequer' in Adonis and Thomas, *Roy Jenkins*, 88.
29 Kenneth Baker, 'A Life in Caricature' in Adonis and Thomas, *Roy Jenkins*, 169.
30 Edmund Dell, *The Chancellors: A History of the Chancellors of the Exchequer, 1945–90* (HarperCollins, 1997), 357.

long time coming. For a time, sterling reserves remained low and foreign confidence uncertain. There were even fears in 1968 that there would be a second devaluation. But eventually, in 1969, the hard slog paid off and the balance of payments was restored. By 1970, a balance-of-payments surplus had been achieved as well as a budget surplus (the only such surplus between the years 1936–7 and 1987–8), while the rate of economic growth in 1970 was to be over 5 per cent. But these achievements had come at the cost of holding down personal consumption because of the need to increase exports. There was also an increase in unemployment of around 1 per cent, although it remained below the definition in the 1944 White Paper on Employment of a 'high and stable level of employment' at 3 per cent. Jenkins's 1970 budget was to be criticised as excessively cautious, and he came to be blamed for Labour's loss of the 1970 election. Later, it was criticised for being insufficiently restrictive, for prices were still rising, and rising prices were a major cause of Labour's defeat.

Whatever the final judgement on Jenkins's economic steward-ship, his time at the Exchequer raised his already high reputation. Most commentators believed that, with the economy recover-ing, Labour would win the 1970 election. In that case, so it was believed, Jenkins would become foreign secretary, and when Wilson retired, Jenkins would appear as the natural successor. Even after Labour's unexpected defeat, Jenkins still appeared the heir apparent. One month after the election, in July 1970, he was elected Labour's deputy leader. But the 1970 election has rightly been called 'a watershed in British history ... It ushered in a period of economic crisis and political polarisation, unprec-edented since the end of the Second World War.'[31] In the Labour Party, that polarisation centred around Europe and was to ruin

---

31 David Marquand, 'The Welsh Wrecker' in Adonis and Thomas, *Roy Jenkins*, 109.

Jenkins's prospects of leadership – though even without Europe, his position would have become weaker in opposition, since Labour, finding itself out of power, would be likely to swing to the left – as indeed it did.

IV

In the 1970s, the issue of Europe was to cause a fundamental cleavage in the Labour Party, a cleavage which at one time seemed to presage the break-up of the party. It took all the political skills of Wilson to hold the party together. But the effect of Wilson's legerdemain was to leave the pro-European right of the party, led by Jenkins, isolated and in retreat.

In government, Labour had sought to join the EC, but the French president, Charles de Gaulle, had vetoed the application in 1967, just as he had done in 1963 when Macmillan had sought to join. Wilson's application, however, remained on the table, and with de Gaulle's resignation in 1969, there seemed a real prospect of British entry. The Conservative prime minister, Heath, persuaded de Gaulle's successor, Georges Pompidou, that Britain had become genuinely European, and he negotiated terms not markedly different from those that Wilson had sought. Labour's left, however, had always been against membership, and in opposition it was joined by others who sought to use the issue to embarrass the Conservative government. In particular, James Callaghan sought to recoup his position, after his failure as chancellor, by opposing entry on the terms negotiated by the Conservatives. Wilson, fearing a threat to his leadership, concurred that the emerging 'Tory terms' were unacceptable. In 1971, a special Labour Party conference came out three to one against entry. Labour MPs voted 159 to 89 against entry and insisted on a three-line whip mandating Labour MPs to vote against the principle of entry by 140 to 111. In his memoirs, Jenkins describes this movement away from support for Europe as being 'like watching someone being sold down the river into slavery, drifting away, depressed but unprotesting'.[32]

Jenkins found himself unable to follow the party line and was not prepared to take refuge in abstention. He regarded the vote on Europe as comparable in importance to 'the first Reform Bill, the repeal of the Corn Laws, Gladstone's Home Rule Bills, the Lloyd George Budget and the Parliament Bill, the Munich Agreement and the May 1940 vote'.[33] How, then, could he abstain? How would it be, he asked rhetorically, if, asked what he had done faced with such a momentous issue, he replied, 'I abstained'? In 1971, therefore, he ignored a three-line whip, leading sixty-eight other Labour MPs to vote in favour of the principle of entry. He was becoming 'the Bevan of the Labour Right'.[34] But Bevan had never voted to keep the Conservatives in power. Yet that was the effect of the vote of the sixty-nine. It kept a Conservative government in office. Had they voted against the government, it would probably have been defeated, and Heath, who had made it a vote of confidence, would have been forced to dissolve Parliament. Jenkins, therefore, had, in effect, rejected the opportunity to force the hated Conservatives from office.

Having taken this stand, Jenkins nevertheless voted with his party on the second reading and in other votes, against the legislation that was necessary for Britain to join. This was a humiliation he later regretted, believing that he should then have resigned as deputy leader. He was in fact to resign six months later, when Wilson conceded to the demand of Benn for a referendum on Europe. That was perhaps the wrong issue on which to go.

32 Jenkins, *A Life at the Centre*, 320.
33 Ibid., 329.
34 Marquand, 'The Welsh Wrecker', 115.

After his resignation, Jenkins made a number of speeches putting forward a programme of government for the Labour right, something he compared to Joseph Chamberlain's Unauthorised Programme of 1885. The speeches were later published in a short book called *What Matters Now*. Jenkins assumed that Labour, veering to the left, would lose the next election; that Wilson would then resign, as indeed he would have done, had the February 1974 election been lost; and that Jenkins would have a good chance of succeeding him: 'Nineteen seventy-four, according to my strategy, was the year in which temporising Labour Party leadership was due to receive its just reward in the shape of a general election'.[35] But, just as in 1970, the voters had declined to support Jenkins's leadership ambitions by re-electing Labour, so, in February 1974, they frustrated him again by declining to defeat Labour. Jenkins wrote in retirement:

> In 1970, I wanted Labour to win and thought it deserved to do so. In 1974 I took a different view on both points … To paraphrase Wilde, getting one election result wrong might have been excused as a misfortune, but to make a mistake about two pointed to carelessness.[36]

It is in fact doubtful whether Jenkins could have become Labour leader, even if the party had failed to win the 1974 election. The circumstances of his resignation in 1972 had annoyed many Labour MPs less committed to Europe than Jenkins, since they believed – correctly, no doubt – that Europe was more important to him than the Labour Party. In addition, Jenkins had failed to cultivate trade-union opinion, a mistake that Callaghan, Wilson's eventual successor, had not made.

---

35 Jenkins, *A Life at the Centre*, 364.
36 Ibid.

The general election of February 1974, which resulted in a minority Labour government, was a defeat not just for Heath's Conservatives but for Jenkins and his vision of social democracy. It gave a great boost to Labour's left, which could now argue that the party could win on a left-wing programme, a thesis that was later to be tested to destruction by Michael Foot in 1983 and Jeremy Corbyn in 2019. In the new Cabinet, Jenkins became home secretary again and once more enacted fundamental legislation extending civic rights – the first Sex Discrimination Act in 1975, prepared against some departmental opposition, and then a new Race Relations Act in 1976, greatly extending protection against discrimination and establishing a Commission for Racial Equality to monitor progress. These reforms were as important as those enacted in his first period at the Home Office and, like them, made Britain a better place to live in.

But Jenkins's heart was no longer in government, and he became increasingly disillusioned by its failure effectively to combat inflation, by the growth of trade-union power, and by the strength of anti-European feeling in the Labour Party. He was, in addition, becoming disenchanted with socialism itself, even the revisionist version of it which his friends Gaitskell and Crosland had championed. He seemed a somewhat semi-detached member of the government, if not also of the Labour Party.

Jenkins was to be given a renewed lease of life, ironically, in the referendum on Europe which was to be held in June 1975. Although called by the anti-Europeans, it yielded a convincing victory, by three to one, for those who wanted Britain to remain in the EC. Jenkins warned that a Britain which rejected Europe would be one dominated by narrow nationalism, an ungenerosity of spirit, and extremist politicians. For Britain, leaving the EC, he declared – thinking, no doubt, of Powell and Benn – would be to go into 'an old people's home for fading nations ... I do not think it would be a very comfortable old people's home. I do not like the look of some of the prospective wardens'.[37] Perhaps the outcome of the 2016 referendum bears out his warning!

For Jenkins personally, the 1975 referendum showed that he had more in common with the pro-European Liberal Party than with his increasingly Eurosceptic Labour colleagues. He was coming to think that the first-past-the-post electoral system was at fault in preventing like-minded people from cooperating with each other, while forcing incompatibles together in what he was to call 'loveless marriages'. Coalition government, as practised on the Continent, would, so he was coming to believe, yield more stable and more centrist government, less susceptible to attack from unrepresentative extremists. It is a paradox that the 1975 referendum, which he had sought to prevent taking place, rein-vigorated him. His Cabinet colleague Barbara Castle had noticed the evolution of Jenkins's thinking on proportional representa-tion and coalition at a Cabinet meeting as early as April 1974, just four weeks into the Wilson minority government, when he wanted the forthcoming Speaker's Conference to consider the single-transferable-vote method of proportional representa-tion, which, according to Willie Ross, the secretary of state for Scotland, 'could see the end of any possibility of a Labour Gov-ernment'. 'It was obviously best,' Barbara Castle commented, 'to let this sleeping dog lie as long as possible. So we sent Roy away with a flea in his coalition ear.' In November 1975, Jenkins tried again. 'These rightists,' Castle complained, 'will go on beavering away ... until they have finally destroyed the Labour Party's inde-pendence and power to govern single-handedly.' By March 1976, she reported Jenkins as saying, 'As you know, I don't think we can continue much longer with the system of "first past the post".'[38]

---

37 Roger Berthoud, 'Mr Jenkins sees cold world outside Nine', *The Times* (28 May 1975).
38 Barbara Castle, *The Castle Diaries 1974–76* (Weidenfeld and Nicolson, 1980), 70, 554, 682.

In March 1976, Wilson finally resigned as prime minister and Jenkins stood for the leadership. But his chances were not high. Indeed, once Labour had lost the 1970 election, it was never really likely that he would become Labour leader. His support was much wider in the country outside Parliament, amongst uncommitted voters and the commentariat, than in the Labour Party, where he faced rivals on the right: Anthony Crosland and Denis Healey, less fervent Europeans than he was. Unlike Wilson, or his successor, James Callaghan, Jenkins had spent little time cosying up to back-benchers, and he had never been elected to Labour's National Executive Committee. His support in Westminster was largely restricted to a comparatively small coterie of pro-Europeans. In the event, he came third on the first ballot, with 56 votes, defeating his two rivals on the right, Healey and Crosland, who had received 30 and 17 votes, respectively. Had they not stood, and had all their votes been transferred to him, Jenkins would have led the field with 103 votes, ahead of Michael Foot, who on the first ballot had led the field with 90 votes. As it was, Jenkins decided not to contest further ballots. With some relief, he decided that it was now time to leave British politics: 'I realised retrospectively how ill the shoe of British politics had been fitting me. I had felt neither at ease in, nor derived pride from my membership of that Government of 1974, and I ought to have got out before.'[39]

V

In January 1977, Jenkins became the first, and indeed the only, British president of the European Commission, proclaiming

---

39 Anthony Lester, 'The Home Office Again' in Adonis and Thomas, *Roy Jenkins*, 162.

himself liberated. In October 1977, he delivered the first Jean
Monnet Lecture, in Florence, in which he proposed the creation
of a European Monetary System so as to revive the idea of economic and monetary union. He was instrumental in persuading
the French president, Giscard d'Estaing (Pompidou's successor),
and the German chancellor, Helmut Schmidt, to support this initiative. The European Monetary System, involving alignment of
exchange rates, came into operation in March 1979. To Jenkins's
regret, the Callaghan government decided that Britain should
remain outside the European Monetary System, and Britain
did not join until October 1990, in the dying days of Margaret Thatcher's government. Margaret Thatcher herself had been
unwilling for Britain to join, and indeed membership proved an
unhappy experience. Britain was to be forced out of the European Monetary System less than two years later, in September
1992 – an event which helped to undermine Major's government.
Nevertheless, Jenkins remains one of just three presidents of the
European Commission to have had a large policy impact, the
others being Walter Hallstein, the first president, and Jacques
Delors, the architect of the single market and full monetary
union. Nevertheless, the president is essentially a persuader;
policy is made not by him but by the leaders of the member
states. So, Jenkins 'might have been the godfather, but Schmidt
and Giscard became the parents'.[40] The presidency was, in the
words of Shirley Williams, a Labour minister who was later to
join Jenkins in the SDP, a hollow crown for one so used to executive decision.[41]

Although Jenkins's engagement with British politics seemed
to have come to an end, a series of contingencies brought him

---

40 Adonis and Thomas, *Roy Jenkins*, 193.
41 Michael Cockerell, 'A Very Social Democrat: A Portrait of Roy Jenkins' [TV
programme], BBC (26 May 1996).

back to the front line in the early 1980s. Margaret Thatcher's government, elected in 1979, seemed to be moving away from the one-nation Toryism of Macmillan and Heath, pursuing economic policies which caused a rapid rise in unemployment. At the same time, Labour in opposition was once again moving to the left, and its policy proposals for the 1983 election included withdrawal from the EC without a further referendum, and unilateral nuclear disarmament.

Jenkins, who had become increasingly disillusioned with his old party and had not voted in the 1979 general election, delivered in the autumn of that year the BBC's Richard Dimbleby Lecture, entitled 'Home Thoughts from Abroad'. He called for a 'strengthening of the radical centre', a term later to be used by Blair, to be achieved by proportional representation and party realignment.[42] This put the creation of a new social-democratic party on to the political agenda. Then, in January 1981, after he had left Brussels, he and the other three members of the 'Gang of Four' – the group of breakaway ex-Labour Cabinet ministers in which Jenkins was joined by David Owen, Shirley Williams, and Bill Rodgers – issued the Limehouse Declaration, advocating a revived form of social democracy. In March, this Gang of Four left the Labour Party and formed a new party, the SDP, which allied itself with the Liberals. A total of twenty-seven Labour MPs defected to the SDP, making it the largest split within a major party since the Liberal Party had been divided over home rule in 1886. But an important section of Labour's right – headed by Denis Healey, John Smith, and Roy Hattersley – remained within the party, taking the view that the swing to the left was a temporary aberration and that Labour would soon return to mainstream policies.

The SDP had hoped to attract some Conservative MPs who

---

42 Jenkins, *A Life at the Centre*, 519.

felt that Margaret Thatcher's government was too extreme. But, while it attracted many previously Conservative voters, it attracted just one Conservative MP, a maverick with no significant following. Tory grandees who might have been thought to be sympathetic – such as the former prime minister Heath and Jenkins's friend Ian Gilmour – took a view parallel to that of many Labour moderates, that Thatcherism was a temporary aberration and that their party would soon return to a more sensible stance.

Nevertheless, it soon became apparent that the SDP was tapping a considerable vein of political disillusionment. Within two months, it had attracted around 45,000 members. These were not only defectors from the Labour Party; there were also ex-Conservatives and ex-Liberals. But the vast majority – seven out of ten – were political virgins, never having belonged to any political party before. In July 1981, Jenkins stood as the first candidate for the new SDP, with Liberal support, at a by-election in Warrington, a seat with hardly any Liberal tradition. He came near to winning the seat, losing by just 1,759 votes. This was, he said after the result was announced, his first election defeat since 1945, but 'by far the greatest victory in which I have ever participated'. The Labour vote was its lowest in the constituency since 1931. The academic and BBC commentator Robert McKenzie said that it was 'the most sensational by-election result of the century'.[43] In March 1982, just before the Falklands War, Jenkins won a second by-election, becoming MP for Glasgow Hillhead, and shortly afterwards he was elected leader of the SDP. The SDP–Liberal Alliance seemed to be enjoying a rapid take-off, and at the end of 1981 it appeared to have the support of around 50 per cent of voters. Before Christmas, *The Economist* dubbed

---

43 Bill Rodgers, 'SDP' in Adonis and Thomas, *Roy Jenkins*, 219.

the Alliance 'Her Majesty's New Opposition'.[44] 'Such an erup-
tion of third-party support,' the psephologist Ivor Crewe later
wrote, 'is unprecedented: for speed, strength and duration there
has been nothing to match it since Britain's modern party system
emerged in the 1920s.'[45]

Then things began to go wrong. There were squabbles
between the SDP and the Liberals over the allocation of seats,
which undermined the image of an alliance dedicated to a new
kind of politics of agreement. Then Britain's victory in the Falklands War, her first major foreign-policy success for many years,
led to an outburst of patriotic feeling, greatly to the benefit of
Margaret Thatcher's Conservatives. Between February and June
1982, Conservative support rose by 11 per cent, and a MORI
poll in 1983 indicated that one-third of the voters were supporting the Conservatives because of Margaret Thatcher's perceived
strong personality. 'We have ceased to be a nation in retreat,' she
declared. 'We have instead a new-found confidence.'[46] Admittedly, Conservative support had been rising slightly before the
Falklands War as inflation seemed under control, but the Falklands factor intensified support for the Conservatives. As the
Marxist historian Eric Hobsbawm put it, the war had 'mobi-
lised a public sentiment which could actually be felt'. He added
that 'anyone of the Left who was not aware of this grass-roots
feeling ... ought seriously to reconsider his or her capacity to
assess politics'.[47]

Compounding these problems, Jenkins proved ineffective
as leader of the Alliance in the Commons. He seemed to have

44 *The Economist* (5 December 1981).

45 Ivor Crewe, 'Is Britain's two-party system really about to crumble? The Social
Democrat–Liberal Alliance and the prospects for realignment', *Electoral Studies*, 1/3
(1982), 275–313, 276.

46 'Nation in retreat' speech at a Conservative rally, Cheltenham, 3 July 1982,
Margaret Thatcher Foundation Archive.

47 Eric Hobsbawm, 'Falklands Fallout', *Marxism Today* (January 1983), 14.

lost his touch, and he was not used to speaking from the back benches, something that he had last done in 1972. He had been, he told David Butler, 'essentially a batsman in the House of Commons. Was now asked to be a bowler!'[48] Although appointed prime minister–designate of the Alliance in the 1983 general-election campaign, opinion polls showed that the Liberal leader, David Steel, was in fact more popular than Jenkins amongst the electorate.

In the 1983 election, the central feature of the economic policy of the SDP–Liberal Alliance as laid out in its manifesto, published under the title *Working Together for Britain: Programme for Government*, was an incomes policy. Such policies had of course been tried by every government since Macmillan's attempt in 1962, including by governments of which Jenkins had been a member. But on each occasion, after some initial success, the policy had failed. Why should the incomes policy of an Alliance government prove any more successful? The Alliance argued that the policy had failed in the past because previous incomes policies had been essentially short-term, designed to resolve immediate crises, not part of long-term strategies, and that they had lacked a mandate from voters. In addition, the introduction of proportional representation would ensure that government had a mandate from a majority of voters, and would not be in hock either to the trade unions or to industrial management, so that it would not be perceived as pursuing sectional interests. Proportional representation would make it easier for a government to follow a consistent line of policy without being subject to the so-called adversary politics of the first-past-the-post electoral system, by which oppositions sought to outbid governments by promising higher wages. In addition to incomes policy, the Alliance proposed selective assistance to industry, greater

---

48 David Butler Election Archive, 11 June 1983.

public expenditure, and lower taxation. But these too had been tried before and had seemingly failed – selective assistance to industry under every government since Macmillan's attempt in 1959, greater public spending and lower taxation under the Reginald Maudling and Anthony Barber booms in 1962–4 and 1972–3, respectively. Britain, so Benn was accustomed to say, had endured an SDP government since 1945 – though perhaps 1962 would have been a better starting date, since it was in that year that the Conservative government of Macmillan began to adopt policies of economic planning and control of incomes hardly distinguishable from those of the Labour Party. Why should the Alliance enjoy greater success?

Jenkins's friend and rival Crosland said in 1960 that the trouble with the Labour Party was that 'some of its leaders are radical but not contemporary – they are discontented, but with a society which no longer exists; while others are contemporary but not radical – they realise that the society has changed, but quite enjoy the present one'.[49] Jenkins had shared this critique. He had hoped that the SDP would be both radical and contemporary – but was it offering, in the mordant words of the sociologist Ralf Dahrendorf, himself a supporter of the Alliance, anything more than a better yesterday?

Although survey evidence in 1983 indicated much sympathy with the policies of the Alliance, such as incomes policy, opposition to Labour's proposals for further nationalisation, and a unilateralist defence policy, the Alliance found itself a victim of the first-past-the-post system in the election. It won 25 per cent of the vote, the largest vote for a third party since 1923, and just 2 per cent less of the vote than Labour. But this was not enough to dent the Conservative–Labour duopoly. Because electoral

49 Anthony Crosland, *The Conservative Enemy: A Programme of Radical Reform for the 1960s* (Jonathan Cape, 1962), 131–2.

support for the Alliance was evenly spread across the country, while Labour's was heavily concentrated in traditional working-class areas, the Alliance secured just 23 seats – of which only 6 were gained by the SDP, as opposed to 17 by the Liberals – while Labour won 207 seats. The Alliance won second place in 332 seats. It had come, as Jenkins declared in his memoirs, 'within a hair's breadth of a breakthrough ... It cannot be wrong to attempt something which so nearly resulted in such spectacular success.'[50] Together with the Liberals, the SDP had provided 'the most serious challenge to the existing two-party hegemony for more than sixty years'.[51]

Immediately after the 1983 election, Jenkins resigned as leader of the SDP, declaring that it would be wrong for the youngest party to be led by the oldest leader. He was succeeded by David Owen, who was to be even less successful than Jenkins in the 1987 election. Jenkins himself was to lose his seat at Hillhead in that election. After 1987, the SDP broke up in mutual recriminations, the bulk of its members merging with the Liberals to form a new party, the Liberal Democrats, in 1988. The SDP, in the words of its chroniclers, 'went up like a rocket but came down like the stick'.[52]

Supporters of the SDP argued that it had helped move Labour to the centre-ground of politics, but that might have happened in any case, once it was clear that the party could not win a general election from the left. Jenkins became a mentor to Blair, who became Labour leader in 1994 and, so Jenkins believed, quickly showed himself to be the most exciting Labour leader since Gaitskell. Jenkins – and, in some moods, Blair – hoped for a realignment so that there would be just one party of the left,

---

50 Jenkins, *A Life at the Centre*, 603.
51 Ivor Crewe and Anthony King, *SDP: The Birth, Life and Death of the Social Democratic Party* (Oxford University Press, 1995), 455.
52 Ibid., vii.

as Jenkins believed would have occurred after 1914, had the First World War not intervened. Had there been a hung parliament in 1997 or 2001, such a realignment might have been possible, but Blair's landslides drove the idea off the political agenda.

The most important consequence of the SDP breakaway was to strengthen the third force in British politics. Although the Liberal Democrats were never to achieve the 25 per cent of the vote that the Alliance had gained in 1983, their vote gradually became more concentrated and they came to benefit from tactical voting against the Conservatives. Under Paddy Ashdown, first leader of the Liberal Democrats, the party won 46 seats in 1997; then, under new leaders, 62 seats in 2005, and 57 in 2010. After the last of these elections, it joined a coalition with the Conservatives under Cameron, marking the first time that Liberals had participated in a peacetime government since 1932. It is, however, unclear whether Jenkins would have supported a coalition with the Conservatives, even though Cameron shared many of his liberal instincts.

The SDP may also have helped to bring constitutional reform to the centre of the political agenda. The Blair government, elected in 1997, enacted devolution and a Human Rights Act and began the process of reforming the House of Lords, all policies championed by the SDP. In addition, Blair established a commission, chaired by Jenkins, to investigate alternatives to the first-past-the-post electoral system. The commission's report in September 1998 advocated the alternative-vote system, modified with a proportional element. The Blair government, however, took no action on the report. Labour was divided on electoral reform, and the large majorities secured by Blair removed an incentive to reform the system, creating a strong constituency of incumbent Labour MPs hostile to change. However, in 2011 when the Cameron coalition government, as part of its agreement with the Liberals, held a referendum on the alternative-vote system, reform was defeated by a margin of three to one, on a turnout of just over 40 per cent. The British public was no longer interested in electoral reform, if indeed it had ever been. The Blair government did, however, introduce proportional representation for elections to the European Parliament, and for elections to sub-national bodies – the Scottish, Welsh, and Northern Irish devolved bodies and the London Assembly. Proportional representation, therefore, even if there was little support for it for Westminster elections, was no longer taboo, as it had been for much of the period since the 1920s. Ironically, however, proportional representation for the European Parliament enabled Farage's United Kingdom Independence Party (UKIP), dedicated to British withdrawal from the EU, to achieve a legislative foothold, so making Brexit more plausible. Jenkins had assumed, however, that proportional representation would strengthen the pro-European forces of the centre.

After being defeated at Hillhead in 1987, Jenkins entered the Lords as Lord Jenkins of Hillhead, of Pontypool in the County of Gwent, a title which he labelled 'a piece of Cymro-Scottish miscegenation'.[53] He remained proud of being the only person to have been an MP for the three major cities of the UK – London, Birmingham, and Glasgow. There was further consolation in his election as chancellor of Oxford University, a largely honorific post, having defeated Heath and the Tory historian Robert Blake. The other three members of the Gang of Four were eventually to join Jenkins in the Lords, a strange conclusion for a radical party which had sought to break the mould.

In retirement, Jenkins continued the career of authorship which he had begun in the 1940s. At the age of eighty, in 2001, he published a massive biography of Churchill, whom he regarded as the greatest figure ever to enter Downing Street. Jenkins,

---

53 Jenkins, *A Life at the Centre*, 614.

indeed, believed that it was harder to be a writer than a minister. He died in January 2003, shortly before the Iraq War, which he would certainly have opposed.

VI

It was said shortly after his death that Jenkins's 'influence on politics was as great as many who held the office of Prime Minister'.[54] He was the leading libertarian and perhaps also the leading internationalist of his age. He showed political courage in twice resigning from Labour's front bench on the issue of Europe, and also in pursuing his reforms as home secretary, reforms which were bound to alienate traditionalists and, in the case of abortion, Roman Catholics. He showed courage also as chancellor in carrying out painful policies to correct the balance of payments. He later displayed vision in attempting to escape the logic of Britain's outdated two-party system by forming and leading the SDP.

Jenkins's legacy, however, now seems far less secure than it did when he died in 2003. Already, in November 1999, he had confessed to his friend, the author Robert Harris, 'I have three great interests left in politics, a single currency, electoral reform and the union of the Liberals with Labour. And all three are languishing'.[55] Britain never appeared likely to join the single currency and has indeed now gone further by leaving the EU. The alternative vote was heavily defeated in a referendum in 2011. The idea of party realignment on the left comes to the surface from time to time and might just possibly be resurrected if a future election yields a hung parliament, rather than a clear

---

54 Andrew Adonis, 'A Biographer's Tale' in Adonis and Thomas, *Roy Jenkins*, 325.
55 Robert Harris, 'A Late Friendship' in Adonis and Thomas, *Roy Jenkins*, 311.

majority for one of the major parties. But at the time of writing, the idea of a realignment of the right, possibly led by Farage, seems more plausible.

In the late 1990s, Jenkins met Major, who asked him whether he regretted not having been prime minister. Jenkins replied, 'Not really,' and was tempted to ask Major whether he ever regretted having been prime minister![56] In his memoirs, Jenkins confessed:

> I always sensed that I would enjoy being Prime Minister more when it was over than while it was taking place. This thought … raises the question of how much I was truly at ease with power. It is not a thought which I suspect much troubled the minds of the great determined leaders of history. Napoleon was not secretly looking forward to writing his memoirs, whether at St. Helena or elsewhere. And even those multi-volume memorialists and politicians of genius, Lloyd George and Churchill, never doubted that they were happier in 10 Downing Street even in the darkest days of war than they ever could be on the hills of Wales or in the painting groves of the South of France.[57]

Jenkins speculated that he might actually have become prime minister had he been more ruthless, perhaps when Wilson was at the depth of his unpopularity in 1968: 'People who effectively seize the prime ministership – Lloyd George, Macmillan, Mrs Thatcher – do not let such moments slip.'[58] He suffered from the handicap that he rather liked Wilson, despite having little respect for him.

Nevertheless, Jenkins may have been mistaken in his belief that he could have seized the premiership. He was, as the former

---

56 Ibid., 313–4.
57 Jenkins, *A Life at the Centre*, 621.
58 Ibid., 260.

MP David Marquand said, 'a quintessential insider in a party founded by and for outsiders'.[59] Therefore, the Liberal Democrat peer Dick Taverne wrote, he 'was always most likely to capture supreme power through succession from within government rather than by assault from outside. He was never a populist politician, the natural leader of a barnstorming campaign, inspiring his troops to raise ladders against castle walls and to brave the burning oil.'[60] If that judgement is right, his best chance of the leadership would have been if Labour had won the 1970 election and Wilson had retired shortly afterwards. In opposition, however, the European issues destroyed his chances.

VII

Whether or not Jenkins could have become prime minister in the late 1960s, there are deeper reasons for his failure and indeed for the failure of the SDP. They lie in the contradictions of social democracy itself.

Jenkins's 'civilised society' reforms accelerated what was already no doubt occurring: a weakening of restraints on social behaviour, particularly sexual behaviour. This was welcomed by social democrats. In their blood, Crosland insisted, there should 'always run a trace of the anarchist and the libertarian'.[61] But a society dominated by individualism and hedonism could hardly be expected to accept the social obligations which underpinned the post-war settlement. The ethic of social democracy, one of fellowship and social service, depended upon self-restraint. Crosland, in his famous book *The Future of Socialism*, had

---

59 Marquand, 'The Welsh Wrecker', 111.
60 Taverne, 'Chancellor of the Exchequer', 105.
61 Anthony Crosland, *The Future of Socialism* (Jonathan Cape, 1956), 522.

'continually invoked the old communitarian catchwords of ethical socialism – whilst at the same time deriding the old culture of Puritanism and stoicism from which such ideals had sprung'.[62] It was a contradiction that neither Jenkins nor Crosland nor other social democrats could resolve.

There were other serious contradictions in Jenkins's approach. Social democrats believed that the state could, through intelligent macroeconomic policy, secure both full employment and price stability using Keynesian methods. The state could also use its ability to control the economy to redistribute income so as to create a fairer society. This belief, though taken for granted across most of the political spectrum, had nevertheless hardly been subject to empirical testing. Indeed, even at the height of the Keynesian era, in 1968, R. C. O. Matthews, Drummond professor of political economy at Oxford, had convincingly argued in an article in the *Economic Journal* that post-war full employment in Britain owed hardly anything to Keynesian techniques of pump-priming.[63] The belief that social-democratic aims could be achieved by fiscal means was, therefore, quite untested. By the time of the International Monetary Fund (IMF) crisis in 1976, Labour's leaders hardly dared test it. They were already convinced that it would not work. At the 1976 Labour Party conference, Prime Minister James Callaghan said:

The cosy world we were told would go on for ever, where full employment would be guaranteed by a stroke of the Chancellor's pen ... that cosy world is gone ... We used to think that you could just spend your way out of a recession ... I tell you in all candour that that option no longer exists, and that

---

62 Jose Harris, 'Political Thought and the State' in S. J. D. Green and R. C. Whiting, *The Boundaries of the State in Modern Britain* (Cambridge University Press, 1996), 27.
63 R. C. O. Matthews, 'Why has Britain Had Full Employment Since the War?', *Economic Journal*, 78/311 (1 September 1968), 556–69.

in so far as it ever did exist, it only worked ... by injecting a
bigger dose of inflation into the economy, followed by a higher
level of unemployment ... That is the history of the last twenty
years.[64]

Social democrats also believed that the British state was
beneficent, efficient, and generally fit for purpose – for the social-
democratic programme, and in particular the redistribution of
income and wealth, could be achieved only by using the state as
its instrument. The power of the state would no doubt expand,
but this, so social democrats believed, need not be a matter of
any particular concern. Indeed, the expansion of the state might
actually strengthen rather than weaken democracy by increasing
the liberty of those who lacked market power. Government was,
after all, responsible to Parliament, and Parliament was responsible to the electorate. The state, therefore, was under the control
of the people.

But by the 1970s, social democrats in general, and Jenkins in
particular, were coming to the view that the limits of taxable
capacity were being reached, and that there was a danger of
the state gaining so much power that the values of a pluralist
society could come under threat. Moreover, it seemed that some
of Labour's supporters, better-off members of the working class
whose votes might be crucial in marginal constituencies, were
themselves coming to be hostile to high taxation, preferring, in
place of what Wilson artfully used to call the 'social wage', to
retain more of their real wage in their pockets. Labour supporters were also becoming sceptical of the motives and behaviour
of some of those on social benefits, financed by public spending.
During the 1920s, Labour MPs had told Ramsay MacDonald

---

64 Quoted in Kenneth O. Morgan, *Callaghan: A Life* (Oxford University Press,
1997), 535.

that their own supporters, men and women in low-paid jobs, were the most stringent in demanding that 'scroungers' be denied benefits.[65] In late 1975, arguing that public-expenditure cuts would not necessarily be unpopular amongst Labour supporters, Denis Healey, Labour's chancellor, told the Cabinet:

> At the Labour clubs you'll find there's an awful lot of support for this policy of cutting public expenditure. They will all tell you about Paddy Murphy up the street who's got eighteen children, has not worked for years, lives on unemployment benefit, has a colour television and goes to Majorca for his holidays.[66]

At the time of the 1976 IMF crisis, therefore, the argument that the economic crisis should be met by a rise in taxation, rather than by cuts in public services, was rapidly dismissed by Callaghan and Healey, and it was pressed, even on the left, in a somewhat lukewarm manner.[67]

It seemed, therefore, that social democrats were facing a completely changed landscape, one dominated by new techniques of economic management, accompanied by considerable scepticism as to the value of government intervention and even of expenditure on public services. After its unexpected defeat in the 1992 general election, the Labour Party drew the lesson, whether rightly or wrongly, that electors, whatever they told the opinion pollsters, would not, in the privacy of the voting booth, support a party which proposed higher taxes to finance public services.

---

65 See Alan Deacon, *In Search of the Scrounger: The Administration of Unemployment Insurance in Britain, 1920–1931* (Bell, 1976).

66 Quoted in Tony Benn, *Against the Tide: Diaries 1973–76* (Hutchinson, 1989), 461.

67 Tom Clark, *The limits of social democracy? Tax and spend under Labour, 1974–1979* [working paper 64/01] (Department of Economic History, London School of Economics and Political Science, 2001). This paper analyses the effects of the 1976 crisis on the ethos of social democracy.

Improvements in public services, therefore, would have to be found in other ways.

In the last quarter of the twentieth century, social democracy faced a further contradiction. Like its ancestor, socialism, it is, in essence, an internationalist doctrine. Yet, in practice, the most favourable conditions for social democracy lie in highly cohesive nation states such as Norway or Sweden before the age of mass migration. Social democracy depends upon a sense of social solidarity, more likely to be present in small and cohesive nations than in large multicultural societies or in an international community. That is because social democracy requires citizens to feel a sufficient sense of social obligation towards their fellows that they are prepared to pay in taxation to secure benefits for them. The stronger the sense of community, the more likely it is that such a sense of social obligation will be felt. Of course, even in a single state, this sense of solidarity is not always easy to achieve, and there are many who feel resentful at contributing in taxation to provide for the welfare of 'spongers'. Social democracy, therefore, is more difficult to achieve in a multicultural country, especially if those from minority communities are not seen as full members of the community, or if recent immigrants are seen as less deserving of benefits because they have not made lifetime contributions to taxation or National Insurance. Social democracy became even more difficult to achieve once Britain jettisoned her protective tariffs and became subject to the market forces of globalisation and the rules of the EU.

In the 1950s, it had seemed that social democrats could pursue policies of their choice untrammelled by foreign opinion. Britain had been a sheltered economy protected by tariffs, Imperial Preference, and exchange controls. During those years, Labour criticised the Conservatives for liberalising the economy too rapidly and for making the pound convertible in 1958. Some looked longingly backwards to the days of the Attlee government, when, so it seemed, intelligent use of controls had helped promote economic recovery, and Britain had appeared an island beacon of social-democratic hope in a largely unsympathetic world.

But those social democrats who followed Jenkins were committed to European integration. Indeed, it has been said that, for Jenkins, 'Europe had become a substitute for the failed god of socialism'.[68] Was social democracy any longer a feasible option for social democrats? François Mitterrand had tried it in France from 1981 to 1983, seeking to expand the economy without regard for the international markets, but its failure had pushed him back to the policy of the *franc fort* and tighter European integration. Gerhard Schröder, when he came to power in Germany in 1998, was determined not to make the same mistake, and he accepted, rapidly and with some gratitude, the resignation of his neo-Keynesian finance minister, Oskar Lafontaine. He too came to see in European integration a substitute for the ideal of social democracy in one country.

But how could the social-democratic value of equality possibly be attained in a globalised world? Globalisation removed from national states many of the policy instruments on which social democrats relied. It became more difficult to tax and regulate capital and wealth in a world in which they had become mobile. The EU would limit the role of national governments in determining interest rates and exchange rates. It would also set constraints limiting the power of national governments to budget for deficits. Numerous studies showed that globalisation, by removing state controls which protected against inequality, had the consequence of increasing inequalities even within a single state, let alone between states. Globalisation allowed the

---

68 Edmund Dell, *A Strange Eventful History: Democratic Socialism in Britain* (HarperCollins, 2000), 412.

few to acquire massive financial rewards, while making life more difficult for those without marketable skills. So, the trends of history seemed to be leading away from social democracy, not towards it. And, while globalisation had increased inequality, it had, at the same time, removed from national states those policy instruments which they would need to redress those inequalities. Such instruments would now be forbidden by the rules of the EU, the World Trade Organization, and similar international bodies. Governments could no longer adopt national macroeconomic policies aimed at boosting demand without risking punishment by the markets in the form of higher interest rates and falling currencies. Blair showed that he understood this when, in his Mais Lecture in 1995, he said:

> We must recognise that the UK is situated in the middle of a global market for capital, a market which is less subject to regulation today than for several decades. An expansionary fiscal or monetary policy that is at odds with other economies in Europe will not be sustained for very long. To that extent the room for manoeuvre of any government in Britain is already heavily circumscribed.[69]

In addition to the constraints of the global economy, Britain, as a member of the EU, was subject to its trading rules and the provisions of the internal market. When Crosland wrote *The Future of Socialism* in 1956, the EC – forerunner of the EU – had not yet come into existence. Gaitskell, then Labour's leader, was, together with some of his leading colleagues such as Douglas Jay and Patrick Gordon Walker, positively hostile to it, largely on the grounds that membership would inhibit the policies of economic planning to which a social-democratic government should

---

69 Cited in Dell, *A Strange Eventful History*, 568.

be committed. Jenkins and his followers never really resolved the conundrum of how social democracy was to be achieved in a globalised world, in which what those on the left used to call 'the commanding heights of the economy' were no longer under national control. Jenkins had, as we have seen, been an early advocate of the European Monetary System and wanted Britain to join its Exchange Rate Mechanism. But that mechanism would have constrained those policies of economic expansion which the SDP was advocating in 1983. The SDP, according to the former MP Edmund Dell, 'did not seem at first to realise that it was not simply socialism that was dead. So was social democratic Keynesianism in one country, in devotion to which they had lived their political lives.'[70] Globalisation had become, in the words of the American commentator Thomas Friedman, a 'golden straitjacket' constraining social democracy.[71]

If it has become vastly more difficult to attain the aims of social democracy because of the transfer of power upwards from national institutions, these difficulties would be compounded by the transfer of powers downwards to devolved bodies, a policy which lay at the forefront of the proposed constitutional reforms of the Liberals and SDP. Indeed, Blair, who implemented devolution to the non-English parts of the UK, seems to have taken some time to grasp its full implications. In 1999, he berated Paddy Ashdown, the Liberal Democrat leader, for the policies that the party was pursuing on student support in Scotland, which were contrary to those being pursued by the government in Westminster:

"You can't have Scotland doing something different from the rest of the country," Blair complained ...

---

70 Dell, *A Strange Eventful History*, 479.
71 Quoted in Sheri Berman, *The Primacy of Politics: Social Democracy and the Making of Europe's Twentieth Century* (Cambridge University Press, 2006), 209.

"Then you shouldn't have given the Scots devolution," Ashdown retorted, "specifically, the power to be different on this issue. You put yourself in a ridiculous position if, having produced the legislation to give power to the Scottish Parliament, you then say it is a matter of principle they can't use it."

Tony Blair (laughing) "Yes, that is a problem. I am beginning to see the defects in all this devolution stuff."[72]

Social democracy presupposed a strong state and a centralised state. That was why devolution had been opposed by leading figures on Labour's left, such as Bevan, who, when establishing the NHS, rigorously set his face against a separate Welsh health service. It was to be a *national* health service, and its benefits would be provided on the basis of need and not of geography. That was also the reason why devolution had been opposed in the 1970s by Neil Kinnock, who then regarded himself as Bevan's disciple, and who declared in 1976 that devolution 'could be an obituary notice for this movement'.[73] For social democrats, only a strong, centralised state could evaluate the needs of different social groups and ensure that redistribution was effective. But devolution would fragment the power of the centralised state and cut it into pieces. There could not, in the ideology of social democracy, be a separate Scottish or Welsh political will, for the problem of securing equality in Scotland or in Wales was no different in principle from the problem of securing it in England. These problems could be resolved not by establishing toytown parliaments in Edinburgh and Cardiff, but only by a strong social-democratic government in Westminster.

---

72 Paddy Ashdown, *The Ashdown Diaries, Vol II: 1997–1999* (Allen Lane/The Penguin Press, 2001), 446.

73 Quoted in Miles Taylor, 'Labour and the Constitution' in Duncan Tanner, Pat Thane, and Nick Tiratsoo (eds.), *Labour's First Century* (Cambridge University Press, 2000), 180.

Devolution, then, strongly advocated by the SDP, would be likely to increase rather than mitigate geographical inequalities in Britain. It therefore ran counter to social democracy, which sought to equalise welfare opportunities between those living in different parts of the country. It is difficult to see how the state can promote social justice if it has been fragmented and cut into pieces by devolution.

So, the failure of Jenkins and the brand of social democracy which he favoured was not simply the result of political vicissitudes and contingencies. It was a result of contradictions inherent in the very nature of social democracy as an ideology.

VIII

Nevertheless, despite the failure of the SDP, Jenkins fundamentally altered Britain, and for the better. He was, as Shirley Williams, his fellow member of the Gang of Four, declared, a politician of great courage, indeed one of those rare politicians who was consistently more courageous in his action than in his speeches.[74] Politics, Jenkins declared, was 'not only the art of the possible ... it is also the art of making possible tomorrow what may seem impossible today'.[75] Liberalising the laws against homosexuality and abortion and protecting by statute the rights of women and ethnic minorities has improved the lives of millions of people. The formation of the SDP–Liberal Alliance lent credibility to the idea that the two-party duopoly could be challenged, even if that insight was later adopted by Farage to a cause that Jenkins strongly opposed, while Jenkins's view that Britain could become an integral part of the EC/EU influenced

---

74 Cockerell, 'A Very Social Democrat'.
75 Adonis and Thomas, *Roy Jenkins*, 192.

establishment thinking for many years, even if it never entirely convinced the British public, who rejected it in 2016.

Jenkins was, above all, a brave and honourable politician, clear in what he believed in and prepared to fight for it. 'He had,' it has been said, 'the four ultimate qualities of the successful liberal political leader – rational optimism, deep humanity, a bold plan for the future, and inspirational perseverance.'[76] A man of great integrity, he was loyal to his friends, and was perhaps the last really literate and civilised member that the House of Commons has seen. If he was not ruthless enough to reach No. 10, he had other great qualities, rare amongst politicians – integrity, consistency, determination, intellectual distinction, considerable sensitivity to the changing winds of politics, and a generous nature. Robert Harris is probably right to suggest that the very qualities that made Jenkins so attractive – 'the lack of rancour, the broad toleration of all points of view, the unhurried pleasures in food and drink and conversation' – were also 'the very qualities which held him back from achieving the supreme office'.[77]

Yet perhaps Jenkins's main legacy lies not so much in the policies he espoused as in his conception of democratic leadership. The courage to take an unpopular line in public was – his hero, Gaitskell, believed – the first qualification for political office. Jenkins often displayed that courage. He wrote of Gaitskell that he had left 'a memory which is in standing contradiction to those who wish to believe that only men with cold hearts and twisted tongues can succeed in politics'.[78] Those words could also be his own political epitaph. Like Bevan, he leaves behind him the thought of what might have been.

---

76 Adonis, 'A Biographer's Tale', 329.
77 Harris, 'A Late Friendship', 314.
78 Cited in Lester, 'The Home Office Again', 163.

4

Keith Joseph and the Market Economy

I

Keith Joseph (1918–1994) was one of the main intellectual influences on Margaret Thatcher – he was a guru of Thatcherism. Yet his influence, unlike that of, for example, Bevan and Jenkins, does not lie in what he did in government. As a minister, he was, by contrast with them, a failure. But – as with Powell and Benn – his significance lies in what he said, in his ideas. From that perspective, he had more influence than most of those who have held the great offices of state. Bevan and Benn failed to gain general acceptance for their socialist ideas, Jenkins failed to achieve realignment, while Powell was for much of his political career a voice in the wilderness. But Joseph very rapidly secured acceptance of his ideas in the Margaret Thatcher governments, and those ideas were tacitly to be endorsed by Blair. Indeed, few now wish totally to undermine the economic framework which he proposed. Judged from that perspective, he has a claim to be thought of as, with Nigel Farage, the most influential politician of the post-war period.

Joseph was remarkable as a politician in another sense, one which marks him out from the other five politicians who 'made the weather', and indeed from almost every other leading politician. Most MPs have a prime minister's baton in their knapsack. They seek to become party leader and prime minister. Of the other five considered in this book, only Jenkins and Farage have been party leaders – albeit of minor parties: Jenkins of the SDP and Farage of UKIP and the Brexit Party/Reform UK. The other three – Bevan, Powell, and Benn – all stood for the leadership of their parties, though unsuccessfully. Joseph, however, deliberately rejected the chance to stand for the leadership of his party in 1974, saying afterwards, in words one cannot imagine any of the other five using, that if he had been prime minister 'it would have been a disaster for the party, the country and for me'.[1] The same self-deprecation prevented him from writing his memoirs. He is indeed the only major figure of the Margaret Thatcher years who did not publish an autobiography.

Joseph is remarkable in yet another way: he was the first Jew to have become a Conservative Cabinet minister. Disraeli, of course, had been prime minister in the nineteenth century, but he was a convert to Christianity – or rather had been converted by his father, following a dispute with the Jewish religious authorities. Had Disraeli not converted, he would not have been able to enter Parliament when he did, in 1837, since MPs at that time had to be members of the Church of England, and Jewish disabilities were not removed until 1858. Leslie Hore-Belisha, who was Jewish, was a Cabinet minister in the Conservative-dominated National Government of the 1930s, but he was a National Liberal, not a Conservative. Joseph was the first genuinely Conservative Jew to become a Cabinet minister, at a time when the Conservative Party was far less sympathetic to Jews than it is today. Joseph, however, was not a particularly observant Jew and never showed the slightest sympathy with Zionism. Nevertheless, he always regarded himself – and was regarded by others – as Jewish. His family, he said, were 'minimally observing, but maximally acknowledging, Jews'.[2]

Joseph's background, however, was very different from that

---

1 'Escaping the Chrysalis of Statism', *Contemporary Record*, 1 (1987), 30.
2 Morrison Halcrow, *Keith Joseph: A Single Mind* (Macmillan, 1989), 2.

of the vast majority of British Jews. In the first thirty years of the twentieth century, most British Jews were children of refugees from Russia or Poland, fleeing discrimination. They lived in rather poor circumstances and tended to be on the left. Most lived in London, primarily in the East End, or in Manchester or Leeds. Joseph, however, was born not in the East End of London but in the West End, in the billiard room of 63 Portland Place, the home of his father, Samuel Joseph. His maternal grandfather, Montague Gluckstein, was a founder of the Lyons company, which was best known for its tea-shops and which in the 1940s was to hire Margaret Thatcher as a research chemist in its food laboratory. Samuel Joseph was a prosperous businessman, who was at the time of his son's birth on active service in the Royal Irish Regiment and was twice mentioned in dispatches for bravery. After the First World War, he was to become a leading figure in the City of London, and in 1933 became a sheriff of the City, defeating A. L. Bateman, Conservative MP for North Camberwell, and overcoming some degree of prejudice in the process. In 1942, he became the sixth Jewish lord mayor of London. Churchill, who admired Samuel, was present at his inauguration, and in 1943 Samuel was created a hereditary baronet. Joseph, therefore, came from the *haute juiverie*, memorably portrayed in C. P. Snow's underrated novel *The Conscience of the Rich*, which gives a good impression of the kind of life that Joseph enjoyed, and was, perhaps not surprisingly, one of his favourite novels.

Joseph was born in 1918 – symbolically, perhaps, a year after the Bolshevik Revolution, which 'began a competition between communism and liberal democracy', a competition that lasted for most of Joseph's life until the collapse of the Berlin Wall in 1989 and set the context for his political career.[3] But the

---

3 A. J. P. Taylor, *The Struggle for Mastery in Europe, 1848–1918* (Clarendon Press, 1954), 568.

conflict that most concerned him was less that between communism and liberal democracy than the conflict between the
market economy and democratic socialism, indeed 'statism'
more generally.

Unlike most English Jews at the time, Joseph was educated
at a public school, Harrow, at which he did not shine. But he
flourished at Oxford, achieving a first-class degree in law, one of
just six in his year. He never practised law; his career was swiftly
interrupted by the Second World War, in which he fought and
was wounded at Monte Cassino. Like his father, he was mentioned in dispatches. Returning to Oxford, he won in 1946 the
accolade of a prize fellowship at All Souls College and began
work on a thesis on toleration, a thesis that was never finished.
Indeed, despite Joseph's academic laurels, his literary output
was confined to a few policy papers. In 1948, he joined the
Young Conservatives, declaring later, 'It never occurred to me
to become a member of any other party.'[4] In 1956, he entered
the House of Commons after winning a by-election in Leeds
North East. While there were at that time seventeen Jewish
Labour MPs, Joseph was one of just two Jewish Conservative
MPs, the other being another equally well-born baronet, Henry
d'Avigdor Goldsmid. Joseph was not slow to display his courage
and independence of mind by showing himself sceptical of the
1956 Suez expedition, even though his constituency contained
a large Jewish population which would have supported it, since
Britain was fighting against Israel's then enemy, Egypt. Joseph
was one of just seventeen Conservative MPs to rebel against the
government by demanding that British troops in Suez be placed
under the orders of the United Nations.

Unfashionably for Conservatives in those days, he was interested less in foreign affairs and defence than in social welfare. 'My

---

4 'Escaping the Chrysalis of Statism', 26.

main motivation was then,' he reminisced in 1987, when asked why he had entered politics, 'as it has been since, the escape of society and of individuals from poverty ... I had arrived anxious to *eliminate* poverty ... I simply arrived in Parliament full of good-will, with passionate concern about poverty'.[5] He retained that passionate concern throughout his career but gradually came to the view that poverty could not be alleviated by the state alone. It also required voluntary action – as indeed William Beveridge, a founder of the welfare state, had foreseen – and, above all, cultural changes, changes in the behaviour of individuals and families.

Joseph was appointed to the Cabinet after just six years in the Commons, becoming minister for housing and local government in Macmillan's government in 1962. He was already being regarded by some as a possible future leader of his party. Thanks to his good looks, it was even suggested that he might be a 'Tory Kennedy', John F. Kennedy having won the American presidential election in 1960. But Joseph lacked the self-assurance and natural confidence of a Kennedy and often appeared tense and uneasy in public. He was, moreover, a politician of great integrity, who would never have countenanced, nor even perhaps understood, the dirty tricks by which Kennedy succeeded in advancing in politics. Nor would he have used his wealth, as Kennedy did, to ease his way into power.

As minister for housing and local government, Joseph was responsible for two major policy initiatives. Characteristically, he was later to repudiate both. The first was the London Government Act, which established a Greater London Council to replace the London County Council. After 1981, this was to provide a laboratory for socialist experimentation by the left wing of the Labour Party, led by Ken Livingstone. It was

---

5 Ibid.

abolished by Margaret Thatcher's government in 1986. The second innovation was to encourage high-rise blocks of flats in which many of those displaced by inner-city redevelopment schemes and removal of slums were rehoused. This came, over time, to be thought of as a major planning disaster, the high-rise flats being regarded as 'ghettoes in the sky'.[6] Joseph was by no means the only nor even the main advocate of this policy, which was supported by many in the planning and architectural professions – indeed, there was a professional consensus in favour of such flats – but, typically, Joseph took much of the blame on himself: 'God forgive me. I did that.'[7] This showed a note of self-deprecation and apology unusual amongst politicians, but which was to become characteristic for him. Joseph was indeed to become noted for the many apologies he uttered for past policies for which he had been responsible. When, in 1978, he gave a speech at the Conservative Party conference on the day after the Jewish Day of Atonement – Yom Kippur – one journalist commented that it was a sign of his 'growing confidence that this is thought to be the first time he has atoned for a speech before making it'.[8]

In 1965, Joseph voted for Heath in the first-ever election among MPs for the Conservative leadership, in preference to Reginald Maudling and Enoch Powell. He persuaded Margaret Thatcher to do the same, on the grounds that 'Ted has a passion to get Britain right'.[9] In 1970, Heath appointed Joseph secretary of state for health and social services; here too he was responsible for policies which he later repudiated. There was the first of many managerial reforms of the NHS, none of which seemed

---

6 Denham and Garnett, *Keith Joseph*, 132.
7 'Profile of Sir Keith Joseph: Prophet without Honour', *New Statesman* (29 October 1976), 59.
8 Denham and Garnett, *Keith Joseph*, 378.
9 Margaret Thatcher, *The Path to Power* (HarperCollins, 1995), 136.

to produce any obvious benefit. Joseph's National Health Service Reorganisation Act of 1973 provided for three layers of appointed boards – 14 regional authorities, 90 area authorities and 200 district authorities. These last would be monitored by community health councils. The aim of the reorganisation was to secure greater delegation downwards and greater account-ability upwards, but critics alleged that it caused maximum confusion everywhere – more Heath Robinson, one wag sug-gested, than Edward Heath. One commentator called the new system 'a Byzantine structure in which there were too many tiers of administration and in which senior executive officials were responsible to authorities which might include among their members one of their own subordinates'.[10] The Labour opposi-tion hoped to repeal the legislation reorganising the NHS, but by the time it came to power in March 1974, it was too late to do so, although the area health authorities were to be abolished in 1982 by Margaret Thatcher's government. Joseph later came to agree that his health service reorganisation, like the London gov-ernment reorganisation and his advocacy of the high-rise flats, was a mistake.

Joseph's period at the Department of Health and Social Ser-vices was characterised by high departmental spending. The 1970 Conservative manifesto had declared, 'The fundamental problem of all Britain's social services ... is the shortage of resources,' and at the 1973 Conservative conference, Joseph boasted:

The real buying power of the NHS and the local authority social service departments in our current four years is rising from year to year at a rate of 40 per cent higher than it was in Labour's central four years, year by year ... In other words, we are spending more in real terms than Labour ever managed to

---

10 Denham and Garnett, *Keith Joseph*, 215–6.

do and increasing our rate of spending on these services faster than Labour did.[11]

Joseph popularised the idea of a 'cycle of deprivation', whereby the social problems of one generation were transmitted to the next, thanks to anti-social behaviour and attitudes. He emphasised the 'Cinderella' services in the NHS – those which were not fashionable and had been ignored: care for the old and the mentally ill. 'This is a very fine country,' he declared, 'to be acutely ill or injured in, but take my advice and do not become old or frail or mentally ill here.'[12] He introduced an attendance allowance for those looking after the severely disabled, and diverted spending to the Cinderella services.

The Heath government of 1970–4 appeared in hindsight to have embodied a more moderate and socially responsible Conservatism than the administrations led by Margaret Thatcher, who defeated Heath in the 1975 Tory leadership election. But as prime minister Heath had been seen rather differently, and had been regarded as somewhat uncaring, especially during the first part of his premiership – the so-called Selsdon period – between 1970 and 1972, when he applied free-market policies not noticeably dissimilar from those which Margaret Thatcher was later to employ with greater success. Joseph, however, escaped much of the opprobrium directed at the Heath government. Partly because he was able to increase spending on the social services, he was seen as the 'statutory humane minister'.[13] In 1973, Michael Fraser, deputy chairman of the Conservative Party, regarded him as 'one of the successes of the government … He had shown an extraordinary genius at Social Services. He was certainly the best

---

11 Ibid., 211.
12 Halcrow, *Keith Joseph*, 45.
13 Denham and Garnett, *Keith Joseph*, 231.

minister there since the war. He had had great flair in finding
ways to deal justly with the people who were hard done by, by
inflation and other injustices of the welfare state.'[14] A Labour
opposition spokesman, Brian O'Malley, referred in 1972 to
Joseph having a reputation as 'a compassionate man who cares
about the problems of the underprivileged'.[15] In March 1973, the
Sunday Mirror, a Labour-supporting paper, called him 'a man
of strange contradictions, the Tory Minister who really cares'.[16]
But here too Joseph was to repudiate his own legacy, since he
came to believe that the problems of social deprivation were not
to be resolved by greater public spending.

II

Joseph's reputation, then, was high when Heath's government
was defeated in the February 1974 general election. Many
believed that his hour had come and that he could be the next
leader of the Conservative Party. It was indeed during the early
period of opposition that he exercised his greatest influence,
laying the basis for what was later to become Thatcherism, while
at the same time disqualifying himself from the Conservative
leadership.

Following the Conservative defeat in February 1974, there was
an intense debate within the party about its future. Heath, a practical politician never very comfortable in the world of doctrine
and ideology, together with most of the party establishment,
did not believe that a fundamental rethink was needed. Instead,
he felt the Conservatives should win over the centre ground of

---

14 David Butler Election Archive, 16 January 1973.
15 Hansard, House of Commons, 28 November 1972, vol. 847, col. 261.
16 Halcrow, *Keith Joseph*, 52.

politics, in particular those who had defected to the Liberals, a
party that had won six million votes in the February 1974 election. Voters who had defected to the Liberals would not, so the
Conservative leadership thought, support a party which shifted
to the right. Conservatives, therefore, should gather around
them all centre and even moderate-centre-left forces to defeat a
Labour government dominated, so most Conservatives believed,
by the left wing of the party.

Joseph, however, took a different view. The main problem
was not only the Labour Party – not even the left of the Labour
Party; it was rather the Conservative Party itself that was a key
part of the problem, since it had refused to address or challenge
head-on the ever-expanding role of the state. Indeed, Joseph
was the first senior Conservative to suggest that *both* political
parties were responsible for Britain's decline, since both were
responsible for the interventionist policies which had led to Britain's decline. Conservatives, he thought, should be seeking to
reduce the role of the state, not accepting it, still less expanding
it, as the Heath government had done with its statutory prices
and incomes policy and programme of industrial intervention.
Joseph, rather like Powell and Benn, was undergoing a political
conversion in mid-career. 'It was only in April 1974,' he was to
say, 'that I was converted to Conservatism. I had thought I was
a Conservative, but I now see that I was not one at all.'[17] He was
later to elaborate on this in an interview by saying:

> I didn't become a Conservative for very many years after I
> became a Conservative Member of Parliament. I was a rather
> thoughtless statist expecting government to solve the problems
> of the world and unaware of the limitations and indeed the
> often perverse implications of depending upon government

---

17 Denham and Garnett, *Keith Joseph*, 250.

… I simply wanted more of what was going on. Heaven help us, I used to think myself a public benefactor in all that slum clearance and all that central area redevelopment and all those high blocks of flats which were then fashionable … We broke up communities, we broke up long-standing architecture and relationships, and all with the best intentions.[18]

The state, he had now come to believe, could not itself resolve social and economic problems. All it could do was to provide a framework through which individual enterprise and community spirit could be brought into play. It was this theme which was to provide the Conservatives with something they had not enjoyed since the days of Joseph Chamberlain at the beginning of the twentieth century: intellectual self-confidence, a conviction that the left could be defeated on the battleground of ideas.

The central theme of the speeches which Joseph made after 1974 was his attack on the post-war consensus, on the middle ground of politics – 'thirty years of interventions, thirty years of good intentions, thirty years of disappointments', as he put it in a speech in Upminster in June 1974.[19] The essence of that middle ground had been a shared belief in the mixed economy encompassing a large nationalised sector and an important role for the state. It implied a regular alternation of power as the pendulum swung between the left and the right, with a central ground which remained unchanged. In practice, however, so Joseph believed, there had been not a pendulum but a ratchet. Each Labour government had expanded the role of the state, while Conservative governments – those of Churchill and Macmillan in the 1950s and Heath in the 1970s – instead of reversing

---

18 'Escaping the Chrysalis of Statism', 26, 28.
19 'Sir Keith Joseph: Four Speeches that Changed the World', Centre for Policy Studies (2014), 2.

Labour's policies had accepted them in the interests of consensus, and, in the case of Heath, had actually expanded the
role of the state. In its later phase, between 1972 and 1974, the
Heath government had adopted a statutory prices and incomes
policy, which many Conservatives felt went against their party's
basic philosophy, and which had in any case proved unsuccessful, leading to a strike by the miners against the policy and
defeat in the 'Who Governs?' election of February 1974. So, the
centre ground shifted further and further to the left. The mixed
economy, Joseph was to argue in 1974, had 'become increasingly
muddled, as we tried our best to make semi-Socialism work.
Its inherent contradictions are intractable'.[20] It was time for the
Conservatives to reverse the process and to entrench what he
called 'common ground' – a new consensus based on recognition of the creative role of private enterprise, the entrepreneur,
and the market economy, a consensus which, so he believed,
the social-democratic parties of the Continent had by and large
accepted but the Labour Party in Britain would not. At the 1975
Conservative Party conference, Joseph declared, 'We are only
trying to achieve by argument what many European social democrats have long understood – that you cannot make the mixed
economy work at all effectively if you cripple the private sector
and lose control of the public sector.'[21] Joseph and Benn alike
perceived that this post-war settlement had run into the sand
and could no longer be sustained; perhaps they were the first to
do so.

In June 1974, Joseph began a series of speeches which first
transformed the Conservative Party and then laid the foundations for a wider transformation in the country. In the first

---

20 Ibid., 10.
21 Speech to Conservative Party conference 1975, reported in the *Daily Telegraph* (8
October 1975).

speech, delivered in Upminster on 22 June, he gave a wide-ranging critique of post-war economic and social policies:

> This is no time to be mealy-mouthed. Since the end of the Second World War we have had altogether too much Socialism ... For half of that thirty years, Conservative governments, for understandable reasons, did not consider it practicable to reverse the vast bulk of the accumulating detritus of Socialism which on each occasion they found when they returned to office. So we tried to build on its uncertain foundations instead.

He then characteristically added, 'I must take my share of the blame for following too many of the fashions.' As a result:

> For thirty years the private sector of our economy has been forced to work with one hand tied behind its back by government and unions. Socialist measures and Socialist legacies have weakened free enterprise – and yet it is Socialists who complain that its performance is not good enough.[22]

No one, he went on to say, had intended to preside over a period of decline. But 'never in the course of this nation's history have so many good intentions by so many people created so many disappointments'. Why had it all gone wrong? Joseph offered four reasons. First, the party had sought 'short cuts to Utopia'. It had overestimated what government could do to reshape the economy and society. In particular, the social services seemed 'to have generated more problems than we have solved'. Attempts to expand the economy had led to inflation, while industry had been hampered by excessive taxation. Governments had sought

---

22 'Four Speeches', 2–3.

to raise Britain's low rate of growth, but the truth was that governments lacked sufficient knowledge to understand what caused low growth, or how the growth rate could be increased. And perhaps the causes of low growth were very long-term and not to be altered during the term of a single government. 'During thirty years,' Joseph declared, 'we have tried to force the pace of growth. Growth is welcome, but we just do not know how to accelerate its pace.'

Second in the list of what had gone wrong was excessive public spending – in particular, subsidies to nationalised industries, financed by heavy taxation, which drew away the wealth created by the private sector. Even so, the public sector remained inefficient and cumbersome. Much public spending was designed to secure social peace, yet instead of peace there was confrontation between trade unionists and employers. In consequence of the misplaced search for economic growth and excessive public spending, Britain had secured 'the worst of all worlds, inefficiency, hence poor performance and hence social discontents'.

Third in this litany of what was wrong, Joseph pointed to the various privileges and immunities enjoyed by the trade unions, which gave them excessive power to wreck the economy. Here he was in tune with a developing national mood, after the industrial-relations disputes of the past decade, that trade-union power needed to be controlled.

Fourth and last was an ideological antagonism on the part of 'a large section of the Socialist leadership' towards wealth producers and the profit motive. But 'low profits today mean low earnings and low pensions tomorrow ... A football team could not perform at its best if it were treated in the way that Socialists have treated British management.' This Upminster speech and those which followed were intended to combat the 'ideological antagonism' towards free enterprise and to persuade not only the Conservatives, but also the Labour Party, to adopt a more friendly attitude towards the market economy.[23]

In his next two speeches – in Leith in August and in Preston in September – Joseph stressed the overriding importance of the conquest of inflation, 'the arch-destroyer', indeed the greatest threat that Britain faced, undermining as it did both its democracy and the economy. Inflation, he argued, was 'threatening to destroy our society ... the savings and plans of each person and family and the working capital of each business and other organisations. The distress and unemployment that will follow unless the trend is stopped will be catastrophic.'[24] While there would undoubtedly be a temporary increase in unemployment during a period of economic stabilisation, this would be as nothing compared to the mass unemployment that would follow if inflation were allowed to persist. So, defeating inflation, rather than reducing unemployment, should be government's first and most immediate priority. In looking at the reasons why governments had not so far adopted the conquest of inflation as their top priority, he characteristically began 'by accepting my full share of collective responsibility' – for inflation, he believed, was 'largely a self-inflicted wound', a wound which successive governments had inflicted upon the British people. It was the result of the Utopian aspirations that he had decried in his Upminster speech, the mistake of 'trying to do too much too quickly'.[25]

Inflation, Joseph continued, needed to be combatted not solely or even primarily by incomes policies – at that time a favourite nostrum of Heathite Conservatives, as well as of Labour:

[Adopting an incomes policy] is like trying to stop water

---

23 Ibid., 5–8.
24 Ibid., 17, 25.
25 Ibid., 27.

coming out of a leaky hose without turning off the tap; if you stop one hole, it will find two others. We tried incomes policy – more than once; Labour tried incomes policy. The great and the good favoured it – and many still do. But bitter experience reinforces elementary economic logic – with excess demand it will not work.[26]

The Conservatives, like Labour, had financed excessive wage rises by increasing the money supply, by printing money. But that simply fuelled further inflation and led to industrial bankruptcies. In addition, incomes policies had given too much power to the trade unions. The key to controlling inflation, Joseph believed, lay not in incomes policies but in controlling the supply of money. That, Joseph argued, perhaps implausibly, would encourage wage restraint, since excessive wage claims would then result in unemployment. The solution to inflation, as with other economic and social problems, lay not in state action but in a greater sense of responsibility on the part of the individual, particularly the individual trade unionist.

Why had governments not done more to defeat inflation? The reason, Joseph believed, was because they had been over-influenced by memories of the inter-war years. The Conservatives had needed to convince voters that they were not a barbarous capitalist party prepared to see millions thrown out of work. But the experience of the 1930s was, he insisted, not relevant to the contemporary problems that Britain now faced:

We were dominated by the fear of unemployment ... Our post-war boom began under the shadow of the 1930s. We were haunted by the fear of long-term mass unemployment, the grim, hopeless dole queues and towns which died. So we

26 Ibid., 29.

talked ourselves into believing that these gaunt, tight-lipped men in caps and mufflers were round the corner, and tailored our policy to match these imaginary conditions. For imaginary is what they were.

The main post-war problem had been inflation, not mass unemployment. Indeed, for much of the time there had been a shortage of labour – over-full employment. It was because of the shortage of labour that Britain had been able to absorb around a million workers from overseas, many of them unskilled or semi-skilled. So it was a mistake 'to fight the battles of the seventies with the weapons of the thirties'. It was a mistake to increase public spending when faced with temporary recessions, as the Heath government and its predecessors had done.[27]

In his next speech, in Luton on 3 October 1975, Joseph linked his economic critique with a social critique. The post-war consensus, he insisted, had not only impoverished Britain; it was also destroying the moral foundations of society:

It was not long ago that we thought utopia was within reach ... What has happened to all this optimism? Has it really crumbled under the weight of rising crime, social decay and the decline of traditional values? Have we really become a nation of hooligans and vandals, bullies and child-batterers, criminals and inadequates? ... Our loud talk about the community overlooks the fact that we have no community. We talk about neighbourhoods and all too often we have no neighbours. We go on about the home, when we only have dwelling places containing television sets. It is the absence of a frame of rules and community, place and belonging, responsibility and neighbourliness, that makes it possible for people to be more lonely

---

27 Ibid., 30–31

than in any previous stage in our history. Vast factories, huge schools, sprawling estates, sky-scraping apartment-blocks; all these work against our community and our common involvement one with another ... There is, moreover, a commercial exploitation of brutality in print and in film which further debases the moral climate. And how is it that a generation that rejects the exploitation of man by man and promises the liberation of women can accept the exploitation of women by pornography? The left, usually so opposed to profitable commerce in trades beneficial to the public, systematically defends the blatant commercialism of the pornographic industry.[28]

He praised Mary Whitehouse – who had launched an organisation called Clean Up TV and was regarded by the liberal left as intolerant and bigoted – as 'a brave woman'. Britain, Joseph concluded, had been ruined in the public sphere by collectivism, in the private sphere by individualism. The connecting link, in his view, was socialism.

Through these speeches, which attracted wide attention, Joseph was mounting a fundamental attack on the post-war settlement in Britain, a settlement which seemed to have brought full employment, higher living standards, and rising standards of welfare. Joseph, like Benn, although for quite different reasons, regarded the settlement as deeply flawed. Powell had for some years similarly questioned the post-war settlement, stressing that priority needed to be given to the control of inflation, which required control of the money supply, but his views on immigration and hostility to the EC repelled some who might otherwise have supported his critique. By 1974, Powell had broken his ties with the Conservative Party and had become a prophet in the

---

28 Speech in Luton, 3 October 1974, quoted in Denham and Garnett, *Keith Joseph*, 262.

wilderness. Joseph, however, spoke as a leading front-bench member of his party, one who had been a loyal member and supporter of the Macmillan and Heath governments.

Joseph's attack on the post-war settlement in his various post-war speeches, like Benn, was strong on assertion but weak on historical detail. Typical of those who looked back to a supposed golden age existing in a not very clearly defined past, he was apt to contrast the best of the past with the worst of the present. Nevertheless, his celebration of the entrepreneur – 'the character who works the magic, the Aladdin who creates the jobs' – was music to the ears of many Conservatives, who also hoped that the more restricted role which the state was to adopt would at the same time somehow contribute to a rediscovery of social obligation and social morality, even though exactly how this was to be achieved was never quite spelled out.[29]

Although Joseph's speeches appealed to many MPs and constituency members precisely because they called for a smaller state, the Conservative establishment felt them to be maladroit, for they were made at a time when a general election was widely expected. After the inconclusive general election of February 1974, which had produced a hung parliament and a Labour minority government under Wilson, a second election was widely anticipated. This second contest occurred in October 1974, just over one month after Joseph's Preston speech and a week after the Luton speech. Heath was fighting the election on a platform of national unity, and there was talk of the Conservatives forming a coalition government even if they secured an absolute majority in the election. Such a government would no doubt have sought to preserve and build upon the post-war settlement, rather than seeking to dismantle it. Joseph's speeches, however, implied that the settlement needed to be radically

---

29 Denham and Garnett, *Keith Joseph*, 420.

recast within a new common ground, to be established by the free-market wing of the Conservative Party. He was therefore intensifying the ideological division among Conservatives by implying that the Heath government had misjudged and misunderstood the fundamental problems facing the country. That was hardly helpful to the cause of party – let alone national – unity. Further, the logic of his Preston speech in particular seemed to imply that the economy needed to be managed at a higher rate of unemployment to function effectively. Joseph himself denied this implication. 'I am not saying,' he insisted, 'and do not believe that we need a certain level of unemployment to avoid inflation.'[30] Full employment was, he believed, compatible with stable prices, free collective bargaining, and a sound balance of payments, but only if the right methods were used to combat inflation. All the same, it was easy to see how his speeches could give rise to misinterpretation, and the Labour spokesmen had a field day arguing that a Conservative government would mean higher unemployment. Joseph had, in the words of an otherwise favourable leading article in *The Times*, 'handled a blunderbuss loaded with duckshot to Mr. Wilson and invited him to blow the Conservative Party's head off'.[31]

In the October 1974 general election, Labour scraped home with a narrow overall majority of three seats. Even though the government remained in a precarious parliamentary position, and was indeed to lose its parliamentary majority as a result of by-election losses and defections by April 1976, it was the position of the Conservative leader, Heath, which now came under strain. He had, after all, now lost three of the four general elections which he had fought – in 1966, February 1974, and October 1974 – and Conservative MPs had found whilst canvassing that

---

30 'Four Speeches', 40.
31 'The Sharp Shock of Truth', *The Times* (6 September 1974).

Heath was, in the minds of many voters, a barrier to Tory success. Although Heath decided to battle on, it was clear that a leadership election could not be long delayed. Joseph, who was emerging as the natural standard bearer of the Tory right, was now coming to be seen as a possible successor. In an article in *The Spectator*, just two weeks before the October election, the Conservative commentator Patrick Cosgrave had labelled Joseph 'the probable next leader of the party'.[32] But Joseph's next speech, delivered in Edgbaston on 19 October, was to destroy whatever chances he may have had.

III

In the Edgbaston speech, as in Luton, Joseph denounced the permissive society which was responsible, he believed, for a wide range of disparate ills – including drugs, drunkenness, teenage pregnancies, hooliganism, violence in schools, illiteracy, and illegitimacy. He asked rhetorically, 'Are we to be destroyed from inside – a country which successfully repelled and destroyed Philip of Spain, Napoleon, the Kaiser, Hitler – are we to be destroyed by ideas, mischievous, wrongheaded, debilitating, yet seductive because they are fashionable and promise so much on the cheap?' He again lauded Mary Whitehouse who had spoken out 'against the BBC, the educators and the false shepherds'.[33] Joseph's sweeping condemnation, it has to be said, was not borne out by the facts. In the 1970s, for example, whilst the murder rate was static, sexual offences and armed robbery were falling, and the burglary rate had been falling since 1973.

---

32 Patrick Cosgrave, 'The Man Who Told the Truth', *The Spectator* (28 September 1974).
33 Speech in Edgbaston, 19 October 1974, Margaret Thatcher Foundation, 9.

After Joseph's litany of woe came the crucial passage of the speech. He declaimed against the large number of pregnancies in young women – particularly unmarried ones – in the working classes. 'Our human stock,' he insisted, 'was threatened by the relatively large proportion of babies being born to women from social classes 4 and 5. The balance of our population, our human stock is threatened.' It was this comment that destroyed his leadership chances. The words 'human stock' carried with it a flavour of eugenics – 'very nasty genetic undertones,' thought Barbara Castle, the health and social services secretary – and the implication seemed to be that government should take forcible steps to prevent women from the lowest social classes having large families, since they were unfit to be parents. Joseph was certainly not advocating this, although in 1970, as social services secretary, he had asked his officials if sterilisation was possible with 'really bad problem families'.[34] Margaret Thatcher, interestingly, refused in 1974 to have anything to do with population policy, though she was urged by Central Office to consider the issue.[35]

Joseph's Edgbaston speech, and in particular his comments about the birth rate, caused a furore. For the first time in his life, Joseph was to find himself a celebrity. He apparently received around 2,000 letters of support, including one from the actor Laurence Olivier, but many misunderstood what he had been saying. One correspondent told Joseph that he was right, since 'too many Irish are breeding'.[36] But such public support as he secured was countered by excoriation in the press and from many other politicians. He was also criticised by many social-science experts. Joseph had made himself an obvious target for

---

34 Halcrow, *Keith Joseph*, 221.
35 Castle, *The Castle Diaries*, 198.
36 Denham and Garnett, *Keith Joseph*, 268.

attack. A headline in the *Evening Standard* declared, 'Sir Keith in "Stop Babies" Sensation'.[37] 'Castrate or conform' was another headline.[38] Joe Gormley, leader of the miners' union, declared that the message of the speech was that 'we should put down the kids produced by what he calls the lower classes'.[39] One journalist called Joseph 'a saloon-bar Malthus'.[40] The inference was made by some that the poor were immoral and so should have their benefits withdrawn, something which, again, Joseph had not advocated. Frank Field, the director of the Child Poverty Action Group, who would later become a Labour MP, declared that the speech 'bore all the marks of deliberately attempting to unleash a national backlash against the poor'.[41] That also was something Joseph had certainly not intended. But it was in vain that Joseph protested, 'I had thought that my record of initiative and concern for problem families and for what I have called "the cycle of deprivation" when I was Secretary of State for Social Services would have protected me from misunderstanding.'[42]

When the dust had settled, it appeared that Joseph had not fully understood the complexities of the research which he had cited. This research had been undertaken by two social researchers, Arthur and Peggy Wynn, and published in the magazine of the Child Poverty Action Group. But the Wynns had been far

---

37 Halcrow, *Keith Joseph*, 74.

38 Denham and Garnett, *Keith Joseph*, 268.

39 John Cunningham, 'Child researchers attack Sir Keith's moral judgment', *Guardian* (21 October 1974).

40 Denham and Garnett, *Keith Joseph*, 270.

41 Cunningham, 'Child researchers'.

42 Denham and Garnett, *Keith Joseph*, 270. In a footnote to page 234 of his book *Seasons in the Sun: The Battle for Britain, 1974-1979* (Allen Lane, 2021), Dominic Sandbrook erroneously claims that Jonathan Sumption, later Lord Sumption and a judge of the Supreme Court, was the author of the speech. Although Sumption was at that time assisting Joseph on a part-time basis, he had nothing whatever to do with the Edgbaston speech. Indeed, in May 2020 he told me, 'The first I knew of it was when I read about it in the press after it had been delivered.'

more circumspect and cautious than Joseph, who was entering, in the words of the *Guardian*, 'a statistician's labyrinth'.[43] The Wynns' research had been based on figures from Scotland only – since, while the Registrar General for Scotland published figures relating the birth rate and births out of wedlock to social class, the General Register Office for England and Wales did not. In Scotland, the population was poorer than in the rest of Britain, with 34 per cent in social classes four and five. Women in those classes were producing 35 per cent of the births, hardly a much greater percentage than in other classes. In addition, the statistics recorded the father's occupation when registering the birth of a married couple, but the mother's occupation when registering a birth for an unmarried woman. It was therefore very possible that, in such cases, the father's social class would be higher than that of the unmarried mother, who might be less likely to be in a skilled job. Even so, just 3 per cent of the births in classes four and five in Scotland were to single mothers, and fewer than 5 per cent to teenagers.[44]

There appeared to be no link between social class and sexual permissiveness. Indeed, Michael Schofield, a former research director of the Central Council for Health Education, told the *Guardian* that the higher up the social scale, the more likely it was that a girl would be sexually experienced.[45] Further, the 1971 census showed that family size was approximately the same in all social classes, the implication being that, with the spread of knowledge of methods of birth control, women in classes four and five were coming to limit the size of their families. Joseph's argument, as so often, was long on sweeping assertions, but weak on facts. Moreover, statistics shortly to be published, which had

43 'Sir Keith's Cosmic Canvas', *Guardian* (21 October 1974).
44 Statistics provided by Barbara Castle, health and social services secretary, in Hansard, House of Commons, 1 November 1974, vol. 880, col. 546.
45 'Mrs. Castle tilts at Sir Keith's Birth Statistics', *Guardian* (26 October 1974).

not been available to the Wynns or to Joseph, would confirm that the pattern was radically changing. Teenage pregnancies were not rising, and fewer babies were being born to girls aged under twenty than in the 1960s. In 1972, just 3 per cent of births were to unmarried girls under twenty. And unmarried pregnancies were spread fairly evenly amongst girls and women of different social classes.

It was not clear whether Joseph attributed the threat to the 'human stock' to 'permissiveness' or, more simply, to an absence of family-planning facilities and advice. If the cause was permissiveness, it was hardly plausible to attribute this to socialism, since similar trends were noticeable in other advanced societies, such as the US, which had not been contaminated by that creed. More plausible culprits were affluence and the rise of individualism, which had speeded up the cause of female emancipation. In any case, if permissiveness was the problem, it was not clear how the provision of contraceptives to the lower classes would assist in alleviating it. It was at this point that Mary Whitehouse, the recipient of Joseph's encomium, parted company with him. She certainly endorsed his view that society needed remoralising but was fervently opposed to free contraception, which, she believed, would simply encourage immorality.

There was, in any case, some irony in Joseph's critique. As health secretary in the Heath government, he had resisted pressures for contraceptive appliances to be free under the NHS, a decision reversed by his Labour successor, Barbara Castle. He had also been unsympathetic to proposals for abortion on demand.

Nevertheless, when all of the considerable caveats and criticisms of the Edgbaston speech have been made, there was a core of truth at its centre which its critics ignored, but which is now accepted as commonplace – Joseph was arguing that social problems were a consequence of individual behaviour as well as social factors and that, in consequence, many social problems are reproduced through vulnerable families from one generation to another. This was, he believed, a prime cause of delinquency, poor educational standards, lack of skills, and unemployment. By April 2000, Blair's New Labour government welcomed a report which declared that 'girls are nine times more likely to become teenage mothers if they come from a low skill background'.[46]

IV

The Edgbaston speech was to be repudiated by many of Joseph's Tory colleagues, while Margaret Thatcher, his only obvious ally in Heath's Shadow Cabinet, came to the understandable conclusion that he lacked sufficient political judgement to be a plausible candidate for the leadership. A little later, in April 1975, Denis Healey, the Labour chancellor, declared in the Commons that 'when the right hon. gentleman started on his crusade he was seen by many as a Moses who would save this country. In twelve short months he has turned into a Malvolio'.[47] Conservatives could hardly elect a leader whose every speech needed to be qualified by amendments or repudiated by an apology. Joseph himself was quite unable to cope with the virulent criticism which the speech had aroused, and he announced that he would not be a candidate in any leadership election. Margaret Thatcher, who had intended to support Joseph for the leadership, felt, after his withdrawal, that there should be a candidate who represented their standpoint. So she then announced her own candidature, something she would not have done had Joseph's hat remained in the ring. To the surprise of many, she succeeded in overthrowing Heath

46 Denham and Garnett, *Keith Joseph*, 429.
47 Quoted in Halcrow, *Keith Joseph*, 99.

and securing the leadership, Joseph being the only member of Heath's Shadow Cabinet to vote for her. But it was Joseph who had first noticed and articulated a new mood, a consequence of the seeming failure of governments both of the left and the right. This failure delegitimised traditional elites. The failure of the Heath government delegitimised one-nation Conservatism; the failure of the Wilson government delegitimised social democracy. Governments of both the right and left seemed increasingly disconnected from the public, as well as inefficient and incapable of coping with such new problems as inflation, excessive trade-union power, mass immigration, globalisation, the EC, and the rise of Scottish nationalism. One consequence was party dealignment – voters became more volatile and less willing to support the two major parties. Another was a search for alternative ideologies, the most prominent of which were Joseph's neoliberalism and Bennite socialism.

So, Joseph's speeches had come at exactly the right time. Conservatives had accepted Heath's policy of industrial intervention and rigid control of prices and incomes very unwillingly. Such departures from traditional Conservative nostrums could only have become acceptable if they had been rewarded with success. But they had twice failed electorally in 1974; they had failed also to control inflation. No doubt incomes restraint was needed to reduce inflation, but the Conservatives seemed unable to achieve it. In any case, Labour, with its close links to the unions, seemed always able to offer trade unionists a better deal than Conservatives could. There was therefore a new mood in the Conservative Party, a mood which Joseph exploited, though it was not a mood that he himself had created. Admittedly, Powell had said similar things about the market economy in the 1960s, but he seemed a maverick. Joseph, by contrast, was a mainstream and front-line politician who had very recently served in Cabinet.

When, in the late 1960s, Wilson and his Labour government

disappointed the hopes of its supporters, disillusioning a whole generation who had expected great things from him, it had been widely expected that this new mood would be articulated not on the right but on the left. Indeed, the seeming failure of moderate social democracy appeared to be giving rise to a radicalism of the left – symbolised by hostility to the Vietnam War and the student revolt of 1968. But the deeper alienation was occurring elsewhere. Its earliest manifestation could have been seen in the widespread enthusiasm for Powell after his speeches on immigration from 1968. This was an early and unexpected indication that the real revolutionaries would come neither from the London School of Economics nor from the University of Essex, but from the right. The impetus came not from the betrayal of socialism but from the failure to conquer inflation, and the failure to control trade-union power. It was a revolt not primarily of the working classes, but of middle Britain, in particular of the self-employed, small businesspeople, and those living on fixed incomes, who were suffering from rising prices and industrial disruption, without powerful unions to protect their interests.

The popular discontent based on cultural and economic frustration which was undermining the consensus did not come – as Bevan had once hoped and Benn still hoped – from the left, but from the right. It was the manifestation of a social mood that was very far from being conservative, and could be exploited only by politicians willing to move beyond conservatism as it had been understood in the years since 1945. The left, whether liberal or socialist, found this new mood difficult to understand. So did many of the more traditional Conservatives. Conservatism had for much of its history been an elite philosophy. Conservative administrations had been accommodationist and defensive. But Joseph and Margaret Thatcher saw themselves in a society saturated with the statism of the post-war consensus, whose morality had been undermined by the 'permissive society' of the 1960s.

They found themselves sceptical of, if not downright opposed to, the status quo rather than being upholders of it. Their enemies lay, they believed, not only on the left but at the heart of the establishment. They sought, therefore, to turn the Conservatives into a popular if not populist party, as both Disraeli and Chamberlain had sought to do. They wanted radically to transform the political culture of which the traditional Conservative Party was so central a part. Just before the 1983 general election, which yielded a Tory landslide, one commentator mischievously wrote that Margaret Thatcher had achieved 'what Labour has been ineffectively talking about for years: the elimination of Britain's old ruling class from the corridors of power'.[48]

Joseph was Margaret Thatcher's closest political associate after she won the Tory leadership in February 1975. The two formed a remarkable political partnership. Their qualities were complementary; Margaret Thatcher had the tactical and political skills that Joseph lacked, but as he put it, 'She was not so much a woman of ideas as of beliefs'.[49] Joseph declared that 'her common sense and instinctive approach had reached the same disenchantment and review of policy that I had come to'.[50] One of her advisers later wrote, 'Lady Thatcher is great theatre as long as someone else is writing her lines.'[51] Joseph supplied the ideas with which to clothe her instincts.

V

In the Conservative government formed after the May 1979 general election, Joseph became industry secretary. He always

---

48 Peregrine Worsthorne, 'Enter the New Men', *Sunday Telegraph* (29 May 1983).
49 *Independent* (23 November 1990).
50 'Escaping the Chrysalis of Statism', 29.
51 'Sir Alfred Sherman' [obituary], *Daily Telegraph* (28 August 2006).

believed that his influence had been greater before than after 1979, by which time 'the work had been done'.[52] The practical work was carried forward less by him than by Margaret Thatcher and her leading paladins, notably, Geoffrey Howe and Nigel Lawson.

Joseph, in truth, proved an unsuccessful minister, and, paradoxically, his creative period in politics was largely over by the time he returned to office. In a sense, it was odd that he became industry secretary, for he believed that the Industry Department over which he presided ought not to exist, since it was dedicated to government intervention. He did, admittedly, have some successes. He began the process of breaking the Post Office's monopoly of the telephone system, preparing it for privatisation, and he sold state shares in British Airways, the National Freight Corporation, and Cable and Wireless. But the failures were more noticeable. He did not follow through on the tough prospectus that he had laid down in opposition. He did not split off or sell British Leyland; instead, he provided public funds for the stricken motor company, as he did for British Steel.

By 1981, the Conservative journal *Crossbow* was calling Joseph 'the most dismal disappointment of this administration', arguing that his 'transfer to a less demanding post is clearly long overdue'.[53] In that year, Margaret Thatcher moved him sideways to the post of education secretary, the role that she herself had held in the Heath government. But here too Joseph was to disappoint his supporters, most of all perhaps his prime minister, who must have hoped that he would bring to bear his reforming zeal on a department that she had regarded as recalcitrant to new thinking. In opposition, Joseph had been sympathetic

---

52 'Escaping the Chrysalis of Statism', 29.
53 Denham and Garnett, *Keith Joseph*, 357.

to the free-market idea of education vouchers, but he did not pursue this with any force as a minister. He tentatively proposed ending the student grant for the most affluent families, so that they would be required to contribute towards tuition fees and increase their contributions towards student maintenance. But he was forced to withdraw by hostility from Conservative MPs and howls of rage from Conservative constituency organisations, whose middle-class supporters – while no doubt favouring the free market in principle – found themselves, when the education of their own offspring was at stake, as tenaciously committed to state subsidies as any trade unionist or benefit recipient. Margaret Thatcher appreciated that, whatever the theoretical merits of Joseph's proposal, it was politically impracticable at that time, and he was forced to withdraw, although his successor, Kenneth Baker, was to introduce a system of student loans in 1990, while the Blair government would introduce a fully fledged scheme of student contributions towards tuition fees.

But Joseph did succeed in articulating a number of issues in addition to tuition fees, which were to become important for future education secretaries. Several of his ideas were put into practice in Baker's wide-ranging Education Reform Act in 1988, with its provisions for greater information about the performance of schools, appraisal, testing, and league tables, as well as the promotion of grant-maintained schools free of local-authority control, and moves towards a core curriculum. But paradoxically, the search for better standards in schools involved a greater, not a smaller, role from the state and a shift from local autonomy to central control – in other words, more rather than less state intervention.

One fundamental issue raised by Joseph was that of non-academic children who, he believed, were gaining little from their eleven years of compulsory education. He argued that schools needed to encourage vocational skills and practical subjects.

He was drawing attention to a fundamental problem that has bedevilled British education since the beginning of the twentieth century if not before. Britain has always done well in educating its elites. In world university league tables, Oxford and Cambridge regularly appear in the top ten. But Britain has historically done much less well in educating those whose skills are technical and vocational rather than academic. The education system focused too much on those already advantaged, rather than on those who needed more help to realise their abilities. Those whose abilities were technical and vocational rather than academic were, as conveyed by the title of a 2016 report by the House of Lords Social Mobility Committee, *Overlooked and Left Behind*. Joseph sought to combat this waste of human resources. In 1986, the General Certificate of Secondary Education (GCSE) was introduced for those leaving school at sixteen, some of whom would not previously have received any qualification at all at the end of their period of compulsory education. This proved a precursor to other very recent initiatives: Technical (T) Levels, enacted by Theresa May's government and introduced in 2020, and the Lifetime Skills Guarantee, introduced by Boris Johnson's government in 2021. Joseph also encouraged a greater concentration on standards in education, and that, perhaps, was an influence on the reforms of Blair's New Labour government after 1997. He helped to set a new agenda on education.

Joseph's most controversial initiative was his 1985 Green Paper, *The Development of Higher Education into the 1990s*, which insisted that higher education must 'become more responsive to changing industrial and commercial circumstances' and develop 'close links between higher education on the one hand and business, the professions, and the public services on the other'.[54] George Walden, Joseph's parliamentary private

---

54 Hansard, House of Commons, 21 May 1985, vol. 79, col. 857.

secretary, remembers a Conservative back-bencher putting the point more pithily: 'Why don't we just make them give up this Shakespeare nonsense and do something useful?'[55]

Just three MPs – a strange trio – spoke out against the Green Paper. Powell, a former professor of Greek, declared that it was 'barbarism to attempt to evaluate the contents of higher education in terms of economic performance or to set a value upon the consequences of higher education in terms of a monetary cost-benefit analysis'.[56] The effect of this attack on Joseph in the House of Commons was, one journalist wrote, like 'some graceful and defenceless animal being brought down by an incredibly long and accurate spear throw. Was ever barbarian so incongruously diffident, charming, donnish and polite, so rueful and hesitant?'[57] Gordon Wilson, then the SNP leader, called Joseph a philistine; Eric Heffer, the left-wing Labour MP for Liverpool Walton, declared that 'man does not live by bread alone'.[58] The House of Commons was thus treated to the piquant spectacle of a fellow of All Souls being roundly and appropriately rebuked for his lack of understanding of education by Eric Heffer, a man who had left school at fourteen. Margaret Thatcher came, in due course, to accept this criticism of Joseph's approach. In her autobiography, *The Downing Street Years*, she declares that, in higher education, 'Many distinguished academics thought that Thatcherism ... meant a philistine subordination of scholarship to the immediate requirements of vocational training. That was no part of my kind of Thatcherism'. Nevertheless, she accepted that her critics 'were genuinely concerned about the future

---

55 George Walden, *Lucky George: Memoirs of an Anti-Politician* (Penguin, 2000), 270.
56 Hansard, House of Commons, 21 May 1985, vol. 79, col. 861.
57 Colin Welch, 'The Donnish, Hesitant Barbarism of Sir Keith Joseph', *The Spectator* (6 July 1985).
58 Hansard, House of Commons, 21 May 1985, vol. 79, col. 864.

autonomy and academic interests of universities' and that they 'had a stronger case than I would have liked'.[59]

In 1986, Joseph left the Department of Education and Science and retired from government. He was interviewed by a reporter from the newspaper of one of the teachers' unions, the Assistant Masters' and Mistresses' Association. The interviewer asked if he 'looked back over his period at Elizabeth House with a sense of achievement'. 'No,' Joseph answered, characteristically.[60] For his period as education secretary a correspondent in *The Jewish Chronicle* rebuked him, saying that he did not have 'a fraction of traditional Jewish respect for teachers and for learning, of Jewish intellectual humility and flexibility'.[61] That would have distressed him greatly, had he read it. But Joseph later suggested that 'against the great national incubus of low standards in education, I had only begun to lay the foundations for improvements, for necessary work'.[62] That was not an unfair judgement.

After leaving the Commons in 1987, he became Lord Joseph of Portsoken. He died in 1994 at the age of seventy-six.

It is perhaps hardly surprising that Joseph was not a particularly successful minister. Like many politicians of an intellectual tendency, he could be hard and ruthless in stating ideas, but soft and pliable in following – or not following – them up. A lion in opposition, he became a lamb in government. He was an indecisive minister, partly because – despite his forceful and intransigent speeches – he was basically a warm-hearted, generous, and kindly man who thought deeply about social and economic problems, yet was seemingly incapable of effective practical action.

---

59 Margaret Thatcher, *The Downing Street Years* (HarperPress, 2011), 599.
60 Halcrow, *Keith Joseph*, 187.
61 Denham and Garnett, *Keith Joseph*, 13.
62 'Escaping the Chrysalis of Statism', 30.

VI

Most politicians exaggerate their successes, boasting about largely non-existent achievements. Joseph was the opposite. His tone was generally one of self-deprecation. 'I was a joke, a useful joke,' he said, 'a convenient madman.'[63]

Margaret Thatcher took a different view. 'I could not have become leader of the Opposition,' she declared in her memoirs, 'or achieved what I did as Prime Minister without Keith'.[64] Her authorised biographer, Charles Moore, concurs. 'From the beginning to the end of her career, Mrs Thatcher maintained an unbounded admiration and affection for Keith Joseph, although when she was prime minister she quite often found him exasperating and spoke rudely to him.'[65] Joseph, Margaret Thatcher declared, was 'a political giant'. He was 'England's greatest man', 'a darling man'. 'You more than anyone else,' she insisted, 'were the architect who, starting from first principles ... shaped the policies which led to victory in two elections ... Our debt to you is great indeed.'[66] And she dedicated a volume of her autobiography to him. Joseph, she believed, gave Conservatives what they had lacked for many years: 'He gave us back our intellectual self-confidence.' For 'it was Keith who really began to turn the intellectual tide back against socialism ... If Keith hadn't been doing all that work with the intellectuals, all the rest of our work would probably never have resulted in success.'[67] Joseph played a similar role to that of left-wing intellectuals such as R. H. Tawney, G. D. H. Cole, Harold Laski, and members of the

---

63 Halcrow, *Keith Joseph*, 149.
64 Thatcher, *The Path to Power*, 251.
65 Charles Moore, *Margaret Thatcher, The Authorised Biography, Vol. One: Not For Turning* (Allen Lane, 2013), 255.
66 Denham and Garnett, *Keith Joseph*, 403–5.
67 Halcrow, *Keith Joseph*, x, 194.

Fabian Society in the 1930s, who had prepared the ground for Labour's election victory in 1945. But he did not influence only the Conservatives. He has, with some justice, been called 'New Labour's Secret Godfather', since it was 'uncanny' how many of New Labour's themes 'were prefigured in his speeches and pamphlets'.[68] Indeed, as early as 1976, the Labour government seemed to have imbibed much of Joseph's critique, when, at the 1976 Labour Party conference, Prime Minister James Callaghan declared that Keynesian techniques of economic management and fine-tuning had led to higher inflation as well as higher unemployment. That is exactly what Joseph had claimed in 1974.

The 1997 general election, which Blair's New Labour won by a landslide, was to be the first since the foundation of the party in which nationalisation was no longer on the party's agenda. Indeed, the question came to be not which industries Labour would nationalise, but which industries Labour would privatise.

Blair's New Labour government accepted the Joseph view that the main aim of macroeconomic policy should be stability based upon continence in monetary policy. It also accepted Joseph's view that supply-side reforms rather than the manipulation of demand were needed if economic growth was to be secured. It accepted Joseph's criticism of the dependency culture. Above all, it adopted Joseph's view of the importance of entrepreneurs: that only they could create the wealth which the country needed. The official document supporting Britain's bid for the 2006 World Cup declared that Britain was 'a nation of entrepreneurs'.[69] Blair's associate Peter Mandelson declared that Labour was relaxed about people becoming 'filthy rich' so long as they paid their taxes.[70] As chancellor of the Exchequer, Labour's

---

68 Charles Leadbeater, 'New Labour's Secret Godfather', *The New Statesman* (10 May 1999).
69 Denham and Garnett, *Keith Joseph*, 428.
70 David Wighton, *Financial Times* (23 October 1998).

Gordon Brown was to devote his first term, from 1997 to 2001, to achieving monetary continence, as Joseph would have done, accepting for three years the spending plans of the previous Conservative chancellor, Kenneth Clarke. Labour also adopted Joseph's view that education should do more to prepare young people for the world of work.

There was, however, a crucial weakness in Joseph's philosophy, and indeed in Thatcherism. For both Joseph and Margaret Thatcher, economic policy was only a part of what they sought to achieve. It was not an end in itself, but a means to other ends. A healthy economy was a means to a healthy society; it would help to heal a broken society. Traditional Conservatives, after all, had been deeply concerned with maintaining the bonds of community. Joseph shared that concern: he believed that obsession with economics in the past two decades and claims to bring about utopia rapidly had been unsuccessful in part because the body politic itself was unhealthy, since thrift, self-reliance, and respect for law had broken down.

Margaret Thatcher put the same point more pithily: 'Economics are the method: the object is to change the soul'.[71] She shared Joseph's view that the market society required a moral framework, but – as her comment 'there is no such thing as society' suggested – she did not seem to understand that it might also require, in addition to self-reliant and responsible individuals, strong independent and intermediate institutions such as local authorities and professional organisations.[72]

Joseph and Margaret Thatcher did succeed in altering society, but not in the way that they hoped. Margaret Thatcher expressed her admiration for Victorian values, although perhaps what she

---

71 *Sunday Times* (3 May 1981).
72 Interview for *Woman's Own*, 23 September 1987, Margaret Thatcher Foundation Archive.

really sought was a return to what the political philosopher John Gray has called 'the bourgeois life of the 1950s – an idealised image of which she aimed to re-create: a middle-class world of secure livelihoods, dutiful families, and prudent saving for the future'.[73] She wanted by using radical methods to recreate a conservative society that had been undermined by overreliance on the state and a 'devil take the hindmost' attitude, particularly by the trade unions. Yet the free market and the growth of individualism would undermine – even more radically, perhaps, than the state socialism which they so deplored – the very communities and family life that the Thatcherites hoped to restore. In destroying the post-war settlement based on an interventionist state, they also delegitimised such bulwarks of society as local government, the professions, and the trade unions, and in so doing helped to sweep away much of what may have helped sustain that settlement. As a result, many who were attached to these institutions did not feel that they had more control over their lives. Instead, they had a feeling of cultural dislocation.

There is a fundamental tension between economic liberalism based on a market economy and a responsible, stable, and secure society. A successful and dynamic private-enterprise system is likely to undermine social stability rather than sustaining it. Characteristically, Joseph was surprised when the divorce rate was higher among those who had their own homes thanks to the assistance of the Mulberry Housing Trust – a grant-making housing association which he had founded to assist in housing the homeless – than among those on the trust's waiting lists.[74] He had failed to appreciate that achieving the long-desired security of a home gave couples the chance to reappraise unsatisfactory relationships. Those who were able to enrich

---

73 John Gray, *Gray's Anatomy* (Penguin, 2016), 510–11.
74 Halcrow, *Keith Joseph*, 36–7.

themselves by embracing the economic precepts of Joseph and
Margaret Thatcher tended to ignore, therefore, their social precepts. The contraceptive pill, household labour-saving devices,
and supermarkets were freeing women from their traditional
role. Women were demanding more of marriage, having
become more independent, less reliant on their husbands, and
less willing to put up with bad treatment. The possibility of
choice which they now enjoyed undermined the very family stability that Joseph sought to restore. Prosperity, therefore, would
not necessarily lead to a more stable society, but to a more
volatile one. And the market economy was also undermining
the traditional British Sunday. In 1994, after Margaret Thatcher's retirement, the Sunday Trading Act was passed, legalising
buying and selling on Sundays. Capitalism was a radicalising
and destabilising force, undermining the props both of traditional community and of family life. In doing so, it would
further undermine traditional conservatism, based on hierarchy,
deference, and respect for community ties.

Joseph regarded entrepreneurs as heroes of the new market-led regime. But many of the beneficiaries of the Thatcher
regime seemed far from heroes, having little regard for wider
social obligations. A powerful image of the late 1980s, following
the deregulation of financial markets in 1986 – the so-called Big
Bang – was that of suddenly rich young financiers or entrepreneurs – yuppies, as they came to be called – drinking heavily and
immoderately at Liverpool Street station late on Friday after-
noons, before travelling home to Essex for the weekend. The
traditionalist Tory journalist Peregrine Worsthorne unkindly
suggested that Margaret Thatcher had wanted to create a society
in the image of her father, the prudent owner of a grocery shop
in provincial Grantham. In fact, so Worsthorne declared, she
had created a society in the image of her son, a speculative
businessman who operated through various offshore financial

centres and had attracted the attention of the tax authorities.[75] Joseph and Margaret Thatcher preached the virtues of saving and investing, but the society which they helped to create seemed more based on borrowing and spending. Indeed, Joseph himself had noticed that the property boom of the early 1970s had led to a number of young men having made 'exceptionally large sums very quickly by speculating in land (and in most cases lost it when the bubble burst)'.[76] The Great Recession of 2008 was to further delegitimise the very rich by showing that some of the wealthy bankers – who had been set free to earn as much as they could by the Big Bang deregulation of the City in October 1986 – were barely competent, and their ethical standards left much to be desired.

Both Joseph and Margaret Thatcher appreciated that a successful private-enterprise society needed a moral framework for markets to be able to work effectively. It needed, in particular, the virtues of mutual trust and self-discipline. But they did not know how to create a society which secured those virtues. And, after all, a market economy could yield, as well as valuable consumer goods – houses, cars, fridges, washing machines, consumer electronics, and the like – the very hedonism and sexualisation of society which Joseph so deplored. To this conundrum Joseph seemed to have no convincing answer. His encomium of Mary Whitehouse suggested that the way forward lay in greater regulation of 'permissive society'. But that involved the paradox that, while the state should be kept away from the adjustment of prices and incomes, industrial intervention, and the fine-tuning of the economy, it could be given a free hand in controlling what went on in people's living rooms and bedrooms. The market should

---

75　Charles Moore, 'Margaret Thatcher & Capitalism' [lecture transcript], *Margaret Thatcher Foundation* (2012), accessed online.
76　Denham and Garnett, *Keith Joseph*, 332.

be unregulated, except when matters of personal behaviour were involved. That was a strange inversion of John Stuart Mill's principle that matters of private behaviour between consenting adults which did not harm others should remain free from state interference.

The truth is that the market philosophy adumbrated by Joseph and Margaret Thatcher undermined rather than reinforcing social cohesion and traditional institutions. Indeed, it swept away many traditional practices which Conservatives believed they were in politics to defend. What, after all, would there be left to conserve in a full market regime which seemed to require endless change, permanent evolution – what John Gray has called a 'Maoism of the Right'?[77] Political theorists have spilled much ink on the cultural and social preconditions needed to secure a stable yet successful market economy. But they have not yet discovered how to achieve it. Joseph may have identified and helped to resolve the problems facing the Conservative Party and the country in the 1970s, but, half a century later, his legacy has raised new questions which have yet to be answered. He and Margaret Thatcher succeeded in creating a new economy, but not a new society – or, rather, the new society that came into existence was in many respects one far removed from what they had hoped.

In a Commons speech on 29 October 1980, Michael Foot, a leading Labour front-bencher shortly to be elected leader of his party, spoke of a 'magician-conjurer' whom he had seen in his youth in Plymouth. The magician-conjurer took a gold watch from a member of the audience and hit it with his mallet, smashing it to smithereens. 'Then on his countenance would come exactly the puzzled look of the secretary of state for industry [Joseph]. He would then step in front of the stage and say, "I

---

77 John Gray, *Enlightenment's Wake* (Routledge, 2007).

am very sorry. I have forgotten the rest of the trick."[78] Indeed, Joseph was never to remember the second half of his trick.

But it would be wrong to conclude on a negative note. Joseph was fond of quoting the following lines from a now-forgotten poet, Arthur O'Shaughnessy:

One man with a dream, at pleasure,
Shall go forth and conquer a crown;
And three with a new song's measure
Can trample a kingdom down.[79]

Joseph both trampled a kingdom down, the kingdom of statism inherited from the war years, and also conquered a crown, by laying down a formula for regenerating Britain through the tenets of economic liberalism. He is crucial to an understanding not only of Thatcherism, but also of New Labour, a product of the new consensus which Joseph, more than anyone else except Margaret Thatcher, helped to create. Joseph had sought to construct a new 'common ground' based on the market economy, and in this – his fundamental aim – he did not fail. His heirs were not only Margaret Thatcher and Howe, but also Blair and Brown. Henry Kissinger was to tell Margaret Thatcher that the greatest tribute to her success was, paradoxically, the election of New Labour under Blair in 1997 – for New Labour sought, as Joseph had done, to marry economic efficiency with social compassion. Indeed, there was, for many years after Blair became leader of the Labour Party in 1994, broad agreement that the fundamental framework proclaimed by Joseph and implemented by Margaret Thatcher – based on a liberal economy, privatisation, and a trade-union movement operating within a framework

---

78 Hansard, House of Commons, 29 October 1980, vol. 991, col. 607.
79 Arthur O'Shaugnessy, 'Ode', available at poetryfoundation.org.

of law – should be maintained. The point at issue at elections after 1992 ceased to be about competing visions of society and came to about which party would administer the Thatcher–Joseph dispensation most effectively. It was not unfair for the former Conservative foreign secretary Douglas Hurd to say that 'the Conservatives lost the 1997 election, having won the fundamental arguments'.[80]

Still, neither Blair nor Brown did any better than Joseph and Margaret Thatcher in resolving the conundrum of how a dynamic economy could be reconciled with social stability and community feeling. Perhaps no reconciliation is possible, and we will all have to learn to live with the social dislocation which the market economy has brought in its train.

The trajectory of Blair shows that the frequently made comment that Thatcherism was divisive needs to be qualified. It is certainly the case that one of Thatcherism's legacies was an increase in economic inequality, divisions between south and north, and the alienation of opinion in Scotland – an important factor in the rise of Scottish nationalism. But much of the 'Thatcher effect' has not been divisive. There is now a broad consensus that there should be no further large extensions of public ownership. There is a consensus that the top rate of income tax should be far lower than the 60 per cent rate that was in place before 1988, when Nigel Lawson's budget reduced it to 40 per cent, although a rate of 45 per cent currently applies for incomes above £125,000. There is broad agreement that the conquest of inflation should be the major economic priority of government. There is broad agreement that trade unions should operate within the framework of the law. In 1979, 29 million working days were lost through strikes. By 2022, the figure was just 822,000. None of the major measures of the Thatcher

---

80 Douglas Hurd, 'His Major Achievements', *Daily Telegraph* (30 June 1997), 18.

government in the areas of privatisation, tax reductions, inflation targets, and trade-union law were to be reversed by Blair or
Brown in thirteen years of Labour government. These matters
seemed settled, just as Attlee's post-war Labour government had
seemed to settle many issues relating to health, education, and
welfare. Most of these issues remain closed today. Some, therefore, of what Margaret Thatcher did, just as some of what Attlee
did, served to unite, not divide, the country. Joseph's imprint
remains firmly stamped on modern Britain.

Joseph's political career was highly paradoxical. He is
undoubtedly the oddest of the six politicians who 'made the
weather', and the least ambitious. He lacked many obvious
political skills. But, despite all that, or perhaps because of it, it
is Joseph – the most unpolitical of the six, in the conventional
sense – who has exercised greater influence than any of the
other five, except perhaps for Farage. In the words of Ferdinand
Mount, the head of Margaret Thatcher's Policy Unit in 1982–3,
who previously worked for Joseph at the Conservative Research
Department:

> [Joseph] changed the language of politics ... All the issues
> he obsessed about are now discussed in terms that he made
> familiar. We take it for granted that the control of inflation is
> a matter not for political manipulation but for strict monetary
> control carried out by experts. We understand that the state is
> not an all-wise, benign master and that we need to watch all its
> activities with a close and sceptical eye. We have no illusions
> about standards in our worst state schools or about the feral
> upbringing so many children suffer. In fact there is scarcely
> anything that Keith Joseph worried about that we aren't still
> worrying about too. I doubt whether that can be said of any
> other post-war politician who never became leader of his or
> her party. Rab Butler and Tony Crosland taught their parties

to accommodate to the consensus of the day. Only Keith attempted something far more difficult.[81]

The Britain we now live in is in large part a Britain that Joseph played a decisive role in creating.

---

81 Ferdinand Mount, *Cold Cream: My Early Life and Other Mistakes* (Bloomsbury, 2008), 289.

5

Tony Benn and Participatory Democracy

I

Tony Benn (1925–2014) saw himself, like Bevan, as a prophet of democratic socialism, and, like Bevan, he was accepted as such by both his allies and his enemies. But he was much less influenced by Marx than Bevan. His socialism, he declared, 'owes more to the teachings of Jesus ... than to the writings of Marx whose analysis seems to lack an understanding of the deeper needs of humanity'.[1] Unlike Marx and other socialists, including evolutionary socialists and 'revisionists' such as Crosland and Gaitskell, Benn never developed any economic theory of socialism; neither did he ever provide a convincing explanation of how it might come about. Instead, he emphasised the injustices of the market economy and insisted that greater democracy, egalitarianism, and the spirit of fraternity would conjure them away. He did not really confront the conundrum that, even with a perfect participatory democracy, socialism might not come about, since, after all, the vast majority of the electorate are not socialists and indeed never have been. As early as 1955, Gaitskell told the psephologist David Butler that workers in industries which Labour hoped to nationalise did not want it.[2] Further, as Bevan used

---

1 Tony Benn, *Arguments for Democracy* (Jonathan Cape, 1981), 130.
2 David Butler Election Archive, 2 June 1955.

ruefully to point out, there was not even a majority of convinced socialists in the Labour Party or in the trade-union movement. Benn's aspirations were no doubt noble, but they were unaccompanied by any serious analysis of how socialism was to be achieved.

In the eyes of the public, Benn was the most prominent advocate of a socialist economy in the 1970s and 1980s, when the ideological tide was flowing the other way – towards the market economy. His economic proposals had little chance of gaining widespread acceptance. And his significance today is quite different – not for his analysis of socialism, which contained little that was new, nor for his economic prospectus, but for his ideas concerning participatory democracy. He belongs less, perhaps, to the socialist tradition than to the radical nonconformist tradition in Britain, which may have begun with the Levellers in the seventeenth century, continuing with John Wilkes in the eighteenth century, and the Chartists in the nineteenth. His concern was fundamentally with the widening of democracy, and his attempts to widen participation led to his interest in constitutional reform. His real significance lies, in the words of his biographer, in that 'he has been responsible for more constitutional change in Britain than any other politician excepting some of those who became Prime Minister'.[3] It was he who secured the right of hereditary peers to renounce their peerage and the right of party members as well as MPs to elect party leaders. Above all, it was he who first suggested that referendums should be part of constitutional practice, with the result that 'a constitutional door was opened which can never again be closed'.[4] He was the first senior politician to preach the virtues of participatory democracy, of 'power to the people'.

---

3 Jad Adams, *Tony Benn* (Biteback, 2011), xiii.
4 Adams, *Tony Benn*, 1.

Benn seems to lie at the opposite pole to Joseph, who laid down much of the ideological groundwork for what became known as Thatcherism. Joseph was one of the most powerful supporters of Margaret Thatcher, while Benn was one of her strongest opponents. Yet they have more in common than might at first sight be supposed. Crucially, both of them rejected the post-war settlement, established by the Attlee government and continued by the Conservative governments in the 1950s, and then by Heath's Conservative government from 1970 to 1974. In February 1981, Benn met Joseph on a train journey – both were travelling in a first-class compartment – and Benn said, 'At least we agree on this, Keith, that the last thirty-five years have been a disaster' – for different reasons, of course.[5] Joseph believed that Britain had succumbed to statism. He saw the free market as an Aladdin's lamp which, when rubbed, would bring prosperity. Benn, however, opposed the post-war consensus for diametrically opposite reasons – because the Labour governments of Attlee, Wilson, and Callaghan had not achieved socialism. Far from securing an irreversible redistribution of income, wealth, and property, they had maintained capitalism largely intact. Both were scornful of the SDP and the idea of a centre party, and Joseph 'agreed' with Benn's analysis of it. Both hoped for a polarised debate between three political groupings – the Conservatives, the SDP–Liberal Alliance, and Labour, representing respectively, as they thought, monetarism, corporatism, and democratic socialism. '[Joseph] talked about crippled capitalism,' Benn wrote, 'and I talked about the log-jam in a market economy – we got on famously!'[6]

Benn was in public life for over sixty years, becoming an MP in 1950 and remaining in the Commons, with one brief exception

5 Tony Benn, *The End of an Era: Diaries 1980–90* (Hutchinson, 1992), 93.
6 Benn, *The End of an Era*, 93.

between 1983 and 1984, until 2001. His career in public life was longer than anyone of his generation, except for Queen Elizabeth II. He held Cabinet office for longer than any of the other five politicians who 'made the weather', except for Joseph. Indeed, Benn served throughout the eleven years of the Labour governments of the 1960s and 1970s – from 1964 to 1970 in the first Wilson government, then from 1974 to 1976 in the second Wilson government, and from 1976 to 1979 in the Callaghan government. Yet, like Joseph, Benn is to be remembered for what he advocated rather than for any achievements in government. Such legislative achievements as he did have came from his role in opposition as a campaigner, not from his time in office.

II

Benn was born as Anthony Wedgwood Benn, in April 1925, into a highly political family of dissenting Gladstonian nonconformists. His father and both of his grandfathers had been Liberal MPs. 'In my family,' Benn tactlessly told the queen in 1979, 'politics is like a hereditary disease, rather like the monarchy.' The queen 'gave a rather slow smile'.[7] Benn's paternal grandfather, John Benn, had become an MP in 1892, and was made a baronet in 1914. His father, William Wedgwood Benn, 'inherited distrust of established authority and the conventional wisdom of the powerful', which greatly influenced Anthony.[8] Like his son, William Benn was not afraid to risk unpopularity by taking a stand on issues on which he felt strongly. In 1950, raising a point of parliamentary privilege in the Lords, he was unable to find a seconder. Unabashed, he quoted from a

---

7 Tony Benn, *Conflicts of Interest: Diaries 1977–80* (Hutchinson, 1990), 498.
8 Tony Benn, 'A Radical in Politics', *The Times* (7 May 1977).

nonconformist hymn the injunction, 'Dare to be a Daniel, dare to stand alone' – which could have been the motto of his son's life.[9] When elected to the Commons in 1906, the year of the great Liberal landslide, Benn senior had been the youngest MP in the House. But in 1926 he had left the Liberal Party and resigned his seat. He returned to the Commons in 1928, as Labour MP for Aberdeen North, and was given office in Ramsay MacDonald's second minority administration in 1929. Taunted by Lloyd George as 'a pocket edition of Moses', he replied, 'At least I did not worship the golden calf.'[10] In 1942, he agreed to become a hereditary peer, taking the title Lord Stansgate, so as to improve Labour's representation in the upper house, which at that time was minimal. He was to become secretary of state for air from 1945–6 in Attlee's post-war Labour government.

At that time, being a peer meant being a hereditary peer. There were no life peerages until the Life Peerages Act of 1958, except for the law lords and the archbishops and bishops of the Church of England. Accordingly, Lord Stansgate's eldest son could not hope for a career in front-line politics, since he would have to go to the Lords when his father died. This did not seem to affect Tony Benn, since he was the second son, and his older brother, Michael, who intended to enter the Church, said that he had no objection to his father taking the peerage.

Benn, therefore, was born into the aristocracy of the Labour Party. As a small boy, he was invited, with his father, to meet the first Labour prime minister, Ramsay MacDonald, who was to be expelled from the party in 1931 after forming a National, predominantly Conservative, government. The young Benn was offered a chocolate biscuit by MacDonald and declared that he had never trusted any Labour leader since! Indeed, he was to find

9 Hansard, House of Lords, 2 May 1950, vol. 167, col. 51.
10 Benn, 'A Radical in Politics', *The Times*.

himself at odds with every Labour leader after Attlee – Gaitskell, Wilson, Callaghan, Foot, Kinnock, Smith, and Blair.

He grew up in Westminster, living next door to Sidney and Beatrice Webb, and attended Westminster public school. The main influence on his political career was his father's words, 'Dare to be a Daniel, dare to stand alone, dare to have a purpose firm, dare to make it known,' advice which was to form the leitmotiv of his political career.[11] His background gave him enormous self-confidence and the toughness required to tolerate being a member of an unpopular minority and to ignore hostile criticism. It also gave him the confidence to ignore sensible advice. He became politically conscious from a very early age. At the age of seventeen, he walked into Labour headquarters at Transport House and joined the party. In 1941, he went to Oxford as an undergraduate. But in 1943, at the age of just eighteen, he joined the RAF and learned to fly, serving as a pilot in South Africa and Rhodesia, now Zimbabwe. His father was already serving; he had joined the RAF in 1940 at age of sixty-three, and at the age of sixty-seven flew as an air gunner. In Africa, Benn saw at first hand how badly the indigenous population was treated, and became a fervent supporter of rapid colonial independence. The treatment of black people was 'appalling', he said. Africa was his first 'introduction to the real world after having had such a limited education ... I learned an enormous amount which I couldn't have learned if the war hadn't occurred. It was my comprehensive school.'[12]

Benn's older brother, Michael, also served in the RAF as a night-fighter pilot, winning the Distinguished Flying Cross for action in North Africa and Europe. But, tragically, he was killed in an air accident in 1944 at the age of twenty-two. In

11 Hansard, House of Lords, 2 May 1950, vol. 167, col. 51.
12 Adams, *Tony Benn*, 33.

consequence, Tony was now set to inherit the peerage when his father died, and so the prospect of a political career in high office seemed to come to an end. Otherwise, his future appeared bright. On returning to Oxford after the war, he established himself as a first-class debater, becoming president of the Oxford Union in 1947. Thirty years later, however, in 1977, he would remove details of his education from *Who's Who*, shortly after adopting the style 'Tony Benn' in place of 'Anthony Wedgwood Benn'; in place of 'Westminster and New College, Oxford', he inserted 'Education: still in progress'.

In November 1950, at the age of just twenty-five, Benn entered the Commons, having been adopted for a by-election in a safe Labour seat, Bristol South East – succeeding the Labour chancellor of the Exchequer, Stafford Cripps. He was the youngest MP in the House, just as his father had been in 1906 when elected as a Liberal.

Benn was not at that time particularly left-wing. Indeed, in the clash between Gaitskell and Bevan in 1951 over health-service charges, he supported Gaitskell, declaring:

> On this question of "principle" of a free health service, it is nonsense … This is not a matter of principle, but to the contrary it is a practical matter. There is only one test we can apply and it is an overall one: "with what we have and can get by way of revenue, how can we lay it to the best advantage of those who need it most?"[13]

In 1955, he voted for Gaitskell as leader rather than Bevan, the hero of the left. He seemed an establishment Labour figure, rising steadily to a position on the opposition front bench – but in 1958 he was to resign from the front bench, quietly and without fuss,

---

13 Benn, *Years of Hope*, 147–8.

since he could not accept a defence policy based on the use of nuclear weapons. He was not, however, at this time a supporter of the Campaign for Nuclear Disarmament, which called for unilateral nuclear disarmament. Benn said he regarded the idea as 'a typical bit of British self-deception', since 'It wasn't going to make the world give them [nuclear weapons] up.'[14]

In 1959, at the age of thirty-four, he became the youngest member of Labour's Shadow Cabinet. As shadow transport minister, he argued for compulsory seat belts and MOT tests, and harsher penalties for drunk drivers, all of which were later to be introduced by Barbara Castle, transport secretary in Wilson's 1966 Labour Cabinet. Benn gradually became hostile to Gaitskell's leadership, since he came to believe that Gaitskell was splitting the party unnecessarily on nuclear weapons and nationalisation. When Benn's proposals for compromise were rejected, he resigned from the Shadow Cabinet in October 1960. He came later to regard this resignation as an impulsive decision and a mistake, since it had no effect. He learned the lesson and never resigned again, remaining a Cabinet minister for eleven years in Labour governments, even though he found himself in deep disagreement with many of their central policies. But his 1960 resignation was brave, since he would need Gaitskell's support for his forthcoming campaign to repudiate his peerage. Still, when Wilson stood, unsuccessfully, for the Labour leadership against Gaitskell in November 1960, on a platform of compromise with the left, Benn voted for Wilson. Benn himself stood unsuccessfully in 1960 for the Shadow Cabinet. *The Times* published a list of the various candidates, with asterisks beside those who were supported by Gaitskell. They did not include Benn. His father rang him to say how glad he was that he was not an 'approved'

---

14 Adams, *Tony Benn*, 135.

candidate.[15] But these were the last words Lord Stansgate ever spoke to his son; shortly after, he suffered a fatal heart attack.

III

The day after his father's death, Benn received his National Insurance card from the Commons, addressed to 'Lord Stansgate'. He was no longer to be allowed to enter the Commons. He protested to the speaker, who responded, 'I have made an order, my Lord, that you are to be kept out of the chamber.' The press began to call him 'the reluctant peer'. He responded that he was the 'persistent commoner', declaring that he lacked blue blood. Indeed, he took a sample of his blood in a vial to prove it. Gaitskell was unsympathetic, saying, 'You can't expect the party to make a fuss over you.'[16] But Benn enjoyed support from a far mightier figure, Churchill, now in retirement, who had written to him in 1955 declaring, 'I am personally strongly in favour of sons having the right to renounce irrevocably the peerage they inherit from their fathers.'[17] Churchill allowed Benn to make public use of his letter.

A report from a Commons select committee on Benn's predicament asked whether Roger le Bygod had 'the legal right to make a valid surrender of the Earldom of Norfolk in 1302'. It went on to quote John Doddridge, a seventeenth-century justice of the King's Bench, who had declared in 1626 that Roger le Bygod had not enjoyed that right, since a peerage was 'a personal dignity annexed to the posterity and fixed in the blood'.[18] Benn responded that this sort of thing would not go down well

---

15 Benn, *Years of Hope*, 353.
16 Ibid., 359.
17 Ibid., 376.
18 Quoted in Adams, *Tony Benn*, 140.

amongst the voters in Bristol! He called on the clerks in the House of Lords to discuss his wish to disclaim his peerage, but found them quite unsympathetic:

> They were very insulted that anybody didn't want to be a peer. If I had arrived with a string around my trousers and a choker scarf, and said I was a dustman but thought I had a strong claim to be the Earl of Dundee, I think they would have treated me with more respect.[19]

Benn fought a by-election in his Bristol constituency on a platform of the right of constituencies to choose who they wished to represent them in the House of Commons. In May 1961, he was re-elected with 70 per cent of the vote; Churchill had sent £10 towards his election expenses.[20] But Benn was still not allowed to enter the Commons. Instead, his Conservative opponent, Malcolm St Clair, was declared elected by an election court and became MP for Bristol South East, even though he had gained just 30 per cent of the vote. St Clair was himself, ironically, heir presumptive to a peerage.

After a long campaign, Benn triumphed, and in 1963 the Peerage Act was passed, allowing peers to renounce their titles and stand for election to the Commons. Benn became the first peer to renounce, and was the first entry in the newly created Register of Renunciation. Malcolm St Clair resigned as an MP, as he had promised to do once Benn became eligible to stand for election, and, facing no Conservative or Liberal opposition, he won the ensuing by-election in August 1963.

This was Benn's first major victory, and it had a deep influence on him. The establishment had been against Benn but he

---

19 Ibid.
20 Benn, *Years of Hope*, 377.

had won by means of the countervailing power of the people. With tenacity and persistence, the establishment could be worn down if one had popular support. It was popular support that was crucial. The crisis taught him that one never got justice from the top; the Privileges Committees of both houses had done little for him, and his party leader, Gaitskell, was lukewarm. But he learned that if he had the people behind him there was no limit to what he could achieve. It was a lesson that Benn drew upon with his two other great constitutional campaigns – on the referendum and on reforms in the Labour Party constitution which would allow party members, and not just MPs, to elect the party leader. Few now wish to overturn these reforms.

The crisis also taught him something else: 'From that moment on, both as an MP and as a minister, I saw through completely new eyes and understood the experience of all those who really suffered from far more serious abuses directed against them by those enjoying authority deriving from wealth or status or power.'[21]

Benn analysed how reform occurred. At first, the establishment had not taken him seriously. He was, after all, trying to alter a rule which had existed for centuries. Then, when he persisted, the establishment said that perhaps there was a case for reform, but it was not an important issue and, in any case, now was not the right time to achieve it. Eventually, however, the establishment crumbled. Once the reform had been accomplished, the establishment would say that it had of course been in favour of it all the time.

Paradoxically, the Lords reform, in the short run at least, appeared to benefit the Conservatives. In 1963, it enabled Lord Home to renounce his peerage to become an MP and, as Alec Douglas-Home, to become prime minister in succession to Macmillan. Indeed, when in October 1963 Benn came to take the

---

21 Tony Benn, *Arguments for Socialism* (Jonathan Cape, 1979), 15–16.

parliamentary oath, having been re-elected for Bristol South West, he was greeted by:

> ... the ironical cheering of the Tories and the waving of their order papers to celebrate Lord Home's appointment as Prime Minister, which my Act has made possible. This discomfitted the Labour Members and confused the nature of the victory. What should have been the celebration of the clear defeat of the Lords by the Commons looked like a victory by a hereditary peer over the dignity and privileges of the Commons.[22]

Perhaps in a slightly longer run, however, the reform benefited Labour. Douglas-Home was of course narrowly to lose the 1964 election. Had he not been eligible, either Rab Butler or Reginald Maudling would have become Conservative leader and prime minister, and either would probably have proved a more effective electoral campaigner than Douglas-Home. So, Labour might then have endured a fourth consecutive electoral defeat.

But was the Peerage Act in fact a victory of the Commons over the Lords? Ironically, and quite contrary to Benn's intentions, the reform, together with the Life Peerages Act of 1958, served to strengthen the Lords by making it more rationally defensible and therefore more legitimate. A House composed entirely of hereditary peers, all of whom were unable to renounce their titles, would have hardly been able to survive the modernising instincts of the last third of the twentieth century. Still, whatever the immediate electoral and political consequences, there can be no doubt that giving peers the ability to renounce was a wholly beneficial reform, and it came about almost entirely thanks to Benn's grit and determination.

---

22 Tony Benn, *Out of the Wilderness: Diaries 1963–67* (Hutchinson, 1987), 71.

IV

Back in the House of Commons, Benn now reverted to one of his main interests, technology. He had been one of the first in his party to recognise the importance of television as a new means of communicating with voters. He had, in consequence, been chosen to front the television coverage of Labour's 1959 general-election campaign, coverage widely recognised as successful, even though in that election the Conservatives had been returned with an increased majority. His mastery of the media led to him being employed both by Gaitskell and Wilson to assist with speeches and television presentations in the 1959 and 1964 elections respectively. But Benn was later to say that he preferred Callaghan, who was to become prime minister in 1976 after Wilson retired, since Wilson gave left-wing speeches at the party conference but was right-wing in government, while Callaghan was right-wing all the time!

After Wilson's 1964 election victory, Benn became postmaster general and, at thirty-nine, the youngest minister in Wilson's first government. He proved a reforming minister, implementing the current system of postcodes and introducing two grades of postage – first- and second-class letters. In October 1965, the Post Office Tower was opened, being at that time the tallest building in London. Benn encouraged journalists to refer to it as 'Big Benn'! It also doubled as a restaurant until a terrorist attack in 1971 forced it to close.

In July 1966, Benn entered the Cabinet as minister of technology, at a time when Wilson was arguing that the 'white heat of the technological revolution' necessitated an enhanced role for the state. Benn took to this theme with enthusiasm. He symbolised the Wilson government's belief in planning and state-led reorganisation of industry to create larger units capable of competing with other advanced industrial societies. He embraced the Anglo-French Concorde project, presenting himself as the minister who was taking Britain into the supersonic age. Many believed these policies ill thought out. Benn's Cabinet colleague Richard Crossman wrote sourly in his diary in May 1968 of the 'lack of success of the interventionist policies of Peter Shore [secretary of state for economic affairs] and Tony Wedgwood Benn, young men who with carefree arrogance think they can enter the business world and help it to be more efficient'.[23] At that time, Benn was a strong supporter of the EC, because it would make possible large technological businesses which could hold their own with companies in the US. It was an era when big was believed to be beautiful.

But if the technological revolution called for an enhanced role for government, it was vital to ensure that the state was made more subject to democratic control. Technology had to be made accountable to Parliament and to the people. Yet, Benn came to believe, the Britain of the 1960s was seeking to control twentieth-century developments with nineteenth-century democratic tools. In 1968, he experienced something of an epiphany. He declared in June of that year, when he attended – inauspiciously – a student teach-in, 'I realised all of a sudden that for three and a half or four years I have done absolutely no basic thinking about politics.'[24]

1968 was the year of the student revolt. The rhetoric of many of the rebels was Marxist, based on the doctrines of contemporary figures such as the German émigré-philosopher Herbert Marcuse, the father of the New Left. But, in reality, the radicals owed more to the ideas of Jean-Jacques Rousseau and radical thinkers of the nineteenth century, such as John Stuart Mill, than to Marx. Their watchword was not so much 'class struggle' as

---

23 Crossman, *The Diaries of a Cabinet Minister*, 57.
24 Benn, *Office Without Power*, 82.

'participation'. The basic message of the revolt was a distrust of the institutions of representative democracy, such as the mass party and other mediating institutions, and a demand that these be placed under popular control. The rebels sought what has been called 'a fuller, and more genuine, version of the old democratic ideal'.[25] They sought, so Benn believed, not only a more humane collectivism, but a more participatory democracy. They claimed that the promise of democracy had not yet been fulfilled and that the people ought to be more directly involved in the processes of government. This New Left was quite distinct not only from Marxism and communism, but also from traditional socialism and social democracy. Benn was one of the first politicians to appreciate its force. His journey to the left had begun. There was, he believed, 'a great gap between the people thinking about the future nature of society and those who are trying to run it at the moment'.[26]

In May 1968, Benn spoke at the Welsh Council of Labour, declaring that much of the discontent – the student riots in the US which had forced President Lyndon Johnson into premature retirement, the riots in France that had almost toppled President de Gaulle and which had been replicated on a smaller and more peaceful scale in Britain – was a protest against the traditional and remote institutions of representative democracy:

> Much of the present wave of anxiety, disenchantment, and discontent is actually directed at the present parliamentary structure. Many people do not think that it is responding quickly enough to the mounting pressure of events or the individual or collective aspirations of the community. It would be

---

25 Michael Steed, 'Participation through Western Democratic Institutions' in Geraint Parry (ed.), *Participation in Politics* (Manchester University Press, 1972), 96.
26 Benn, *Office without Power*, 65.

foolish to assume that people will be satisfied for much longer with a system which confines their national political role to the marking of a ballot paper with a single cross once every five years. People want a much greater say. That certainly explains some of the student protests against the authoritarian hierarchies in some of our universities and their sense of isolation from the problems of real life. Much of the industrial unrest – especially in unofficial strikes – stems from worker resentment and their sense of exclusion from the decision-making process, whether by their employers or, sometimes, by their union leaders.

Frustration was also the driving force, he believed, behind the Scottish and Welsh nationalist movements, then just beginning to secure by-election victories, as well as the Black Power movement, which he believed was an indication that immigrants of colour were 'not prepared to rely entirely on white liberals to champion their cause ... All these causes,' he concluded, 'are indications of a general – and inevitable trend away from authoritarianism and towards personal responsibility.' As remedies, Benn called for more open government and an end to secrecy, reform of the media so that it would become open to those not belonging to the political establishment, and the introduction of the referendum, since 'the five-yearly cross on the ballot paper is just not going to be enough'. But the Labour Party too had to become more participatory, otherwise 'the widening gulf between the Labour Party and those who supported it last time could well be an index of the party's own obsolescence'.

Benn concluded with a peroration. It was wrong to believe that 'the parliamentary system of government – as now constituted' was 'the finest expression of man's constitutional genius':

[Without reform,] discontent, expressing itself in despairing apathy or violent protest, could engulf us all in bloodshed. It is no good saying that it could never happen here. It could ... In a world where authoritarianism of the Left or Right is a very real possibility, the question of whether ordinary people can govern themselves by consent is still on trial ... Beyond parliamentary democracy as we know it, we shall have to find a new popular democracy to replace it.[27]

Benn's speech could easily be interpreted as a breach of collective responsibility and a criticism of the Wilson government, the hallmark of which seemed to be a bureaucratic collectivism satisfying neither demands for a more humane society nor those for greater participation; it did not even seem particularly effective in combatting Britain's economic problems. In Cabinet, the foreign secretary, Michael Stewart, inquired 'whether the role of lecturer in political science was compatible with Cabinet office'. Wilson rapidly dissociated himself and the government from the speech in the Commons, remarking that Benn 'was giving some personal reflections on current political trends', the first time apparently that a public speech by a Cabinet minister was not treated as a statement of government policy.[28] But Benn was adamant. On 6 June 1968, he wrote an open letter to his Bristol South East Labour Party, reiterating his theme: 'The keynote of party reconstruction must start with a search for a greater participation in decision-making. People today are not prepared to have policy handed down to them from on high – even from a Labour government.' He believed that the biggest single issue for the future would be the need for democratisation of power.

---

27 The speech is reprinted in the *Guardian* (27 May 1968) and in shortened form in Benn, *Office without Power*, 70–3.
28 Benn, *Office Without Power*, 73.

Later in 1968, the American magazine *Newsweek* described Benn as 'the only European statesman who has so far made a public attempt to apply the lessons of the new French revolution [in 1968] to his own country'.[29] It was not often that Benn would be called a statesman!

The idea of wider participation was to be the key theme of the rest of his political career. Individuals, he believed, wanted to renegotiate the social contract, so providing a new dimension to the idea of government by consent. Benn regarded worker control as particularly important, since he believed that trade unions currently had a merely negative power – a veto power – to strike and seek to dislocate the system. Benn wanted to convert that into a positive power of participation. His ideas had much in common with earlier theories of guild socialism and syndicalism, which had been fashionable before the General Strike of 1926, at a time when some socialists, fearful of making the state too powerful as a result of policies of wholesale nationalisation, had believed that workers could themselves manage their workplaces. Guild socialism envisaged the self-government of workers as producers, a form of communal ownership which did not involve the state. They insisted that industry should provide permanent full employment, regardless of economic conditions. Wages, they believed, should be determined not by supply and demand but by the criterion of service to the community. But the guild socialists never answered the question of how much, in the absence of market signals, each firm should produce and how much workers should be paid. They argued that production should be for the common good, not for profit. How, then, would it be determined how much should be produced and how much invested? It is hardly surprising that when, as industry secretary after 1974, Benn put his ideas into practice through

---

29 Adams, *Tony Benn*, 231.

encouraging various workers' cooperatives, known as 'Benn's follies', to rescue loss-making businesses, all of them failed, and the businesses could not be saved from bankruptcy.[30] And Wilson poured scorn on Benn's proposals for wholesale nationalisation: 'Who's going to tell me that we should nationalise Marks and Spencer in the hope that it will be as efficient as the Co-op?'[31]

V

In 1970, Benn moved into opposition following the defeat of the Labour government in the general election. He was now a leadership contender and stood for the deputy leadership of the party in 1971, but came bottom of the poll, with just 46 votes against 96 for Michael Foot and 140 for Jenkins. He was one of the few ministers, if not the only one, who left government more radical, and indeed more socialist, than when he had joined it. He told David Butler in 1974 that 'like other Labour politicians he had tried to make the system work, but he now recognised that fundamental and irreversible changes had to be made in a socialist direction'.[32] He believed that where there had been conflict between the Labour government and party members, the government had been wrong: on policies such as deflating in 1964, in a futile attempt to avoid devaluation; on the failed attempt to maintain bases east of Suez; and on supporting the Americans in Vietnam.

Benn came to be fond of saying that his trajectory was to be the opposite of most Labour MPs. They began on the left but ended up in the House of Lords. He, by contrast, began in the

---

30 Joel Barnett, *Inside the Treasury* (Andre Deutsch, 1982), 35.
31 Philip Ziegler, *Wilson: The Authorised Life of Lord Wilson of Rievaulx* (HarperCollins, 1995), 393.
32 David Butler Election Archive, 12 January 1974.

Lords but was to end up on the left. Benn also claimed that he was following in the footsteps of his beloved father, who also moved to the left as he got older. He said that the family had an unusual gene, which, instead of making them more conservative as they aged, made them more radical.

In opposition, Benn reiterated the need for participation and democratic accountability, believing that 'one of the underlying causes of Labour's defeat in 1970 could well have been that we did not appreciate the changing nature of our relationship with the people'.[33] Labour was now swinging to the left and was in danger of being split over the issue of British membership of the Common Market, as the EC was then widely known. In 1967, Wilson had made a second British application to join, following the failed first application by Macmillan in the early 1960s. This second application, like the first, was vetoed by France's president, Charles de Gaulle. But Wilson refused to accept defeat and declared that the application remained on the table. In 1969, de Gaulle had resigned the presidency, having been defeated in a referendum on constitutional reform, and was succeeded by Georges Pompidou, who seemed better disposed to British membership. Labour's application was taken up in 1970 by the victorious Conservative government led by Heath, an enthusiast for Europe, and there now seemed a real chance that the application to join would at last be successful.

The Labour Party, it would seem, had little alternative but to support Heath's application. But the left argued that Labour should oppose entry to what it regarded as a capitalist and market-based institution which would inhibit socialist planning. Benn was, at this stage, favourable to entry, provided that it was democratically approved – so he persisted with his idea of holding a referendum, arguing that so fundamental an issue

---

33 Benn, *Office without Power*, 505 ff.

could not be decided by the House of Commons alone. Both parties, after all, were divided on the issue – Labour obviously so, but also the Conservatives, whose anti-marketeers were now led by the formidable figure of Powell. Further, in the general election of 1970, since all three party leaders had declared their support for EC membership, there was no way in which an opponent of entry could express that opposition through a vote. In his September 1970 Fabian tract, *The New Politics: A Socialist Reconnaissance*, Benn declared:

> A decision taken by the House of Commons that committed Britain to membership of the EEC might or might not conform to the popular view as ascertained by the (somewhat discredited) public opinion polls [which had failed to predict the outcome of the 1970 election.] But if it did not, and those who are opposed to entry refuse to accept the reasons given for joining (or vice versa) something like a breakdown in the social contract might occur.[34]

In other words, the issue was of such fundamental importance that securing legitimacy for it required the participation of the people, as well as that of MPs.

Nevertheless, in April 1971, Benn failed to find a seconder for his European Community (Referendum) Bill; he could not find a seconder for the referendum proposal at Labour's National Executive Committee in 1971 either; and in that year Labour's conference rejected the referendum by a majority of more than two to one, calling for a general election instead. However, at a Shadow Cabinet meeting, Callaghan had, apparently, presciently remarked that the referendum was 'a rubber dinghy into which

---

34 Ibid., 517.

we may well all have to climb'.[35] It was a device which would hold warring factions in the Labour Party together, since both left and right could declare that they would abide by the outcome of a popular vote. There was no need, therefore, for the Labour Party to pronounce on whether it favoured membership or not on the terms to be negotiated by Heath. It could say simply that the issue would be put to the people to decide. The other states proposing to enter the EC – Denmark, Ireland, and Norway – all held referendums before joining, and in Norway the people voted not to join. In March 1972, Pompidou, primarily for domestic political reasons, proposed a referendum in France on whether British entry should be approved – something which was, in fact, hardly in doubt. This made it appear absurd that British voters were not to be consulted. It was under the impact of these developments that Labour performed a U-turn and committed itself to a referendum on British membership.

The purpose of this commitment in the minds of many was to hold the Labour Party together. But the immediate effect was divisive. Jenkins, deputy leader of the party, together with two other pro-European members of the Shadow Cabinet, resigned from the front bench as a result, declaring that the referendum commitment was a piece of political opportunism. However, for Wilson and Callaghan, it was the only way to avoid a successful campaign spearheaded by the left and the trade unions, committing the next Labour government to withdrawal from the EC. And the Labour government elected in February 1974 could not have held together without the referendum commitment. Perhaps Labour would not, in fact, have been elected without it, since it enabled both supporters and opponents of entry to vote Labour with an easy conscience. It also seemed in line with

---

35 Michael Hatfield, *The House the Left Built: Inside Labour's Policy-Making, 1970–1975* (Gollancz, 1978), 70.

the feelings of the British people, who, from February 1971, had been – if survey evidence was to be believed – in favour by a large majority of holding a referendum. So the referendum commitment may also have helped defuse, as Benn had predicted, a dangerous populist resentment against politicians were they to deny voters the opportunity to pronounce on so fundamental an issue.

In June 1975, Britain's first national referendum was duly held on the question of whether Britain should remain in the EC on the terms renegotiated by Wilson's Labour government. In presenting the bill providing for the referendum, Edward Short, the leader of the Commons, declared in March 1975 that 'the issue [of Europe] continues to divide the country. The decision to go in has not been accepted. That is the essence of the case for having a referendum.'[36] That was precisely the case that Benn had put, and it was very much in accordance with liberal doctrine. 'The Legislative,' John Locke had declared in his *Second Treatise of Government*, 'cannot transfer the power of making laws to any other hands. For it being but a delegated power from the people, they who have it cannot pass it to others.' Voters entrust MPs with legislative powers as their agents, but they do not give MPs authority to transfer those powers to another body such as the EC. For that, MPs require specific authority, a specific mandate from the people in the form of a referendum. Therefore, far from being alien to the British constitution, the referendum appeared to be in accordance with traditional British liberal doctrine.

This, then, was Benn's second success. In a Commons debate on the referendum on 18 April 1972, he had predicted the course of events:

The arguments against the Referendum are the very same

---

36 Hansard, House of Commons, 11 March 1975, vol. 888, col. 292.

arguments as have been used against every extension of the people's rights for 140 years. It follows the same pattern. First, the argument is ignored. It is described as a fringe issue. It is then described as trendy. Then it is mocked. Then it is laughed at. Then hon. Members who do not support the Referendum laugh at their own constituents and laugh at those who advocate the referendum. Then they warn against the referendum and against its dangers. Then they denounce it. Then they capitulate. Then they forget and hope that everyone else forgets too.[37]

When he first proposed the referendum, Benn had been in favour of British entry into the EC, believing, as he told the University of Manchester in April 1970, that it had been established 'because you cannot run a modern industrial system effectively unless certain economic decisions are taken internationally'.[38] In a later interview, in September 1990, he explained his support for Europe:

By April 1967 [the Wilson government was] a totally demoralised cabinet. We had tried the National Plan and it had failed. We had tried to hold the pound and it had failed, we were going to have to devalue. We had tried everything. I thought we didn't have a choice. I also thought at that time that the only way you could deal with multinational companies was by multinational political structures.[39]

However, by the time the commitment to the referendum had been made, Benn had become hostile to membership. For this

---

37 Hansard, House of Commons, 18 April 1972, vol. 835, cols. 311–12.
38 Benn, *Office without Power*, 500.
39 Adams, *Tony Benn*, 277.

there were two reasons. The first was that he had come to believe that the EC, by forcing Britain to share economic sovereignty with others, would prevent policies of state planning and therefore act as a barrier to socialism. Interestingly enough, Margaret Thatcher was to come to the quite opposite view in the late 1980s, that the EC would impose an unacceptable degree of supranational regulation and intervention on the British economy, so inhibiting the free-market policies necessary for economic success. 'We haven't worked all these years to free Britain from the paralysis of Socialism,' she was to declare in her Bruges speech of 1988, 'only to see it creep in through the back door of central control and bureaucracy from Brussels.'[40] Both Margaret Thatcher and Powell were fundamentally concerned, however, with the issue of sovereignty. Benn, by contrast, was concerned with power – the power that Parliament needed to retain and exercise to secure fundamental changes to the British economy. In 1976, during the IMF crisis, he was to propose that instead of cutting public spending the government should pursue an alternative economic strategy comprising import controls, restrictions on the export of capital, and control of the banks and insurance companies. But such policies could not have been lawfully implemented by a member state of the EC.

Benn's opponents believed that this strategy amounted to a siege economy; it was not clear how such an economy could advance socialism, which most regarded as an internationalist doctrine.

Benn's second reason for becoming hostile to the EC was even more fundamental: he came to see it as undemocratic. In his last speech in the Commons, on 22 March 2001, he said that there were five essential questions to be asked of anyone with power:

---

40 Margaret Thatcher, speech to College of Europe (Bruges Speech), 20 September 1988, Margaret Thatcher Foundation.

What power have you got? Where did you get it from? In whose interests do you exercise it? To whom are you accountable? And how can we get rid of you? If you cannot get rid of the people who govern you, you do not live in a democratic system.[41]

In Benn's view, the institutions of the EC, now the EU, were not accountable, and electors could not get rid of those who ran them. European institutions, therefore, could not provide convincing answers to his five essential questions. It is indeed admitted, even by many defenders of the EU, that it continues to suffer from a democratic deficit.

Ironically, as with the renunciation of his peerage, the immediate result of Benn's second constitutional reform, the referendum, appeared to benefit his opponents. In the June 1975 referendum, there was a two-to-one majority for remaining in the EC. The referendum indeed legitimised membership. In the words of one of Wilson's advisers, it had been a Conservative prime minister, Heath, who had taken the British establishment into Europe, but it had been left to Labour's Wilson to lead the British people into Europe. Benn felt himself compelled to declare:

I have been in receipt of a very big message from the British people. I read it loud and clear ... By an overwhelming majority the British people have voted to stay in and I am sure that everybody would want to accept that. That has been the principle of all of us who have advocated the referendum.[42]

---

41 Hansard, House of Commons, 22 March 2001, vol. 365, col. 510.
42 Quoted in David Butler and Uwe Kitzinger, *The 1975 Referendum* (Macmillan, 1976), 273.

Benn believed that the referendum had been the equivalent of a general election which the Labour government had won, but the Labour Party, a majority of which was opposed to entry, had lost. It was indeed a triumph of the Cabinet over the Labour Party and the trade unions.[43] The left of the Labour Party was weakened, and Benn's political career suffered a setback when, immediately after the referendum, he was demoted from industry secretary to energy secretary. The Treasury then took control of industrial strategy, which became not dissimilar to that of Heath's Conservatives between 1972 and 1974. And, although the referendum was held because of the supposedly unique nature of the European issue, in 1979 further referendums came to be held on devolution in Scotland and Wales. These led to the defeat of devolution and then the defeat of the Labour government, which was in a minority in the Commons and dependent on nationalist votes, in a vote of no confidence in March 1979.

VI

In 1976, Wilson resigned as prime minister, and Callaghan was elected as his successor. Benn stood for the leadership but received just thirty-seven votes, dropping out after the first ballot. Benn regarded Callaghan as the third revisionist Labour leader in a row, after Gaitskell and Wilson. Even worse, Callaghan, so Benn believed, was not a socialist at all. When the Callaghan government accepted a bail-out loan from the IMF entailing reductions in public spending, Benn believed that this signalled the death of social democracy, since it destroyed the idea that capitalism could be successfully managed by means of a high level of public expenditure.[44]

---

43 David Butler Election Archive, 28 June 1978.
44 Ibid.

Labour was defeated in the 1979 election, and Benn, leaving ministerial office for the last time in 1979, had to hand in his seals of office to the queen. He told her, 'Whereas twenty-five years ago we were an empire, now we are a colony with the IMF running our financial affairs and the Common Market Commission running our legislation and NATO running our armed forces.'[45] The queen rapidly changed the subject!

After the 1979 defeat, Benn moved even further to the left. 'I have the freedom now to speak my mind, and this is probably the beginning of the most creative period of my life,' he wrote in his diaries. 'I am one of the few ex-Ministers who enjoys opposition and I intend to take full advantage of it.'[46] He claimed that he was now leading a third wave of 'struggles against revisionism' in the Labour Party. The first had been after the 1959 election defeat, when the party leader, Gaitskell, had unsuccessfully attempted to remove from the party's constitution its commitment to the nationalisation of the means of production, distribution, and exchange. The second had been, in the late 1960s, the failed attempt to bring the trade unions within the framework of criminal law through the proposals in Barbara Castle's White Paper *In Place of Strife*, though Benn had in fact supported these proposals at the time.[47] The third 'wave of revisionism' had been under the Callaghan government, which, Benn believed, had betrayed the 1974 manifesto on which Labour had been elected.

Benn now proposed to 'take full advantage' of opposition by not standing for election to the Shadow Cabinet, which would have bound him through the convention of collective responsibility.[48] Benn's opponents attributed his shift to the left as

---

45 Benn, *Conflicts of Interest*, 425.
46 Ibid., 422.
47 Eric Hobsbawm, Martin Jacques, and Francis Mulhern, *The Forward March of Labour Halted* (Verso, 1981), 81–2.
48 Benn, *Conflicts of Interest*, 494.

opportunism, but it can be argued that it was a natural result of his analysis of the causes not only of Labour's defeat but of its failure to satisfy its supporters in office. Many party members felt, indeed, that the Labour governments had not only failed to advance Britain towards socialism but had not even moved Britain towards a more egalitarian society. Without economic growth, it had not been possible to secure much redistribution, and advances in public services had been halted even before the 1976 crisis, when the IMF had insisted on cuts in public spending as a condition of its supporting the pound. All this had discredited traditional social democracy and, in Benn's view, meant that the only alternative to economic orthodoxy was now socialism. The Thatcher government seemed to be breaking the post-war consensus which both the Conservatives – Churchill and Macmillan – as well as Labour under Attlee and Wilson had accepted. And in the Labour Party, the spirit of 1968 was becoming even stronger. The decline of deference meant that neither the party leadership nor trade-union leaders could count on automatic respect flowing from their positions. In the trade unions, the decline of deference was manifested in the growing power of the shop floor and the rise of unofficial strikes. Disillusionment with the Labour Party was manifested in falling membership. By 1980, the party had just 348,000 individual members as compared with 675,000 in 1975 and 817,000 in 1965. In 1964, there were 66 Labour constituency parties with over 2,000 members; by 1970, just 22. This decline in membership gave more influence to small groups of activists with the time and energy to spend long hours at party meetings, and these activists tended to drive away older members, who had treasured the party's traditional sociability and camaraderie. Noticeably, the greatest decline in membership was in London, where the takeover by radical activists was most complete. By 1979, 36 per cent of conference delegates could describe themselves as aligned with Militant, a

Trotskyist group which had infiltrated the Labour Party, while a further 24 per cent described themselves as being aligned with *Tribune*, a journal of the soft left.[49] At that time, 46 per cent of the conference delegates favoured Benn as Labour leader, 13 per cent Michael Foot, from the moderate left, and 30 per cent Denis Healey, from the right. The traditional right–left battle in the Labour Party was taking on a different character. In the past, the party had been an alliance between those who agreed about ends but disagreed about pace and timing. It had now become an uneasy alliance between the Labour left and revolutionaries such as the Militant group, whose commitment to democracy was perhaps somewhat dubious. Benn and his supporters, who were not revolutionary, did not – unlike Bevan – disdain the revolutionaries' support, which they used in an attempt to defeat the Labour right. Benn neither condemned nor dissociated himself from their activities.

Benn had come to believe that there was no point in Labour drawing up socialist proposals in opposition if the party's right-wing leadership refused to implement them in office. Therefore, the structure of the party had to be changed to ensure that the leadership could be more accountable to its members and become a more effective instrument of radical change. For this, so he believed, three reforms to the Labour Party constitution were needed. The first was to give party members a vote in the election of the leader, rather than restricting the election to a secret ballot of MPs. The second was to give constituency parties the right to reselect parliamentary candidates once in each Parliament. The third was to have the party's general election manifesto drawn up by the National Executive Committee alone, not, as hitherto,

---

49 Philip Williams, 'The Labour Party: The Rise of the Left' in Hugh Berrington (ed.), *Change in British Politics* (Frank Cass, 1984), 28, 36. This chapter gives an authoritative account of the rise of the left after 1979.

jointly by the Cabinet or Shadow Cabinet together with the National Executive Committee, with the leader enjoying a veto.

Two of Benn's three proposed reforms eventually came to fruition. The first was mandatory reselection, endorsed by Labour's 1980 conference. This was to have much less effect than the left had hoped for, but it did assist in the election of Michael Foot as party leader in 1980: some MPs were so fearful of being deselected that instead of voting for their preferred candidate – Healey, from the right of the party – they voted for Foot, who won by a narrow majority of ten votes. It is entirely possible that, without the threat of deselection, Healey would have won the leadership. In that case, fewer MPs and members would have defected from Labour to the SDP. Foot proved a disastrous leader, and one Shadow Cabinet minister was to declare that the day Labour elected Foot was the day it lost the 1983 election.

Benn's second constitutional reform – that the leader be elected not solely by MPs, as hitherto, but by an electoral college comprising MPs alongside the trade unions and individual members – was endorsed by a special Labour conference in January 1981. His third proposed reform – that the manifesto be drawn up solely by the National Executive Committee alone, rather than by the leader in conjunction with the National Executive Committee – was not adopted.

These reforms were anathema to many Labour MPs, who felt that Benn sought to appeal to Labour Party members over their heads and over the heads of the trade-union leaders. As a result of a muddle by various trade-union delegations, the formula agreed at the 1981 special conference provided for the composition of the electoral college for electing the leader to be 40 per cent trade unions and other affiliated organisations, 30 per cent the parliamentary party, and 30 per cent the constituency parties. This led to fears that the party might become subject to trade-union domination and was a prime cause of the defection of twenty-seven Labour MPs to the newly created SDP. Paradoxically, the leader of the SDP was also to be elected by its members, as the leader of the Liberals had been since 1976, but, by contrast with Labour, the leaders of those two parties were chosen by means of a 'one person, one vote' system, which Labour also would adopt in 1993 under the leadership of John Smith, when the party also adopted a 33–33–33 division in the electoral college. In addition, the trade-union block vote for the election of the Labour leader was abolished, the unions now being required to ballot members individually in leadership elections and divide their votes accordingly.

As with Benn's constitutional reforms, his two internal Labour Party reforms helped his opponents even more than his supporters, or indeed Benn himself. In 1981, Benn stood, against the advice of his wife, for the deputy leadership of the party, but was narrowly defeated by Healey, who secured 50.4 per cent of the vote as compared with Benn's 49.6 per cent. Healey had huge majorities amongst the trade unions and the parliamentary party, but Benn had an even larger majority amongst the constituency parties.[50] Benn could legitimately complain about the outcome that Healey's majority was ensured by the votes of MPs shortly to leave for the SDP. He could also complain that if the electoral college had been divided 33–33–33, rather than 40–30–30, he would have won.

Benn was the victim also of an ill-thought-out voting procedure. Labour's National Executive Committee had decided that the allocation of votes should ignore abstentions rather than be based on votes actually cast. But, as was pointed out in the *Guardian* by George Cunningham, Labour MP for Islington South and Finsbury – though shortly to join the SDP – this was irrational. Suppose, to take a reductio ad absurdum, just one MP

---

50 The youthful Tony Blair was one of his constituency supporters.

had voted, casting her vote for Healey. Would it then be rational for Healey to be allocated the whole 30 per cent of the MPs' vote? In fact, around one-sixth of MPs abstained. Had the allocation in the three electoral colleges been based on those actually voting, Benn, not Healey, would have won a narrow victory by 47 per cent to 46 per cent. Ironically, the rules had been devised by the National Executive Committee, which was Bennite and decided to ignore abstentions, believing the issue to be of little importance.[51]

In the event, Benn's narrow defeat was a result of 37 MPs who abstained, including 17 from the so-called soft left, such as Neil Kinnock, who believed that a Foot/Benn leadership would destroy the Labour Party and cause it to be beaten into third place in a general election by the newly formed SDP–Liberal Alliance. As it was, in 1983, although Labour won 209 seats, as opposed to just 23 for the Alliance, it was only 2 per cent ahead of the Alliance in terms of votes – 27 per cent to 25 per cent. Labour was saved by the first-past-the-post electoral system. Benn himself lost his Bristol seat but was returned in a by-election in 1984 for the constituency of Chesterfield.

1981 was to prove the high-water mark of Benn's influence in the Labour Party. After that, there was a slow but steady right-wing recovery until Labour's election victory in 1997. After Labour's catastrophic defeat in 1983, Michael Foot resigned the leadership and Labour elected in his place Neil Kinnock, from the soft left, who had abstained in the vote between Benn and Healey in 1981, allowing Healey to scrape home. Under Kinnock's leadership, Labour gradually discarded much of the left-wing detritus of the past. This was but a prelude to the more revisionist leadership of John Smith in 1992, and New Labour after Blair was elected leader, upon the death of John Smith, in

---

51 See also Michael Dummett, *Electoral Procedures* (Clarendon Press, 1984), 1–3.

1994. Although Benn was to remain in the Commons until 2001, he was shorn of influence. Already in 1985 he was complaining that all his supporters had deserted him for Kinnock: 'I am now alone with Dennis Skinner [the maverick MP for Bolsover] and the headbangers.'[52] In 1988, he contested the Labour leadership under the new rules that he had himself proposed, but he garnered only a pathetic share of the vote – 11.3 per cent to Kinnock's 88.6 per cent. Benn's day was now over. In 1995, Blair secured the removal of the party's constitutional commitment to the nationalisation of the means of production, distribution, and exchange. Socialism was now definitely in retreat.

VII

In 2001, Benn declared that he was leaving the Commons to 'devote more time to politics'.[53] In the general election, his Chesterfield constituency, hitherto a safe Labour seat, was won by a Liberal Democrat, who held it until it returned to Labour in 2010.

In virtue of Benn's long and distinguished membership of the Commons since 1950 with just one break, between 1983 and 1984, the Speaker gave him the freedom to use the Commons Library and the tea rooms, and to sit in the peers' gallery to listen to debates 'without the humiliation of being a Lord'.[54] He campaigned in opposition to the Iraq War in 2003, becoming president of the Stop the War Coalition and travelling to Baghdad to meet Saddam Hussein in an unavailing attempt to prevent war. He then embarked on a career of public speaking,

---

52 Benn, *The End of an Era*, 405.
53 'More Time for Politics' is the title of the volume of Benn's diaries covering the years 2001 to 2007, published by Hutchinson in 2007.
54 Tony Benn, *More Time for Politics: Diaries 2001–7* (Hutchinson, 2007), ix.

which attracted huge audiences, entrancing supporters and opponents alike. In 2003, at the age of seventy-eight, he held 142 meetings, gave 235 radio broadcasts, and made 150 TV appearances. In 2005, he collapsed at the Labour Party conference after addressing five fringe meetings in a day, and had to be put in an oxygen mask. When his son – Hilary, a Labour MP returned in a by-election in 1999 – arrived at the hospital, Benn removed his mask and said, 'Now, about your speech to conference.'[55] In February 2013, the year before his death, he supported the People's Assembly against Austerity, opposing the austerity of the Conservative–Liberal Democrats coalition government, together with, amongst others, Jeremy Corbyn, whose leadership of the Labour Party Benn would certainly have supported had he lived beyond 2014.

In January 2007, on the BBC programme *Daily Politics*, 38 per cent of viewers voted for Benn as Britain's 'political hero'. Just 35 per cent voted for Margaret Thatcher. Benn felt himself in danger of becoming a national treasure. When, in September 2008, he received a death threat, he said:

> I was very chuffed as I've not had one for years. Once I was called the most dangerous man in Britain; now I'm told I'm a national treasure. That's the final corruption in life: you become a kindly, harmless old gentleman. I am kindly, I am old and I can be a gentleman, but I'm not harmless.[56]

In July 2009, he had a pacemaker fitted: 'The battery lasts 10 years, so I think it will see me out.'[57] He was to receive an encomium from an unexpected source at the Woodstock

---

55 Adams, *Tony Benn*, 400.
56 Tony Benn, 'There's nothing like a death threat to cheer me up', *Sunday Times* (21 September 2008).
57 Adams, *Tony Benn*, 400.

Literary Festival in September 2009: when I interviewed David Cameron, then the leader of the opposition, but shortly to become Conservative prime minister, Cameron declared that Benn's *Arguments for Democracy* was one of the books that had most influenced him. Benn died in March 2014 at the age of eighty-eight.

VIII

Benn had one posthumous victory. The 1975 referendum had seemed to legitimise Britain's membership of the EC. It did not do so for long. By 1983, Labour, now in opposition, was proposing Brexit without any further referendum, a proposal which Benn supported and had indeed advocated, laying himself open to the charge of hypocrisy. The argument over Britain's relationship with Europe continued to simmer, and Euroscepticism was given a boost after Britain's ejection from the Exchange Rate Mechanism of the European Monetary System in September 1992. Finally, in January 2013, Cameron accepted the case for a further in/out referendum on Europe, following a further renegotiation of Britain's terms of membership. This commitment was intended to scupper UKIP, but in fact it gave legitimacy to demands for Britain to leave the EU. The referendum, held in June 2016, resulted in a narrow majority of 52 per cent to 48 per cent in favour of departure. There is no immediate prospect of Britain rejoining – but had the referendum not become part of the British constitution, Britain would probably still be a member of the EU.

Despite Brexit, which Benn would almost certainly have supported, his political career seems, in conventional terms, to have been a failure. He had confessed to his friend David Butler in 1971 that he 'wanted to be leader of the party and ... was not afraid to say so'.[58] But he had twice failed, in 1976 and 1988, to become leader, and had also failed twice to become deputy leader, in 1971 and 1981, albeit in the latter case very narrowly. Although he was a Cabinet minister for eleven years, there is no major government legislation which attaches itself to his name. He pioneered workers' cooperatives, but they all failed. His Industry Bill, giving far greater powers to government over the regulation of industry, failed to yield any discernible benefit. His alternative economic strategy was never tried, and there was no reason to believe that it would have proved successful. Healey waspishly remarked:

[Benn's ministerial career] left only two monuments behind – the uranium mine in Namibia he authorised as Energy Secretary, which helps to support Apartheid and is in territory illegally occupied by South Africa, and an aircraft [Concorde] that is used by wealthy people on their expense accounts, whose fares are subsidised by much poorer taxpayers.[59]

Concorde was taken out of service in 2001.

Benn's philosophy, now contemptuously labelled as Old Labour, has long been superseded by Blair's New Labour, an idea for which Benn had little time. Indeed, in one of his post-Commons meetings, he mocked the Blair government by saying that any supporters of New Labour present should leave by the door at the far right! It is difficult to imagine that any of the Old Labour policies associated with Benn – such as extensive state intervention, workers' control, import controls, and a siege economy – will ever again form part of Labour's electoral platform. If the Liberal William Harcourt could declare in 1887 that

58 David Butler Election Archive, 17 December 1971.
59 Denis Healey, *The Story of My Life* (Politico's, 1989), 409.

'we are all socialists now', Blair – and Starmer, for that matter – can win elections only by insisting that they are none of them socialists now.[60]

Benn's central insight was his perception that the world of deference and respect for authority was passing away. He was one of the first to perceive a trend of the future whereby authority needed to become more accountable to those upon whose support it depended. The key theme of Benn's political career was indeed his challenge to accepted authority – whether that authority was the House of Lords, the Labour leadership, the EU, or global capital. But his wider proposals for reform appeared unrealistic in a modern industrial society. There seemed little demand for workers' control from the workforce, and the trade unions were unsympathetic, since they saw their relationship with management as adversarial. They were not there to take part in managerial decisions but to secure the best deal that they could for their members. An obsessive politician, Benn overestimated the enthusiasm of the public for political involvement. Politics has always remained, and will no doubt always remain, a minority interest. Indeed, despite all the rhetoric of participation, turnout in post-war general elections in Britain has fallen from a high point of 84 per cent in 1950 to under 70 per cent in every general election since 1997. Turnout in local-government elections remains amongst the lowest in Western Europe. When people have the chance to participate, they often fail to do so. The sense of civic duty seems to be weaker today than in the immediate post-war period, when perhaps party membership was one of the few communal leisure activities available. It was indeed widely believed in the immediate post-war years that the Young Conservatives in particular offered an excellent opportunity for young people to socialise with each other. Now, of

60 Hansard, House of Commons, 11 August 1887, vol. 319, col. 140.

course, there are numerous other opportunities. The availabil-
ity of more leisure opportunities has no doubt affected the left
as well. The central weakness of socialism, Oscar Wilde is supposed to have said, was that it took up too many evenings![61]

Benn believed that industry should become accountable to the
workers who actually produced the goods and services. In fact,
accountability has been secured in a quite different way – not to
producers but to consumers, through the market-led policies of
Margaret Thatcher, Major, and Blair encouraging competition
in the public services, as well as private industry, a programme
that included breaking up the large nationalised monopolies
which Benn had championed. Industry has become accountable through competition in a market economy, not through
producer cooperatives or workers' control. The Left would have
done better to take the side of consumers rather than producers.

Benn was more successful in securing constitutional reform.
The aim of his internal Labour Party reforms was to make the
leadership more accountable to party members. This, he thought,
would prevent successive 'betrayals' by right-wing Labour leaders
in government. But the reforms may not have served the interests
of the Labour Party – for, with the membership of the party
rapidly diminishing, those who remained seemed to become
less and less representative of Labour voters, or potential voters
whose support Labour needed if it were to be able to form a
government. In 2010, the party elected Ed Miliband as leader,
rather than his brother, David, the majority choice of MPs. In
2015, the party elected Jeremy Corbyn from the far left; hitherto
seen as an extreme maverick rather than a serious candidate for
the leadership, he was the choice of only a very small minority
of Labour MPs. In June 2016, Labour MPs passed a vote of no
confidence in Corbyn by 172 votes to 40, but Corbyn refused to

---

61 Barry Day (ed.), *Oscar Wilde: A Life in Quotes* (Metro, 2000), 238.

resign, declaring that he was accountable to the members who had elected him rather than the parliamentary party. He denied that the vote by MPs had any 'constitutional legitimacy', declaring that, were he to resign, he would be 'betraying' the party members who had voted for him.[62] Admittedly, Labour succeeded in gaining thirty seats in the 2017 general election and was able to deprive the Conservative prime minister, Theresa May, of her parliamentary majority, but in 2019 the party went down to its worst defeat, in terms of percentage of the vote, since 1935. An alternative leader, more in tune with the wishes of voters, might well have won the 2017 election and would probably have limited the disastrous losses of 2019. As it was, for much of the period of the Corbyn leadership, the party seemed to be talking to itself, not to the country.

Towards the end of Benn's political career, he came to believe that much wider constitutional change was needed. Under both Wilson and Margaret Thatcher, so he believed, the prime minister had become an elective monarch with powers of patronage greater than those of medieval kings, such as the power to appoint ministers, peers, and senior civil servants – powers which, under the prerogative, could not be supervised by Parliament. The uncodified constitution, therefore, buttressed the power of the privileged at the expense of that of the people. In 1992, Benn presented to Parliament his Commonwealth of Britain Bill, proposing a codified constitution with a Charter of Rights, devolution, an elected second chamber, disestablishment of the church, and a republic in place of the monarchy. Ironically, all of this – with the exception of disestablishment and the republic – had been advocated by the breakaway SDP in the 1980s. The one reform Benn did not support was proportional

---

62 'Labour MPs Pass Non-Confidence Vote in Jeremy Corbyn', *BBC News* (28 June 2016), accessed online.

representation, a favourite reform not only of the centrists of the SDP, but of some on the left such as Ken Livingstone and Arthur Scargill, the miners' leader.[63] They hoped that proportional representation would allow a new and genuinely socialist party, distinct from Labour, to secure seats in the Commons, as in the Scandinavian countries. Benn said that he was opposed to proportional representation since it would increase the power of the Labour leadership, especially if proportional representation were to be based on party lists. The party leadership would ensure that Benn would be number 599 out of 600 candidates. As Benn added on a number of occasions, Neil Kinnock replied, 'Do you want that in writing?'

Some of the reforms proposed by Benn were to be implemented by the Blair government, which he disliked, if anything, even more than the SDP. Proposals for a codified constitution had little resonance with the British public – though some believed that Brexit might become a constitutional moment. But the more limited reforms, of the House of Lords and the Labour Party, as well as the referendum, have survived and are now generally accepted. No one today suggests that a hereditary peer should not be able to renounce his peerage. Few dispute the need for referendums on major constitutional issues. Few believe that party members should not have a role to play in the election of a party leader. From this point of view, Benn did indeed 'make the weather'.

But he would not have been satisfied with this. He believed that, above all, the real function of a politician was to be a teacher. Speaking towards the end of his life, he declared:

I have divided politicians into two categories: the Signposts and the Weathercocks. The Signpost says, 'This is the way we should go'. And you don't have to follow them, but if you come

---

63 For Livingstone, see Benn, *The End of an Era*, 578.

back in ten years' time, the Signpost is still there. The Weath-
ercock hasn't got an opinion until they've looked at the polls,
talked to the focus groups, discussed it with the spin doctors.
And I've no time for the Weathercocks. I'm a signpost man.
And, in fairness, although I disagreed with everything she did,
Mrs Thatcher was a signpost. She said what she meant. She
meant what she said ... And I think that we do need a few
more Signposts and a few fewer Weathercocks.[64]

Yet the signposts seem no longer there. And, as the history of
New Labour has shown, Benn became a teacher who had hardly
any pupils; a Starmer government, if one comes about, will
prove more Blairite than Bennite. In October 1976, Callaghan
had apparently told Benn, 'I can see you as leader of the Labour
Party in opposition, and ten years in opposition you will be.'[65]
The history of the Corbyn leadership, which Benn would certainly have supported, shows that, far from being a signpost to
the future, Bennite reforms and the Bennite outlook had hin-
dered the left in facing the changed conditions of the first part
of the twenty-first century. Benn, like Bevan, had been a teacher
who had stopped listening to his audience – or rather the audience he was listening to consisted primarily of Labour activists
in constituency parties, an audience quite unrepresentative of
the average voter. Like Bevan, there was an element of wilful
self-blindness in his character. So, if it is to become once again a
successful governing party, Labour needs to overcome and repudiate Benn's legacy, not build upon it – for Benn, like Bevan, far
from being a prophet of the future, had become a throwback to
an unusable past.

---

64 'Tony Benn Talks Signposts and Weathercocks' [video], at
youtu.be/VBvMQPiDZ3k.
65 Tony Benn, *Against the Tide: Diaries 1973–76* (Hutchinson, 1989), 624.

6

Nigel Farage and Brexit

I

Nigel Farage (1964–) was leader of UKIP from 2006 to its demise in 2016, with one brief interval between 2009 and 2010. He then became leader of the Brexit Party, founded in November 2018 to campaign for a no-deal Brexit. This party was renamed Reform UK in January 2021 and Farage became its leader in June 2024, shortly before the general election of that year. He is also, it has been suggested, 'the most influential politician of the modern era' and a 'modern day Wat Tyler'. This is because he 'is responsible for mainstream Euroscepticism, bringing about the 2016 referendum and then delivering the vote for Brexit', all before he ever reached the House of Commons.[1] Farage's biographer, Michael Crick, has claimed:

> He's been … more influential than quite a few prime ministers. Nigel Farage is the only man ever to have won a nationwide election as leader of an insurgent party … He will go down as one of the great political communicators of our age, a man with a rare instinctive feel for public opinion.[2]

---

1 Mark D'Arcy, 'Nigel Farage: The Story of "Mr Brexit"', *BBC News* (29 November 2019), accessed online; Michael Crick, *One Party After Another: The Disruptive Life of Nigel Farage* (Simon and Schuster, 2022), 400.
2 Crick, *One Party After Another*, 3.

A journalist who initially found it difficult to take Farage seriously has nevertheless concluded:

> The major political event of our times was the EU referendum. Its impact will be felt for decades. And it was called only because of the pressure Nigel Farage put on David Cameron. So I don't think it's any exaggeration to say that – for good or ill – Mr. Farage will come to be seen as the most influential British politician since Margaret Thatcher.[3]

Farage seems to possess an instinctive understanding of an electorate increasingly disenchanted and alienated from the political system. 'We are run,' he would say, 'by a bunch of college kids who've never done a day of work in their lives!'[4] Another commentator opposed to Farage believes:

> It seems perverse not to acknowledge the extraordinary influence he has had. This is the force that has already changed British history several times this century. It was the menacing presence of Farage's UKIP ... that forced the prime minister to make a manifesto commitment in 2015 to hold an in–out referendum. In 2019 it was Farage who brought down Theresa May. The Brexit Party won the European Parliament elections in 2019 and the Tories brought in Boris Johnson.[5]

Farage is unique in two respects. First, he is the only politician in modern times who has exerted great influence from outside

3 Michael Deacon, 'Nigel Farage was a clown. But he was also the most important politician of our age', *Daily Telegraph* (16 September 2016).
4 Matthew Goodwin and Caitlin Milazzo, *UKIP: Inside the Campaign to Redraw the Map of British Politics* (Oxford University Press, 2015), 7.
5 Iain Martin, 'Farage and Reform give Tories sleepless nights', *The Times* (22 November 2023).

the main political parties. He began his political career as a member of the Conservative Party, but from 1993 he belonged to and led parties dedicated first to taking Britain out of the EU and then to making a success of Brexit. 'It is hard,' his biographer comments, 'to think of any other politician in the last 150 years who has had so much impact on British history without being a senior member of one of the major parties at the time.'[6]

Second, Farage is unique because his influence has until now been exercised entirely outside Westminster. UKIP never held more than two seats in Parliament. These were both held by MPs who defected from the Conservative Party: Mark Reckless and Douglas Carswell, both of whom left the Conservatives in 2014 but lost their seats in 2015 and 2017, respectively. No UKIP member except for Carswell was ever elected at a general election in his or her own right, even though in the 2015 election the party secured one-eighth of the total vote.

UKIP's main policy was, of course, Brexit, though it was not to be defined solely by that. It also had policies on such matters as grammar schools – in favour – and HS2, the high-speed rail line – against. Farage has, however, largely been driven by a single cause. He has not been a politician who seeks office for its own sake. He describes himself in his profile for GB News, of which he is a commentator, as 'more of a campaigner than a career politician'.[7] Carswell has said:

If you asked Cameron or Brown, or Theresa May, why they wanted to be prime minister, they would give you vague answers about being good at the job. Nigel genuinely went into politics to get us out of the EU. He's the only other leader

---

6 Crick, *One Party After Another*, 404.
7 Nigel Farage, gbnews.com.

in my lifetime, apart from Margaret Thatcher, who had a sense of mission which extended beyond themselves.[8]

II

Farage's early days were unremarkable, except for his ability to irritate liberals and those on the left. Born in 1964 in the Kent village of Downe, near Bromley, he attended Dulwich College, where he discovered 'a passionate loathing for received opinion'.[9] A journalist once asked him 'how he could claim to be an anti-Establishment outsider, when he'd been educated at the same posh private school as P. G. Wodehouse'. 'Ah yes,' Farage replied in jocular fashion. 'He was two years below me'![10]

At school, Farage made an impact as a powerful debater and as someone determined to get himself noticed. On his leaving Dulwich, one of the masters told him, 'I have a feeling you will go far in life, but whether in fame or infamy, I don't really know.' Farage replied, 'Sir, as long as it's far, I don't care which.'[11]

He was influenced at school by two politicians who are the subjects of earlier chapters in this book: Powell, whom he was to regard as 'a singularly great man' and his political hero; and Joseph, who spoke at the school in 1978. Farage recalled, 'It was then, in the Great Hall at Dulwich College listening to him, that I converted to the model of economic liberalism that would dominate Thatcherite policy for the next decade ... The Britain that Keith Joseph described was a meritocracy, and that had enormous appeal to me.'[12] Farage found Joseph's 'vision' 'limpid and

---

8 Mark D'Arcy, 'Nigel Farage'.
9 Crick, *One Party After Another*, 18.
10 Deacon, 'Nigel Farage was a clown'.
11 Crick, *One Party After Another*, 18.
12 Nigel Farage, *The Purple Revolution: The Year That Changed Everything*

beautiful' and said that although he 'had never joined anything in my life', the day after Joseph's speech, he became a member of his local Conservative Party.[13]

Farage was 'never to be an ardent Conservative activist', he said, but 'As an individualist and a libertarian ... I was an enthusiastic supporter of Maggie [Thatcher] and a believer in the self-reliant, self-determining society which she envisaged'.[14] Margaret Thatcher became prime minister in 1979, when Farage was aged fifteen. He has always shared her views on the market economy and the need for lower levels of taxation. He also claims adherence to the principle of John Stuart Mill that an individual should have the freedom to live her life as she chooses, provided that she does not harm others.

Some of Farage's fellow pupils remember him at school for racist and anti-Semitic remarks.[15] One teacher claimed that he marched through a quiet Sussex village late at night during a school camp, singing Hitler Youth songs. Farage denies this and insists that any comments he made which appeared racist were uttered in jest and intended to provoke. Some believe he was merely an attention-seeker, and point to the fact that one of his close friends was black, but many – both amongst the staff and his fellow pupils – found his comments and attitudes offensive. Some members of staff wanted to expel him, but his headmaster thought his activities were 'naughtiness rather than racism' and, remarkably, made him a prefect in his final year, saying later, 'I saw good in him ... I saw considerable potential in the chap and I was proved right.'[16] Farage denies having been racist, and some of those who knew him say that they never heard him utter

---

(Biteback, 2015), 28.

13 Nigel Farage, *Flying Free* (Biteback, 2011), 27.

14 Ibid., 25.

15 Crick, *One Party After Another*, 24.

16 Ibid., 20, 21.

anything particularly untoward. His biographer believes that 'the picture is confused'.[17] A Eurosceptic journalist, Richard North, who later fell out with Farage, believed that a personal alignment with historical values would have been at the heart of any alleged racist statements on Farage's part, as he explained in an interview with Farage's biographer:

> He was racist in a Churchillian sense. He believed in the supe- riority of the white Englishman – King and Empire ... In a sense he's a white supremacist on a King and Country basis, rather than overt hatred of [people of colour]. He would have made a wonderful subaltern in the Indian Army.[18]

Upon leaving school, Farage decided not to apply for university. He considered the army, but instead decided to join the London Metal Exchange as a commodity broker. In 1989, he founded a lunch club, the criteria for membership of which were 'an appre- ciation of things British (with particular reference to cricket), a resilient liver and a hearty appetite, and a deep mistrust of the European Union'.[19] He remained a loyal Conservative until October 1990, when Britain, in the dying days of Margaret Thatcher's government, joined the Exchange Rate Mechanism of the European Monetary System. Margaret Thatcher had, in fact, always been deeply sceptical of the Exchange Rate Mecha- nism, but had been overborne by her foreign secretary, Douglas Hurd, and her chancellor, John Major, shortly to be her suc- cessor. Farage believed that fixed-currency arrangements were doomed to failure, since they could not take account of changing economic circumstances in the individual member states, and his

---

17 Ibid., 24.
18 Ibid., 47.
19 Ibid., 52.

view seemed to be confirmed when Britain was forced ignominiously to leave the Exchange Rate Mechanism in September 1992, under the premiership of Major.

Joining the Exchange Rate Mechanism had been, for Farage, 'the defining moment'.[20] He regarded it as the first step towards a single currency: 'I could not believe that we had done something so stupid – and that it was the Conservative Party – my party – that had done it. It triggered a huge break with the Tories for me.'[21] But, since Labour and the Liberal Democrats also supported membership of the Exchange Rate Mechanism – and had indeed pressed the Conservatives to join – he could not support them either.

To protest against Britain's joining, Farage attended a meeting of the Campaign for an Independent Britain, a cross-party campaign formed in 1976 to secure the repeal of the European Communities Act of 1972. At the meeting, he heard the Labour ex-minister Peter Shore and the Conservative ex-minister John Biffen speak against the EC, as the EU then was. Someone from the floor asked what those hostile to the EC should now do. Peter Shore said that the answer was to vote Labour; John Biffen said the answer was to vote Conservative! Farage found neither of these answers convincing, and he decided that the anti-European cause needed an organisation not beholden to the major parties. He therefore joined a small cross-party organisation, the Anti-Federalist League, modelled on the Anti-Corn Law League of the nineteenth century – and a forerunner of UKIP.

Farage's view that neither the Conservative nor Labour Party could be relied upon to campaign against Europe was confirmed by the parliamentary votes on the Maastricht Treaty, by which the EC became the EU and the euro was confirmed as the currency of

---

20 Ibid., 44.
21 Farage, *The Purple Revolution*, 73.

the Union. Recalcitrant Conservative MPs were brought into line by Major's insistence that support for the treaty was a matter of confidence.

Farage believed that the majority of British people were opposed both to the euro, and more generally to the 'ever closer union' heralded in the Treaty of Rome, which had established the EC and had been signed in 1957. He therefore demanded a referendum.[22] Margaret Thatcher, now in retirement, also called for a referendum on the treaty, declaring, 'To hand over the people's parliamentary rights on the scale of the Maastricht Treaty without the consent of the people in a referendum would be to betray the trust – as guardians of the parliamentary institutions, of the courts and of the constitution – that they have placed in us.'[23]

Labour had by this time renounced its previous Euroscepticism, which had climaxed in its 1983 election manifesto, when, under the leadership of Michael Foot, the party had called for withdrawal from the EC without a referendum. After Labour's defeat in that election, Foot's successor, Neil Kinnock, had gradually moved the party towards a pro-European stance, and under Kinnock's successor Labour became even more pro-European. The Conservatives could clearly not be relied upon either. Farage had hoped that Eurosceptics in the Conservative Party would support the call to reject the treaty, but they did not. This confirmed Farage's view that the Conservatives would always, as he saw it, put party before country. In addition, he regarded the Conservative Eurosceptics as an ageing group who had little real chance of gaining control of the party. In fact, Euroscepticism in the Conservative Party was coming to be legitimised after

---

22 Perhaps I should add that I too favoured a referendum on the Maastricht Treaty, though for quite different reasons. I hoped that a referendum would yield a majority in favour of the treaty and so legitimise Britain's membership of the EU. But most of those favouring a referendum were hostile to the treaty.

23 Hansard, House of Lords, 7 June 1993, vol. 546, col. 566.

Britain left the Exchange Rate Mechanism in September 1992. This began a shift of opinion which was to culminate in the general election of 2019, when only those prepared to accept the outcome of the 2016 Brexit referendum were allowed to stand as Conservative candidates. So while in 1992 it was the Eurosceptics in the Conservative Party who were marginalised, by 2019 it was the pro-Europeans in the party who had become marginalised. This, of course, could not have been foreseen in 1992, and Farage decided at that time that nothing could be hoped for from the Conservatives.

The Anti-Federalist League, which Farage had joined, had been set up in 1991 by Alan Sked, a London School of Economics academic, to campaign against ratification of the Maastricht Treaty. Once the treaty was passed, the league began to campaign for British withdrawal from the EU. In 1993, Sked and others established UKIP, which – by contrast with the Anti-Federalist League, a pressure group – was an independent political party. Although Farage did not become leader of the party until 2006, he was, from the beginning, a dominant figure in it.

III

Brexit appeared, for some years, as very much a narrow if not cranky minority interest, and UKIP's campaign for a referendum on EU membership seemed unlikely to succeed. Indeed, there had been a referendum on Europe in 1975, which had resulted in a two-to-one majority for remaining in the EC. That referendum was seen as a unique event and the outcome as irrevocable. 'It means,' Prime Minister Wilson had declared at the time, 'that fourteen years of national argument are over.'[24]

---

24 Quoted in Philip Goodhart, *Full-Hearted Consent* (Davis-Poynter, 1976), 181.

Three things changed this situation. The first was the commitment made by all three parties to a referendum before Britain joined the euro. The second was the massive immigration from the new Central and Eastern European member states of the EU after they were admitted in 2004 and 2007; this made explicit the fact that parliamentary sovereignty had been lost. The idea of 'taking back control' stemmed, indeed, from the increasing scope of European legislation after 1975. The third was the general disillusionment with mainstream politicians following the financial crisis of 2008 and the MPs' expenses scandal of 2009.

In negotiating the Maastricht Treaty, Major had secured an opt-out from the euro to the effect that Britain would be under no obligation to join. Eurosceptic Conservatives, emboldened by Britain's withdrawal from the Exchange Rate Mechanism in 1992, began to demand that a referendum be held before any future decision to adopt the currency, even though no one believed that such a prospect was likely to arise in the near future. In November 1994, however, the foreign secretary, Hurd, with Major's approval, urged just such a referendum so as to pacify Conservative Eurosceptics and hold the party together. Eventually in 1996, despite strong resistance from the chancellor of the Exchequer, Kenneth Clarke, the government accepted a commitment to a referendum, though only for the next Parliament and not as a permanent commitment. This compromise did little to secure Conservative unity. Nevertheless, Labour and the Liberal Democrats also felt impelled to come out in favour of a referendum. It is said that the press tycoon Rupert Murdoch pressed Blair to commit himself to a referendum as the price for his support. Blair, in any case, probably had little alternative once the Conservatives had committed themselves. The effect of the referendum-commitment proposal was to kill any chance of Britain entering the euro, since no opinion poll ever indicated majority support for it. Later, Clarke, as well as his pro-European colleague the deputy prime minister, Michael Heseltine, came to believe, in Clarke's words, that 'this was the biggest single mistake that either of us has ever made in our political careers', since they 'had allowed the idea of a referendum to be given legitimacy again'.[25] Clarke believed that once a referendum on the euro was conceded, the Eurosceptics would in time demand another on the wider question of EU membership itself. He was right. The 1975 referendum could no longer be regarded as a unique or definitive event.

The second factor which brought Brexit to the forefront of political debate was the huge increase in immigration following the admission of the ex-communist states of Central and Eastern Europe into the EU in 2004 and 2007. Until that time, immigration had not seemed a particularly salient issue. Indeed, it was not even mentioned in UKIP's 1999 manifesto for the European Parliament elections, which focused on the threat to the pound posed by the euro, an issue which seemed of little immediate concern to most British voters. But after 2004, the issues of immigration and Brexit came to be intertwined. The freedom-of-movement provisions of the EU treaties prevented the UK Parliament restricting immigration from elsewhere in the EU. Mass immigration made concrete what had hitherto been a somewhat abstract argument about sovereignty. It was clear that many MPs and many voters – perhaps a majority – wished to limit EU immigration, but they were prevented from doing so by laws which their Parliament had not made and which they could not alter, even though they flowed from treaties which Parliament had ratified.

Although citizens of the EU's new member states would enjoy an automatic right to enter Britain, the EU had provided for a transitional period, allowing member states to phase in the right of free movement. All but three member states took advantage

---

25 Kenneth Clarke, *Kind of Blue: A Political Memoir* (Macmillan, 2016), 372.

of this transitional period. Britain was one of the three, together with Ireland and Sweden. This was in large part because Britain needed skilled workers to help service a booming economy. Nevertheless, not to invoke the transitional clause was to sow the seeds of Brexit, and has been described as 'probably the single most important event in the rise of UKIP, and on the road to Brexit'.[26]

Between 2004 and 2016, immigration increased at a faster rate than ever before in British history. An early Home Office report had predicted that EU migration would not be higher than around 13,000, but between 2005 and 2010, annual net migration was regularly above 200,000.[27] Total net immigration between 2004 and 2012 was around 423,000. In the year ending in June 2016, when the Brexit referendum was held, net immigration reached a peak of 321,000, the highest figure on record until then, though over half was from outside the EU. In Powell's day, net immigration had never been higher than around 50,000 a year. Between 2004 and 2017, there was probably a net increase of EU-born people in the British population of just over 2 million – nearly 170,000 per year – most of whom, just over 130,000 a year, came from Central and Eastern Europe. This compares with a total immigration of 325,000 Jews between 1881 and 1914, and of around 600,000 Commonwealth citizens before 1971. By the time of the referendum, immigration had become the issue of greatest concern to the British public. As early as 2011, a survey by the polling company YouGov showed that four-fifths of those questioned believed that the country was overcrowded.[28] Cameron had promised to reduce EU migration to 'tens of thousands', namely to under 100,000 a year, but was clearly very far from

---

26 Crick, *One Party After Another*, 107.
27 Goodwin and Milazzo, *UKIP*, 28.
28 'Migrationwatch UK Petition on Immigration Tops 100,000,' *BBC News* (7 November 2011), accessed online.

achieving that aim.[29] Indeed, the free-movement provisions of the EU made it impossible for him to do so. Even worse, from 2011, there was a mass exodus of refugees leaving Syria to escape the civil war there and the repression which accompanied it. In 2015, a total of one million refugees entered the EU. The refugee crisis made immigration even more salient, even though it was a problem of migration from places external to the EU, not from within it. The EU mitigated the problem by an agreement with Turkey, according to which the latter would, in exchange for massive EU grants, admit the refugees. Turkey was a candidate for EU membership, and even though the chance of her entering the EU in the near future was remote, and Britain in any case had a veto on her admission, the possibility of millions of Turks entering Britain was to provide a new rallying cry for the Brexit campaign.

Farage emphasised fears of mass immigration. During the party leaders' TV debate before the 2015 election, he claimed that within the 7,000 diagnoses a year of those who were HIV-positive, 60 per cent of those diagnosed were not British nationals, implying that HIV-positive immigrants imposed an unacceptable cost on the health service. This prompted a response by Leanne Wood, leader of Plaid Cymru: 'You should be ashamed of yourself.'[30] Shortly before the referendum vote, Farage argued that a Remain vote would threaten Britain's security, since 'Isis promise to flood the Continent with jihadists'.[31] He then stood in front of a UKIP poster showing a line of refugees, almost all of whom appeared to be non-white, on the verge of entering

---

29 David Cameron, speech on immigration, University Campus Suffolk, 25 March 2013, gov.uk.
30 Goodwin and Milazzo, *UKIP*, 240–1.
31 'Nigel Farage says that British women will be at risk of mass sex attacks by gangs of migrants if we vote to stay in the European Union', *Daily Mail online* (4 June 2015).

Britain, which read 'Breaking Point: The EU has failed us all', with the subtitle 'We must break free of the EU and take back control of our borders'.[32] Many regarded this poster as racist, and Boris Johnson dissociated himself from it. The Archbishop of Canterbury, Justin Welby, claimed that Farage's remarks – that staying in the EU could lead to sexual attacks such as had been perpetrated in Cologne on New Year's Eve by young migrants, and that sexual assaults by migrants were the 'nuclear bomb' of the referendum – were also racist.[33] The UKIP poster was unfortunately unveiled just ninety minutes before the murder of Jo Cox, the Labour MP for Batley and Spen, by a neo-Nazi white supremacist, which some unfairly attributed to the atmosphere created by Farage.

Immigration admittedly did not seem a problem for the elite, which could secure hard-working and inexpensive Polish builders and Latvian cleaners. But poorer members of the community believed that immigrants kept wages low and were responsible for pressures on public services such as education, housing, and the NHS. Farage declared:

> I accept that open door immigration and mass cheap labour is good for rich people because it means cheaper nannies and cheaper chauffeurs and cheaper gardeners. And it is good for very big businesses and it is good for big landowners because it keeps their wage bills down. But it has been a disaster for millions of ordinary decent families in this country and surely it is the primary duty of a British government to put the interests of our own people first.[34]

---

32 Harold D. Clarke, Matthew Goodwin, and Paul Whiteley, *Brexit: Why Britain Voted to Leave the European Union* (Cambridge University Press, 2017), 55.

33 'Nigel Farage helping to legitimise racism, Justin Welby says', *Guardian* (7 June 2016).

34 Goodwin and Milazzo, *UKIP*, 88.

Most economists believe that immigration brings a net benefit to the country, though arguably at the cost of suppressing wages, and perhaps productivity also. Yet at the time of Farage's campaigning a large part of the benefit secured by immigration in the form of higher tax revenues was hidden, while the disadvantages seemed, to the low paid, very visible. In addition, many living in the more deprived areas of the country found it difficult to cope with the social consequences of immigration, which, so they believed, had transformed their communities without their consent. Mass immigration, therefore, created a gulf between a meritocratic elite – the exam-passing classes – and the rest. It was those who did not belong to that elite who were to be at the forefront of the vote for Brexit. It was also ironically those who lived in areas where immigration had been low which were to yield the heaviest pro-Brexit votes. Areas with high levels of immigration were far less eager for Brexit. It seems, therefore, that it was the fear of immigration rather than immigration itself which encouraged votes for Brexit. Immigration made the issue of EU membership salient in a way it had not been before. 'The goal,' Farage explained shortly before the 2014 European parliamentary elections, 'was to get into people's heads that immigration and Europe are the same thing and that we are impotent.'[35]

While mainstream parties had emphasised the economic benefits of immigration, Farage was more in tune with the cultural concern of voters that their identity was being undermined by mass immigration; such concern seems to have been felt most strongly by those left behind by social and economic change. The elite felt themselves at home in the conurbations towards which the ambitious had moved – London, Newcastle, and Manchester, all of which were to vote Remain in 2016 – rather

---

35 Ibid., 40.

than those areas of the country left behind by social and economic change – declining small towns, rural areas, and coastal communities. Indeed, the elite probably felt more at home in Brussels or Biarritz than in Bolton or Bolsover. Brexit was in part a revolt of those living in provincial England against the domination of London – the only region of England to vote Remain – and Farage was able skilfully to channel the frustrations of the left behind.

This disconnect between the people and the elite was increased by the third factor, arguably the most important of all, which helped UKIP: the financial crisis and recession of 2008. The recession caused a fall in most people's standard of living, but the banking and financial elite who appeared responsible for it seemed to have escaped unscathed. The justification for the high earnings of this elite had been that they would benefit the less well off. That justification was exploded by the crisis, which seemed to show that the elite were not only less proficient than people had been led to believe, but also less ethical in their financial practices. The crisis also seemed to cast doubt on the wisdom of those experts who had justified the huge rewards of bankers and financiers. During the Brexit referendum, Michael Gove, the justice secretary, was to declare that the country had had enough of experts, a sentiment which gained widespread acceptance amongst those suffering in the wake of the recession.

The crisis of 2008 discredited those internationalist political ideologies which had sought to justify the existing financial dispensation – the market philosophy of Margaret Thatcher and social democracy in the form of Blair's New Labour. The principal beneficiaries in Britain, on the Continent, and in the US, were nationalist and protectionist parties. The crisis led to a renewed emphasis on identity politics, which was to benefit both UKIP and, in Scotland, the SNP. The distinctive cry of UKIP, after all, was not that the other parties were too left wing or too right wing, but that they were insufficiently British. In 2010, Farage declared:

> There is a rebirth of identity politics in this country ... We've seen it in Scotland and it's happening in England but no one has noticed. It's little things. It's the turnout at Remembrance Day parades. They go up every year! A younger generation, an under-45 generation is hungry to know about their history and what their grandparents did and where they come from.[36]

UKIP was to gain further support as a result of the European debt crisis after 2009, when a number of members of the eurozone, primarily the Mediterranean members, and in particular Greece, found themselves unable to repay debt. The crisis seemed to show that the foundations of the eurozone were shaky, and indeed at one point it looked as if Greece might have to leave it. The EU seemed to have played into the hands of Eurosceptics by extending free movement to the ex-communist states of Central and Eastern Europe and by prematurely granting Greece eurozone membership.

IV

UKIP was able to take advantage of fundamental changes in British society and politics. Cameron, prime minister from 2010 to 2016, was a liberal conservative who had sought to modernise the party so as to secure the support of graduates and the professional classes. His approach alienated older working-class Conservative voters, who were largely social conservatives,

---

36 Robert Ford and Matthew Goodwin, *Revolt on the Right: Explaining Support for the Radical Right in Britain* (Routledge, 2014), 90–1.

sought drastic curbs on immigration, and had little sympathy with modern cultural trends. In May 2013, Farage told voters that Cameron was 'not a Tory. He's a socialist. Tory voters feel much closer to me than their own leader. His priorities are gay marriage, foreign aid and wind farms. They're not mine.'[37] The world of these traditional Conservatives 'was under assault and they wanted somebody – anybody – to preserve it'.[38]

Labour too, under Blair's New Labour, had sought to 'modernise' itself, and in doing so had distanced itself from its working-class roots. Blair appealed less to the voters of the traditional working class, who were now a minority of the electorate, than to those aspiring to escape from it. Many working-class voters were coming to feel that a party now dominated by professionals and university graduates was no longer the party that they had grown up with. 'Patriotic Old Labour, working people, working families,' Farage declared, 'these are the people who have been hurt by uncontrolled mass immigration.'[39] He observed, 'I have concluded from my experience that much of what UKIP is saying is not too dissimilar to what the Old Labour voters are looking for.'[40] In 2014, two psephologists concluded that UKIP's base was 'more working class than that of any of the main parties'. UKIP's revolt was in fact 'a working-class phenomenon'.[41] Brexit proved to have particular resonance in working-class areas such as the North East and the North West, areas of industrial decline, which, outside the main conurbations, were to vote heavily for Brexit in 2016.

Both the Conservatives and Labour were preoccupied with

---

37 'Stupidity of Cameron's priorities', *Daily Mail online* (4 May 2013).
38 Goodwin and Milazzo, *UKIP*, 63, 5.
39 Ibid., 63–4.
40 Ford and Goodwin, *Revolt on the Right*, 109.
41 Ibid., 109, 152, 270.

swing voters in marginal seats; they bothered less with those voters living in safe seats. But in the Brexit referendum of 2016, there were no safe seats. Every vote counted. So those living in safe Labour seats in the North East and safe Conservative seats in the South of England were in effect able to take their revenge on the elite which had ignored them. Both Cameron and Blair belonged to the exam-passing classes and welcomed globalisation, multiculturalism, neoliberal economics, and – with their support for gay marriage – alternative lifestyles. That was not an agenda with much appeal for those left behind, more worried about such matters as immigration and crime. So, the traditional loyalties of those who had previously voted for the major parties were fading. They were more ready than they had ever been to consider unorthodox political alternatives.

The journalist Simon Heffer believed that Farage had a particular appeal to 'Essex Man', a category that Heffer claimed to have first detected – namely working-class Conservatives who had in the past supported Margaret Thatcher. In fact, UKIP was strongest in those areas that contained elderly, white, and less well-off voters with low levels of education – left-behind Britain. UKIP, according to the British Election Study, 'had the largest share of voters who were aged over 54 years old and the lowest share of 18–24 year olds ... They were also the most likely to have left school before their seventeenth birthday.' UKIP voters were disproportionately drawn from 'the more financially insecure working class, the lower middle class, and the self-employed – the same social groups that have fuelled many other radical-right revolts in Europe'.[42] Likewise, UKIP members also came from less well-off backgrounds, as the political authors Harold D. Clarke, Matthew Goodwin, and Paul Whiteley have explained: 'Contrary to the popular portrayal of UKIP members as affluent

---

42 Ibid., 79, 81.

Tories who live on wealthy country estates, most of them are not rich.'[43]

These voters were also deeply discontented with the way government was working – believing that it was not working for them – and with the political class, a feeling intensified by the effects of the financial crisis which began in 2008 and the parliamentary expenses crisis of 2009, which showed that many MPs were abusing their allowances. Even though two of UKIP's own MEPs, elected in 2004, had been found guilty of financial dishonesty and given custodial sentences, Farage's party seemed untainted by what had happened in Westminster, where it was not represented. So, what had begun 'as a single-issue, anti-EU rebellion has grown into a potent force by consolidating voters who say "no" three times: no to Brussels, no to political elites in Westminster, and no to immigration'.[44]

The expenses crisis broke in the middle of the 2009 European Parliament election campaign. Polls at the start of the campaign suggested that 80 per cent would vote for one of the three major parties. In the event, only 57 per cent did so.[45] UKIP highlighted reforms designed to make government more accountable, reforms usually the property of the liberal left. These included not only proportional representation but also the recall of MPs and locally elected sheriffs and police, education, and health boards. Here too, as with proportional representation, UKIP was turning the weapons of its liberal-left opponents against them.

---

43 Clarke et al., *Brexit*, 93.
44 Ford and Goodwin, *Revolt on the Right*, 198.
45 Crick, *One Party After Another*, 154.

V

Three factors, then – admission of the referendum to constitutional respectability, the huge increase in immigration, and the financial and expenses crises – were coming together to put Brexit on the agenda, having created, in UKIP's view, a 'gulf' that had 'opened between the ruling elite and the public'.[46] In the twenty-first century, UKIP's progress was rapid. Back in 1999, it had succeeded in gaining representation for the first time in a legislature, winning three seats in the European Parliament elections on 6.5 per cent of the vote. One of its MEPs was Farage, who remained in the European Parliament as an irritant until Britain finally left the EU in 2020. In 2004, UKIP secured twelve MEPs, winning 16 per cent of the vote and pushing the Liberal Democrats into fourth place. In 2009, it came second to the Conservatives, with 16 per cent of the vote and thirteen seats, while in 2014 – in the last European Parliament elections held before the Brexit referendum in 2016 – UKIP won first place, with 27 per cent of the vote and twenty-six seats. In the year 2000, the journalist Fraser Nelson had attended a UKIP meeting in Cornwall at which just one person had appeared. But in 2013, a UKIP meeting he attended at the Worcester Guildhall was standing room only! The meeting at Worcester, Nelson wrote, 'felt like the Tory party in the days when grass-roots members actually turned up. They were young couples, families [and] no one seemed even vaguely to conform to the Prime Minister's now infamous description in 2006 of UKIP supporters as "fruitcakes, loonies and closet racists".'[47] In his autobiography,

---

46 Karine Tournier-Sol, 'The Ambivalence of UKIP towards Enoch Powell's legacy' in Esteves and Porion, *The Lives and Afterlives*, 170.
47 Fraser Nelson, 'Thatcher listened to voters – now it's Farage who hears their despair', *Daily Telegraph* (12 April 2013).

published in 2019, Cameron called that comment a mistake.[48]

When Farage entered the European Parliament in 1999, he was asked on television, 'Next week you'll be off on Eurostar to the European Parliament, and you'll find a never-ending round of invitations to lunches, dinners, champagne receptions; do you think you'll become corrupted by the lifestyle?' Farage replied, 'No, I've always lived like that.'[49] Farage and other UKIP MEPs were to be regularly criticised for their poor attendance record at the European Parliament and for not being present for committee discussions and key votes. The response of the UKIP MEPs would have been that constructive legislative activity was pointless for a party seeking to take Britain out of the EU. They were instead using the Parliament for the purpose of putting forward their case rather than securing new EU legislation carrying Britain further along the road to integration.

Farage specialised in colourful, if provocative, speeches. Indeed, in 2016 the journal *Politico* was to declare that he was 'one of the two most effective speakers in the chamber'.[50] In addition, UKIP benefited from the financial and in-kind resources available to them as a result of being the largest contingent in the political group of hard Eurosceptics which Farage led. His most notorious intervention had occurred in March 2010, on the maiden appearance in the Parliament of Herman Van Rompuy, the newly chosen president of the European Council and outgoing prime minister of Belgium. Van Rompuy, Farage declared, had 'the charisma of a damp rag and the appearance of a low-grade bank clerk'. He asked who had voted for Van Rompuy and how he could be removed. He then concluded that Van Rompuy would be 'the quiet assassin of European democracy' and that he

---

48 Ford and Goodwin, *Revolt on the Right*, 3; David Cameron, *For the Record* (William Collins, 2019), 512.
49 Crick, *One Party After Another*, 72–3.
50 '40 MEPS Who Actually Matter', politico.eu.

lacked legitimacy, adding for good measure that Van Rompuy's hostility to the nation state was due to the fact that he came from Belgium, which was a 'non-country'. Farage was summoned by the president of the European Parliament, Jerzy Buzek, to apologise, but said that his only apology should be to bank clerks: 'If I have offended them, I am very sorry'. He was then fined €3,000, to be deducted from his parliamentary allowance, since he had 'insulted the dignity' of the president of the Council.[51]

From its earliest days, UKIP was dogged by accusations of racism, and these accusations multiplied once it won seats in the European Parliament. Farage did his best to insulate UKIP against such charges, and excluded former members of the British National Party (BNP) and the English Defence League from membership. In the European Parliament, UKIP did not sit with the far-right group containing such figures as Marine Le Pen and Geert Wilders. Farage claimed that UKIP was 'a non-racist, non-sectarian alternative to the British National Party'.[52] He argued that, unless UKIP had a strong presence in the European Parliament, the anti-European cause there would have been left to the tender mercies of racist parties. In 2016, Farage declared proudly that the collapse of the BNP was largely due to competition from the non-racist UKIP. 'I destroyed the British National Party,' he said in 2016.[53] If so, that is a not-insignificant achievement – though there were in fact other reasons for the BNP's demise.

In 2004, Farage became co-leader of the Independence/Democracy Group in the European Parliament, whose other members included two anti-Semitic MEPs from Greece and Poland, and another from Italy who would in 2005 be convicted for setting

51 Crick, *One Party After Another*, 229–230.
52 Ford and Goodwin, *Revolt on the Right*, 93.
53 Crick, *One Party After Another*, 180.

fire to wooden pallets on which migrants were sleeping under a railway bridge in Turin.[54] In 2014, after UKIP had come first in the European Parliament elections in Britain, it joined forces in the European Parliament with the Europe of Freedom and Democracy group – which included, amongst others, the Sweden Democrats, a party founded by white supremacists, including a former member of the Waffen-SS. But the two MEPs from that party wrote to Farage distancing themselves from its past; the Sweden Democrats have now attained respectability, being allied with parties of the moderate right in Sweden, which it sustains in government. A French MEP from Marine Le Pen's Front National, now named the National Rally, also became a member, having distanced herself from the party. So did a Polish MEP who was accused of Holocaust denial and misogyny. This political group was renamed Europe of Freedom and Direct Democracy in 2017, and Farage was for a while its sole leader. Nevertheless, two academic analysts of the party groups in the European Parliament have concluded that 'UKIP was not in the same ideological camp as many of these parties [such as the Front National and the Greek neo-Nazi party Golden Dawn]. It was rooted in a long British tradition of Euroscepticism rather than anti-Semitism, ethnic nationalism, Nazism or Islamophobia'.[55] All the same, Farage did endorse Marine Le Pen against Emmanuel Macron in the 2017 presidential election, and in the same year he spoke at an Alternative für Deutschland election meeting. In 2019, he was to propose that the Brexit Party, a successor to UKIP which he was by then leading, should form part of a new group containing both Marine Le Pen's National Rally and Alternative für Deutschland. This proposal came to nothing, in part because it was rejected by the Brexit Party MEPs, who were more ethnically

54 Ibid., 118.
55 Goodwin and Milazzo, *UKIP*, 115.

diverse than UKIP had been. They included at least one Jewish member and at least one black and gay member. Admittedly, many members of UKIP seem to hold unreconstructed views more appropriate to the Britain of the 1950s than the Britain of the twenty-first century, but such views are better characterised as ultra-conservative than racist.

It would, of course, be difficult to deny that there were racists in UKIP. But there are also, no doubt, racists in the other parties as well. UKIP has never faced accusations of racism in the form of anti-Semitism of the kind that were found by the Equality and Human Rights Commission in 2020 to be justified in relation to the Labour Party. Indeed, one Jewish Labour MP, Margaret Hodge, declared that the anti-Semitism she suffered under Labour was greater than that she had suffered at the hands of the BNP in her Barking constituency. The Equality and Human Rights Commission concluded that there had been 'unlawful acts of harassment and discrimination [against Jews] for which the Labour Party is responsible' under the leadership of Jeremy Corbyn between 2015 and 2019.[56] More recently, in 2022, a report on the Labour Party by the lawyer Martin Forde found that, in addition to anti-Semitism, there was 'overt and underlying racism and sexism' in the Labour Party.[57] Forde's findings are perhaps not as widely known as they might be, since the Forde report has been, on the whole, ignored by the media. Had similar findings been made about UKIP, or for that matter the Conservative Party, it is unlikely that the media would have been quite so passive in reporting on it.

---

56 Equality and Human Rights Commission, 'Investigation into antisemitism in the Labour Party', October 2020, 6.
57 Martin Forde, 'Forde Report', labour.org.uk, 81.

VI

UKIP's success in gaining representation in the European Parliament was largely due to the fact that from 1999 onwards elections to the Parliament were held under proportional representation rather than the traditional first-past-the-post system – under which, so Farage believed, tribal loyalties and fear of a 'wasted vote' will always prevail. In the European elections, Farage said, voters could feel free to express their personal views and preferences, so that Brexiteers would vote for UKIP rather than, for example, the Conservatives as the lesser evil. The use of proportional representation for elections to the European Parliament and for various sub-national bodies – the London Assembly and the devolved bodies in Scotland, Wales, and Northern Ireland – may have helped UKIP in another way, since it enabled voters to get into the habit of voting for smaller parties. That habit may have transferred itself to Westminster voting, though here the party suffered even more than the Liberals and Liberal Democrats had done from the first-past-the-post system. The UKIP vote, like the Liberal vote, has tended to be fairly evenly spread across the country, rather than concentrated – as, for example, the Plaid Cymru vote is concentrated in the Welsh-speaking areas of Wales. The extent to which UKIP was disadvantaged was to be graphically shown in the general election of 2015, when, with 12.6 per cent of the vote, it secured just one seat in the House of Commons. It is hardly surprising, therefore, that UKIP favoured proportional representation and that Reform UK does so as well. With proportional representation, votes for UKIP would no longer be wasted votes, so the party would be able to win seats at Westminster and would be in a position to join a coalition with other parties, as some anti-European parties have done on the Continent.

It is a paradox that direct elections for the European Parliament, intended to create and strengthen a European consciousness amongst voters, in fact helped to create a legislative platform for Eurosceptic parties such as UKIP and, in France, the National Rally, so helping to delegitimise the European cause and leading to the exit of a member state. It is a paradox also that proportional representation, which so many of its advocates hoped would strengthen the Liberal Democrats and, more broadly, centrist politics, actually benefitted UKIP more than any other single party. Farage believes that without proportional representation for the European Parliament elections, UKIP would have found it far more difficult to secure popular support. His party, he declared in a lecture in 2014, had 'always taken the European elections desperately seriously because without them and without proportional representation UKIP never had a chance, frankly, of winning any elective representation in the House of Commons'.[58] One historian of UKIP's early years agrees, and has said that if proportional representation had not been adopted by the European Parliament 'there would have been no UK Independence Party after [the European Parliament elections in] June 1999'.[59]

Nevertheless, UKIP seemed for many years, despite its success in European Parliament elections, to be no nearer to achieving its goal of getting Britain out of the EU. As recently as the 2010 general election, the party secured just 3.2 per cent of the vote, and Europe seemed not to be an issue. Still, 3.2 per cent of the vote was the highest national vote secured in modern times by any party not allied to one of the major parties. And the neofascist BNP, also in favour of Brexit, secured 2 per cent of the vote – so one in twenty voters were supporting parties opposed to EU membership. In a proportional system, UKIP's 3.2 per cent

---

58 Quoted in Martin Westlake, *Slipping Loose: The UK's Long Drift Away from the European Union* (Agenda Publishing, 2020), 106.
59 Peter Gardner, *Hard Pounding: The Story of the UK Independence Party* (June Press, 2006), 84.

share of the vote would have given it around twenty seats in the Commons. UKIP had won nearly as many votes as the Greens, Plaid Cymru, and SNP combined – but these three parties won ten seats between them. Under first-past-the-post, however, UKIP won no seats at all despite having received nearly one million votes. Nevertheless, it may not have been entirely without influence in the election, for in twenty-one constituencies the total of the UKIP and Conservative vote was higher than that of the winning Labour or Liberal Democrat. If UKIP's voters would have been supporting the Conservatives in the absence of UKIP candidates, then the intervention of UKIP cost the Conservatives their overall majority. If that is so, then, ironically, the intervention of the most anti-European of the parties fighting the election handed the balance of power to the most pro-European of the parties fighting the election, namely the Liberal Democrats.

Nevertheless, Europe did not seem very high on the political agenda. Had it been, the coalition between the Eurosceptic Conservatives and the Europhile Liberal Democrats – the first peacetime coalition in Britain since 1931 – would not have been possible. In 2006, in his first speech as Conservative leader, Cameron had said that he wanted the Conservatives to stop 'banging on about Europe, to forget about an issue which was dividing the party and which appeared to have so little resonance with the British public'.[60] Nevertheless, the coalition created a new political space which UKIP could occupy, for it was committed to a programme of economic austerity, which meant cuts in public spending and in welfare benefits, a programme with little appeal to those left behind. The coalition pushed the Conservatives towards the centre ground; the Conservative right seemingly had nowhere else to go. But UKIP, which became 'a multi-flavoured receptacle for disillusioned Conservatives' would

---

60 Andrew Adonis (ed.), *Half In, Half Out* (Biteback, 2018), 221.

provide them with a home. In addition, the coalition 'helped UKIP to become a refuge for Britain's growing "angry" tendency of people who simply want to poke a tired political establishment in the eye'.[61] The coalition benefited UKIP by removing any claim by the Liberal Democrats to be a protest party against 'the system'. The Liberal Democrats had now become part of the system, part of the establishment. Farage's biographer has described the coming of the coalition as 'arguably as important to UKIP's history as the advent of proportional representation in European elections eleven years before'.[62]

In 2011, the Cameron government established a petition system providing that any petition on a matter of governmental responsibility which attracted 100,000 signatures would be eligible for debate at Westminster Hall. The first such petition demanded a Brexit referendum, the second a curb on immigration. In October 2011, the Commons debated the petition calling for an in/out referendum. Eighty-one Conservative MPs – nearly half of all Conservative MPs not on the government payroll – defied a three-line whip by voting for a referendum; in January 2013, Cameron, under pressure both from his own MPs and from UKIP, made the fateful commitment to hold an in/out referendum after securing 'fundamental reform' of the EU. In the event, whilst he was able to secure various benefits for Britain, he did not secure anything approaching the 'fundamental reform' which he sought. In particular, as he himself has admitted, he failed to secure sufficient concessions on the free movement of people within the EU to meet his promise that net migration into Britain could be reduced to the 'tens of thousands'. He may well have underestimated the importance of the immigration issue,

---

61 Tim Montgomerie, 'David Cameron ignores UKIP at his peril', *The Times* (11 April 2012).
62 Crick, *One Party After Another*, 172.

which, remarkably, he did not even mention in his Bloomberg speech of January 2013, in which he committed the Conservatives to a referendum.[63] 'I didn't see,' Cameron has confessed, 'how deep the disillusion was – in some cases outrage – about our inability to control immigration'.[64]

The commitment to an in/out referendum did nothing to stem the Eurosceptic tide. In 2014, UKIP won the European Parliament elections with 27 per cent of the vote – the first time in British history that any party other than the Conservatives, Labour, or the Liberals had come first in a national election. In 2014, *The Times* made Farage its Briton of the Year. In the 2015 general election, UKIP won 12 per cent of the vote, pushing the Liberal Democrats into fourth place. All this was but a prelude to the Brexit referendum on 23 June 2016, which Farage labelled 'Independence Day'. Yet, oddly enough, after the Brexit victory, Farage aligned himself with some of the Remainers and, alone in UKIP, showed sympathy for the idea of a second referendum. This was not, of course, because it would – as the Remainers hoped – reverse the outcome of the Brexit referendum, but because it would, so he believed, yield a larger majority for Brexit and thus 'kill [the pressure to reverse Brexit] off for a generation. The percentage that would vote to leave next time would be very much better than it was last time round, and we may just finish the whole thing off.'[65]

The outcome of the referendum was a moment of triumph for Farage. But he probably had less impact on the voters' decision than Boris Johnson, the former mayor of London, who was at that time a more popular figure than the prime minister, Cameron. Indeed, one leading Eurosceptic, Dominic Cummings,

63 Clarke et al., *Brexit*, 25.
64 Cameron, *For the Record*, 279.
65 Crick, *One Party After Another*, 324.

later to become a chief adviser to Boris Johnson as prime minister, felt that Farage had actually damaged the Brexit cause by
around 6 per cent, since he had put off middle-class and business
voters deterred by what they saw as appeals to prejudice during
the campaign. Analysts of the campaign have concluded:

> Although the close division of the vote ... means that ... it is
> not possible to conclude that "it was Boris wot won it" ... his
> boisterous and widely covered presence on the campaign trail
> was clearly very advantageous to the Leave side, whose only
> other salient leader was the much less popular Nigel Farage.

The analysts believe:

> As a very high-profile establishment Conservative represent
> ing the official Vote Leave campaign, Boris Johnson helped to
> attract "polite Eurosceptics", who otherwise might have been
> put off voting Leave because it involved acknowledgment – to
> themselves, if not others – that they were siding with the highly
> controversial Nigel Farage and assorted other "deplorables".

Farage's image, by contrast, 'was an influential, but longer-term,
factor in the set of forces driving referendum voting'.[66]

Nevertheless, UKIP had showed itself as the most significant
new party in Britain since the birth of the Labour Party. In the
1980s, the SDP had boasted that it would 'break the mould' of
British politics. In the early twenty-first century, UKIP actually succeeded in doing so.[67] 'Nobody in this country has come
closer than me to smashing the system,' Farage has said.[68] The

---

66 Clarke et al., *Brexit*, 173, 207, 239.
67 'The new party's programme include a demand for electoral reform and a
commitment to "breaking the mould"', *Guardian* (27 March 1981).
68 Crick, *One Party After Another*, 400.

SDP, moreover, was an insurgency from the top by members of the political establishment, led as it was by four former Labour Cabinet ministers, and was the result of a split in a major political party. UKIP was a grass-roots insurgency led by a man who had never held any national political office at all. And, while the effect of the SDP–Liberal Alliance had been to push Labour to the centre, and the effect of the Liberal Democrats had been to push the Conservatives to the centre, the effect of UKIP would be to push the Conservatives to the right, away from the centre ground.

Brexit had triumphed, even though all three party leaders and most of the British financial and educational elite had been against it. That result owed as much to years of steady campaigning as to activities during the period of the referendum itself. And the electoral strength of UKIP had, no doubt, been one of the factors persuading Cameron to promise a referendum on continued EU membership in 2013. In the referendum campaign itself, the existence of UKIP prevented the Eurosceptic case being seen as almost entirely Conservative. Some Leave voters might well have been unwilling to support a cause which was seen as being too closely associated with the Conservative Party.

VII

After the referendum, it seemed that UKIP's task was done, and Farage resigned the leadership of the party, though he remained an MEP. But he rapidly came to deplore the tactics of the new leader, Gerard Batten, who seemed to be aligning the party with extremists. At the 2018 annual UKIP conference, Farage announced that 'with a heavy heart' he was resigning from the party, since Batten was working with former members of extremist organisations obsessed with Islamophobia, as well as with those with criminal records. He told the conference that 'one of the reasons for UKIP's success was that we'd excluded extremists ... I warned that any change to this policy would damage the party beyond repair.' As he walked back to his seat, he later recalled, 'I was met by several angry young men, red in the face and mildly abusive, who all seemed to be obsessed with Islam and Tommy Robinson [a former BNP member and a co-founder of the English Defence League].'[69]

Nevertheless, Farage still had work to do in ensuring that Brexit was actually delivered. Before and during the referendum campaign, he had been happy to argue for what was later to be called a 'soft' Brexit on the Norwegian model, by which Britain would remain in the EU's internal market. That, however, would have meant accepting the EU's principle of freedom of movement. After the referendum, Farage changed tack, arguing for a 'hard' Brexit, with Britain outside both the internal market and the EU customs union. After resigning from UKIP in January 2019, Farage led a new party, the Brexit Party. This had been formed in November 2018 to campaign for a clean break with the EU, in contradistinction to Theresa May's form of Brexit, which would have kept Britain within the EU's customs union and replicated the single market, and which its opponents characterised as BRINO: Brexit in name only. Even worse, Labour and the Liberal Democrats seemed to be campaigning for a reversal of the referendum decision. Farage was worried lest the whole Brexit project be unravelled. But the 2019 European Parliament elections provided him with a window of opportunity. Seven months after the Brexit Party was formed, it won the elections for the European Parliament, with 31 per cent of the

69 Nigel Farage, 'With a heavy heart, I am leaving UKIP. It is not the Brexit party our nation so badly needs', *Daily Telegraph* (4 December 2018).

vote. Farage had now triumphed in two European Parliament elections as the leader of two different parties. The Brexit Party, with twenty-nine seats, was now the largest single national-party delegation in that Parliament. This success, Farage later told GB News, was his proudest moment, since it ensured that Brexit would now be on track. The Conservatives secured just 9 per cent of the vote, and this reverse contributed significantly to the end of Theresa May's hold on power. Farage's capacity to drive out a sitting Conservative prime minister made him appear, according to his biographer, as 'the most powerful man in British politics'.[70] Johnson was chosen to succeed Theresa May as leader of the Conservative Party and prime minister, with a mandate to 'get Brexit done'.[71] In the 2019 general election, the Brexit Party had intended to put up 600 candidates, but, after Johnson agreed that there would be no regulatory alignment with the EU and that Britain would definitely leave the EU in 2020, it withdrew from 317 seats which had been won by the Conservatives in the 2017 general election. This was to avoid splitting the pro-Brexit vote and reduce the risk that Labour, many of whose MPs favoured a second referendum – which Farage now opposed – might form a government, perhaps in alliance with the Liberal Democrats, who proposed rejoining the EU without a further referendum. Farage's decision to withdraw candidates helped ensure that Brexit came about. When Britain finally left the EU in January 2020, Farage told a crowd in Parliament Square that 'the people have beaten the establishment ... This is the greatest moment in the modern history of our great nation.'[72]

In November 2020, the Brexit Party changed its name to Reform UK, declaring that, with Brexit achieved, its focus would

---

70 Crick, *One Party After Another*, 343.

71 '"Get Brexit Done". The 3 words that helped Boris Johnson win Britain's 2019 election', *Time Magazine* (13 December 2019).

72 Crick, *One Party After Another*, 363.

now become the reform of British institutions and the preservation of civil liberties. In March 2021, Farage declared that he would stand down from active politics. He was to be replaced by Richard Tice as party leader, though he became the party's president.

VIII

Brexit has not so far achieved the beneficial results that its supporters hoped for. Indeed, in 2023, survey evidence indicated that many Brexiteers suffered from 'Bregret', and that a majority of respondents wanted Britain to rejoin the EU, something unlikely to happen in the foreseeable future. But many Brexiteers, including Farage, argue that Brexit has not so far yielded the hoped-for benefits since it has not been accompanied by the measures needed to make it a success. In particular, Brexit has not led to Britain 'taking back control', since immigration is higher today than it has ever been. In addition, Farage would argue, there has been no push towards greater liberalisation of the economy. His views on economics have always been Thatcherite. He, together with a number of Conservative cheerleaders of Brexit such as John Redwood and Jacob Rees-Mogg, hoped that Brexit would be accompanied by moves towards a low-tax and deregulated market economy, free of the restrictions of the EU. What they wanted was a more globalised world. But that has not come about. Indeed, the rate of taxation in Britain is now the highest it has been since the time of the Attlee government, immediately after the end of the Second World War. Attempts to introduce a more Thatcherite economy were, it is true, attempted by Liz Truss, though she had been a Remainer, in her inglorious forty-nine-day premiership in 2022, but proved disastrous, largely because she was proposing unfunded tax cuts.

Many used the analogy of Singapore as the best post-Brexit future for Britain. But Singapore is an authoritarian state with a powerful role for government. A better analogy would be Australia and New Zealand. They were faced with the loss of their traditional British markets when Britain entered the EC in 1973. They responded with precisely the same policies of reducing subsidies, tariffs, and regulations that Farage and his supporters favoured for Britain. Such policies did prove successful after a period of time, but at ruinous cost, particularly to the farming community suddenly deprived of its subsidies.

It is very doubtful whether such hard-line, free-market policies would ever have been able to secure electoral support in Britain, especially given the pressures in the early 2020s for a larger role for the state during and after the Covid pandemic. They certainly enjoyed little support in the left-behind areas in the North East and North West, which voted heavily for Brexit in the 2016 referendum. These foot soldiers of Brexit held views which had little in common with the cheerleaders. Their main concerns were with security – economic security, social security, a better NHS and social care, cultural security against large-scale immigration. These concerns would not be met by a return to a market economy. Farage had been able skilfully to blend incompatible elements together in the Brexit campaign, but post-Brexit the coalition could not hold. So, perhaps the Brexiteers were doomed to disappointment, though Farage maintains his belief that free-market economic policies still offer the best chance of making Brexit a success.

In 2024, Farage finally became an MP, for the Essex constituency of Clacton, and replaced Richard Tice as leader of Reform UK. His aim had been to ensure that the Conservatives suffered a heavy defeat. He had attended the 2023 Conservative conference, but found it a dispiriting experience. He blames the Conservatives for not securing the benefits of Brexit. In the

2024 general election, his party put up candidates in almost all of the 650 constituencies rather than, as in 2019, standing aside for Conservatives sympathetic to Brexit. In 2019, Farage and the Conservatives under Johnson wanted the same thing: delivery of a hard Brexit. In that election, many Brexit Party supporters voted for the Conservatives, and the Brexit Party won just 2 per cent of the vote. But now the paths of the two parties had diverged. In 2019, 59 per cent of Brexit Party supporters had a favourable view of the Conservatives and 84 per cent had a favourable view of Johnson, but by October 2023, just 21 per cent of Reform UK supporters had a favourable view of the Conservatives and just 21 per cent a favourable view of the prime minister, Rishi Sunak.[73] In addition, as the political commentator Iain Martin has written, 'Reform [UK] and Farage hate the Tory party and want to destroy it. Their ambition is to replace it and help secure proportional representation to break the Conservatives forever,' which puts them in accord, ironically, with many pro-Europeans on the left.[74]

Farage believed that the Conservatives largely wasted their years in office. But electoral defeat, he believes, might rejuvenate the party. It is not perhaps beyond the bounds of possibility that he might eventually rejoin the Conservatives. Attending the 2023 Conservative Party conference, he was more enthusiastically received than any Conservative. On the BBC's *Sunday with Laura Kuenssberg* on 11 June 2023, Farage declared that there was a huge gap in the political market and that prospects for an insurgent party were even greater now than they had been when Reform UK was founded – and certainly greater than in 2015, when, by contrast with Sunak, Cameron had enjoyed a mandate

73 Adam McDonnell, 'Conservatives unlikely to win over Reform UK supporters at next election', *YouGov* (2 November 2023), accessed online.
74 Iain Martin, 'Farage and Reform'.

both from party members and from voters. The thirteen years of Conservative rule, he said, were now seen by many as a period of incompetent government, which, in conjunction with Covid and the Russo-Ukrainian War, had led to the sharpest drop in living standards for seventy years. In addition, there was, Farage went on, scope for realignment on the centre-right, which could, he believed, be achieved were Britain to adopt a system of proportional representation for Westminster elections.

Persistence, Farage has told me, has been the secret of his political success. The same was true, as we have seen, of Benn.

In the first part of the twentieth century, the operatic soprano Nellie Melba became notorious for her endless series of farewell performances. Farage has become the Nellie Melba of the politics of the twenty-first century. He has 'retired' from politics on many occasions, but he has always returned.

So, his period of influence is by no means over; he will continue to 'make the weather' for some years yet. He succeeded in turning UKIP from a crank party into a powerful campaigning force and, despite blemishes, removing from it the taint of racism so that it did not become an outlaw party like the BNP. He succeeded also in melding incompatible elements together into the electoral coalition which sustained UKIP, then the Brexit Party, then Reform UK, and his decision not to oppose the Conservatives in 2019 ensured that Johnson could 'get Brexit done'. He has been largely responsible for the destruction of three Conservative leaders – David Cameron, Theresa May, and Rishi Sunak, in the latter case helping to turn the 2024 Conservative defeat into a rout. In doing so, he helped to turn Reform UK into a dynamic force in British politics and ensured that it has a role to play in the coming debate on the future of the right. These acts have all altered the way we live, though whether for better or for worse will remain a matter of argument for many years to come.

Farage's political future remains a mystery. His story is as yet unfinished. But whatever the future holds, his reputation is secure as perhaps the most influential of the six politicians studied in this book, since he was in large part responsible for the most consequential foreign-policy decision that Britain has taken since the war.

Conclusion

This book has analysed the careers of six politicians who 'made the weather'. Because they made the weather, their influence is still felt today, even although only one of the six – Farage – is still alive. Bevan's conception of the NHS still dominates thinking about health care in Britain, which is deemed untouchable by mainstream politicians. Powell, Benn, Jenkins, and, of course, Farage are all highly relevant to the debate on Britain's relations with the EU. Powell and Farage remain highly relevant to debates about immigration and the sovereignty of Parliament – 'take back control' was, after all, the slogan used by the Brexiteers in the 2016 referendum. Immigration once again came to the forefront of political debate when, in November 2023, it was revealed that net immigration the year before had been 745,000, over two and a half times what it had been at its peak when Britain had been a member of the EU, though the bulk of the immigration was now from outside the EU.

Powell's constitutional arguments concerning the incompatibility of devolution with parliamentary sovereignty also have a continuing resonance in light of the strains caused by Scottish devolution. The jury is indeed still out on Powell's contention that devolution has put Scotland on the slippery slope to separation. Jenkins remains part of the debate about electoral reform and the future of the left, while Farage too favours electoral reform and is relevant to the debate on the future of the right. Benn's ideas concerning participation and democracy still resonate with many. Joseph was in some ways the most prescient of all. The problems he emphasised after 1974 – inflation, the role of the trade unions, the quality of education, the breakdown of families – are also the problems of today. The six, therefore, are by no means of merely historical interest.

Leaders who can 'make the weather', as Henry Kissinger pointed out in his book *Leadership*, are particularly needed when old certainties dissolve. They see themselves as unconstrained by these traditional certainties. In the past, they were generally reflective politicians with a historical perspective, often derived from extensive reading and reflection. In the more visual culture in which we live now – a culture which has, to a considerable extent, replaced the verbal culture of the past – different qualities are perhaps needed, qualities manifested by Farage, with his quick-fire and witty responses to embarrassing questions.

The six who 'made the weather' all, except for Jenkins, reacted against the post-war settlement based on a mixed economy managed by government with the aid of what were assumed to be Keynesian methods, and secured through consultation with the trade unions, which, in the post-war years, were to become an estate of the realm. Wartime experience had given the post-war generation tremendous confidence in the power of government to resolve economic and social problems. When, in 1954, Wilson, as a member of Labour's Shadow Cabinet, produced plans on the future of the cotton industry, Raymond Streat, chairman of the Cotton Board, found himself 'absolutely frightened about what Wilson would do if he became, shall we say, Chancellor of the Exchequer or Prime Minister. He has a fantastic belief in the power of the government and individual Ministers to supervise and decide things for the public good'.[1] By intelligent state action – piecemeal social engineering, to use Karl Popper's

---

1 Nick Thomas-Symonds, *Harold Wilson: The Winner* (Weidenfeld and Nicolson, 2022), 126–7.

phrase – governments could iron out economic fluctuations and ensure full employment, stable prices, and economic progress, as well as social welfare. Through the delivery of prosperity, class tensions would be eased. 'Life's better with the Conservatives. Don't let Labour ruin it' was the party's election slogan in the 1959 general election. After that election, which gave the Conservatives an increased majority, Prime Minister Macmillan declared that the class war was over. Economic progress, so it was believed, obviated the need to make difficult strategic or ideological choices.

In addition, the post-war settlement accepted traditional assumptions about Britain's place in the world. There was confidence that Britain would remain a global power, since, as Churchill was to insist, she alone remained at the centre of three circles of influence:

> The first circle for us is naturally the British Commonwealth and Empire, with all that that comprises. Then there is also the English-speaking world in which we, Canada, and the other British Dominions and the United States play so important a part. And finally, there is United Europe. These three majestic circles are co-existent and if they are linked together there is no force or combination which could overthrow them or ever challenge them. Now if you think of the three inter-linked circles you will see that we are the only country which has a great part in every one of them. We stand, in fact, at the very point of junction, and here in this Island at the centre of the seaways and perhaps of the airways also, we have the opportunity of joining them all together.[2]

---

2 Quoted in Kenneth Waltz, *Foreign Policy and Democratic Politics: The American and British Experience* (Little Brown, 1967), 226–7.

The 'three circles' doctrine made it impossible to contemplate merging sovereignty with the emerging EC. But, with the end of empire and the realisation at Suez in 1956 that Britain was subordinate to the US, choices could no longer be avoided. The decision to seek entry to the EC, first made by Macmillan in 1961 and later endorsed by the Labour Party, introduced into British politics a new issue, one that would come to break up both major parties. Powell's Euroscepticism after 1969 laid the groundwork for a civil war in the Conservative Party after Britain left the Exchange Rate Mechanism in 1992, a civil war which gave Farage his chance, while Jenkins's enthusiasm for the EC was a main factor in the Labour split in 1981 and the establishment of the SDP.

In economic policy, Bevan and Benn reacted against the post-war settlement from the left, seeking to push it in a socialist direction. Powell, Joseph, and Farage reacted against it from the right, seeking to push it in a market direction. Jenkins was the only one amongst the six who endorsed the economic settlement. But he believed it could only be preserved through constitutional reforms, especially proportional representation, and a realignment of the left. In the words of the 1983 SDP–Liberal election manifesto, *Working Together for Britain*:

> Alone of the political parties the Liberal Party and the SDP recognise that our economic crisis is rooted in our political system. As class-based parties, Labour and Conservative represent and intensify our divisions. The 'first-past-the-post' voting system ensures the under-representation of all those who reject class as the basis of politics. Electoral reform is thus a pre-condition of healing Britain's divisions and creating a sense of community.

Oddly enough, Farage could say the same!

By the 1970s, if not earlier, the settlement seemed exhausted. It had been causing discomfort for some time. It had first come to be questioned after Suez, in 1956, when it appeared that, far from being a world power, Britain had become heavily dependent on the US. Then, in the early 1960s, it seemed that the rate of economic growth in Britain was lagging behind its continental competitors. The first response to Britain's economic worries, under Macmillan's government in 1961, was to seek to buttress and reform the settlement. There were, so the government believed, two magic solutions – planning and Europe. State planning and an incomes policy would make economic policy more effective. Entry to the EC would benefit British industry by exposing it to the cold shower of competition. These two measures, so it was argued, would boost economic growth, and put the settlement back on its feet again. Wilson's Labour Party, elected in 1964, declared that it rather than the Conservatives held the secret to economic success, because only Labour could secure the consent of the organised working class – the trade unions – without which economic planning was bound to fail. Labour would ensure, to use a phrase current after 1974, a social contract with the trade unions. But attempts to buttress and reform the settlement did not succeed in remedying the sense of decline. By 1976, Callaghan, in his first broadcast as prime minister, could ask, 'Do you, like me, feel that we have been slipping?'[3] Unemployment was rising, and inflation at 16 per cent was five times higher than in 1964, while the flimsiness of the 'social contract' with the trade unions was to be shown by the 'winter of discontent' of public-sector strikes of 1978–9, which brought down the Labour government and led to its replacement in the general election of 1979 by the Conservatives, led by Margaret Thatcher. By 1983, The SDP–Liberal election manifesto claimed

---

3 'Call for National Effort on Inflation', The Times (7 April 1976).

that 'the Conservative and Labour parties between them' had 'made an industrial wasteland out of a country which was once the workshop of the world', with unemployment still rising and manufacturing output 'back to the level of nearly 20 years ago'.

Benn, Jenkins, Powell, and Joseph all responded to political crises engendered by growing disillusionment with the post-war settlement, a disillusionment which caused a crisis in the party system. Disillusionment began after the devaluation of the pound in 1967 and the period of austerity required to make devaluation work. It was after this that Benn argued that greater participation was needed to ensure that socialist promises were kept by Labour governments. Powell declared that the political class had failed the nation by not coming to terms with the end of empire and controlling immigration from the Commonwealth.

The 1970s intensified the political crisis, which had begun in the late 1960s. Neither Wilson nor Heath, leaders of the two major parties, seemed capable of rejuvenating the settlement. Wilson's main concerns had been pragmatic: to keep the ship afloat and to ensure that he remained the captain. Heath, like Macmillan, sought to buttress the settlement with an incomes policy and government intervention in industry, policies quite incompatible with the traditional philosophy of the Conservative Party. Heath's instinct when he saw that the settlement was in trouble was to repair it. It did not occur to him that the settlement itself might have outlived its usefulness. Jenkins thought that only a heroic effort of realignment could preserve the settlement. But the SDP–Liberal Alliance found that it lacked sufficient electoral support to put the settlement on firmer foundations. So, the 1970s and 1980s were to prove a historic defeat both for social democracy and for one-nation conservatism. These two philosophies had relied upon a sense of civic cohesion which was rapidly passing away. Both were paternalistic philosophies which relied on the leaders leading and the followers following. But by the 1970s, the followers were ceasing to follow. Authority was under challenge, primarily from militant trade unions but also from Scottish nationalists, Irish republicans, students, and sexual and racial minorities. It is hardly surprising that the desperate attempts made in the 1970s by Heath, Wilson, and Callaghan to rescue the settlement did not succeed. Indeed, during the time of the miners' strike in 1974 and the 'Who Governs?' election of February 1974, and then again during the period of public-sector strikes in the 'winter of discontent' of 1978–9, it appeared that the country might be becoming ungovernable. The state seemed too weak to control powerful sectional groups, while the public became disillusioned with the settlement as the habits of the immediate post-war period which had sustained it – deference, respect for authority, and social cohesion – gradually fell away. A specific historic era was, it appeared, coming to an end, as Callaghan declared ruefully in 1979, in the face of electoral defeat:

> There are times, perhaps once every thirty years, when there is a sea-change in politics. It then does not matter what you say or what you do. There is a shift in what the public wants and what it approves of. I suspect there is now such a sea-change – and it is for Mrs. Thatcher.[4]

In the 1970s, Joseph, almost alone among front-line politicians, saw that the settlement had reached the end of its useful life. The challenge to it came not from the left but from the right, and it was the right, not the left, that proved to be the beneficiary of its collapse. That surprised many, since, for much of the post-war period, it had appeared that the crucial challenge to the settlement came from the left. The main challengers had seemed to be Bevan and Benn. But the left, though possessed of high ideals

---

4 Morgan, *Callaghan*, 697.

and good intentions, failed to understand those for whom it claimed to speak. Both Bevan and Benn held a romanticised view of the working class, a view that was remote from reality. Indeed, in many ways, Powell, Farage, and Joseph's heroine, Margaret Thatcher, understood the working class better than those on the left. So the high ideals of the left proved insufficient. It had forgotten that only the fullest understanding of popular feeling and a willingness ruthlessly to jettison outdated shibboleths would bring political success.

Alienation from the post-war settlement was to be channelled not by Bevan or Benn, but by Powell. Enthusiasm for Powell was an early and unexpected indication that popular discontent, hostility to immigration, and fear of inflation would undermine the settlement from the right rather than the left. The revolutionaries turned out to be what Richard Nixon, in the US, called the 'silent majority', the non-militant constituency of small businesspeople, those on fixed incomes threatened by inflation, small shopkeepers, and the aspirational working class.[5] These groups, since they lacked large corporate institutions to defend their interests, had always felt unrepresented by the dominant institutions of the post-war settlement. It was this constituency that gave large majorities to Margaret Thatcher in the general elections of the 1980s and then, in 1997, transferred its allegiance to Blair when it could be assured that he would not disturb the new settlement which Margaret Thatcher had inaugurated.

It may be that the historical era inaugurated by Margaret Thatcher in 1979 is itself now coming to an end, a long-term consequence perhaps of the economic and financial crisis of 2008 and then of Covid, which have collectively altered attitudes to the state and led to a demand for government intervention to

---

5 Richard Nixon, 'Address to the Nation on the War in Vietnam', 3 November 1969, Miller Center for Public Affairs Presidential Speeches.

protect the victims of untrammelled economic and social forces. It is too early to tell; a historical era becomes clear only in hindsight. The philosopher, Hegel, said that the owl of Minerva spreads its wings only at dusk. What he meant was that one can only understand a historical era when its way of life is so well established as to be already ending. But what can be said with some assurance is that the future will be shaped not primarily by those conventional politicians whose policies are conditioned by an era that is passing away, but by those unconventional politicians who, by challenging the orthodoxy of their times, succeed in 'making the weather'.

Suggestions for Further Reading

There are interesting general reflections on some of the themes discussed in this book in Henry Kissinger's *Leadership: Six Studies in World Strategy*.

Aneurin Bevan

The authorised biography of Bevan by Michael Foot, *Aneurin Bevan: A Biography*, has rightly been labelled by Jenkins as 'inspired hagiography'.[1] It is unreliable in its interpretation and occasionally even on matters of fact. It does, however, convey the ideological atmosphere surrounding Bevan. The best biography is by John Campbell, *Aneurin Bevan and the Mirage of British Socialism*, reprinted as *Nye Bevan: A Biography*, which is severely critical of Bevan's ideas, though less so of the man.

More recently, the Labour shadow minister Nicklaus Thomas-Symonds has written a biography, *Nye: The Political Life of Aneurin Bevan*, which is accurate and reliable, though it adds little new. There is also a shorter but still valuable biography by Francis Beckett and Clare Beckett, titled *Bevan: Creator of the NHS*. In 1997, just after New Labour's electoral victory, Blair wrote a foreword to a book of essays edited by Geoffrey Goodman entitled *The State of the Nation: The Political Legacy of Aneurin Bevan*, calling Bevan 'a genuine hero'.

---

1 Jenkins, 'Six Men of Power', *The Times* (10 April 1993).

Of great value is a collection of Bevan's speeches, *Aneurin Bevan on the National Health Service*, edited by Charles Webster and published in 1991.

The shelves groan with books on the history of the NHS. The official history of the NHS is by Charles Webster, *The Health Services since the War*, the first volume of which is entitled *Problems of Health Care: The National Health Service Before 1957*. This is authoritative but hardly a pleasure to read, being, like most official histories, top-heavy with detail. But Webster has written a shorter, more readable volume summarising his official history, *The National Health Service: A Political History*.

Enoch Powell

There are a large number of biographies of Powell. The authorised one, *Like the Roman: The Life of Enoch Powell*, is by Simon Heffer, and was published in 1998. It is an impressive and scholarly account. Though favourable to Powell, it is far from being a hagiography – but it is, in my view, unfair to Heath. A more neutral account can be found in Robert Shepherd's *Enoch Powell: A Biography*, published in 1997. There is a vigorous polemic, *The Rise of Enoch Powell* by Paul Foot, which regards Powell as entirely opportunistic. Although it is in my view unfair, the book is well worth reading and contains much interesting material on Powell's early career. Douglas E. Schoen's *Enoch Powell and the Powellites* is an impressive analysis of Powell's thought and of his electoral influence. Powell refused to cooperate with Schoen and, interestingly, this book is not listed in the bibliography accompanying the Powell website.

Rex Collings's *Reflections of a Statesman: The Writings and Speeches of Enoch Powell*, published in 1991, comprises material not only on politics, but on Powell's widespread interests outside politics, as well as valuable autobiographical material. Powell's speeches have also been collected in a number of books: three volumes edited by John Wood, *A Nation not Afraid: The Thinking of Enoch Powell, Freedom and Reality*, and *Still to Decide*; *Immigration and Enoch Powell*, edited by Tom Stacey; *Enoch Powell: No Easy Answers*, published in 1973 by Sheldon Press; *The Common Market: Renegotiate or Come Out*, published in 1973 by Elliot Right Way Books; and two further volumes edited by Powell's archivist, Richard Ritchie, *A Nation or No Nation?: Six Years in British Politics*, and *Enoch Powell on 1992* (the year set for the completion of the EC single market). But every surviving speech made by Powell between the 1950s and 1990s is now available on the *John Enoch Powell Speech Archive* website (www.enochpowell.info). Powell's own writings are also, of course, important in studying his career – in particular a book he wrote with Angus Maude in 1955, *Biography of a Nation*, and his biography *Joseph Chamberlain*, published in 1977, in which Powell restates the case against devolution and federalism.

There is a good scholarly study of immigration policy by Randall Hansen, *Citizenship and Immigration in Postwar Britain*. There is also an important PhD thesis completed in 2022 by David Clarke Shiels, *Enoch Powell and the 'crisis' of the British Nation, c. 1939–71*, which I hope will be published.

Roy Jenkins

Jenkins wrote a wonderful autobiography, *A Life at the Centre*. There is also an excellent biography by John Campbell, *Roy Jenkins: A Well-Rounded Life*, and a most valuable collection of essays edited by Keith Thomas and Andrew Adonis, titled *Roy Jenkins: A Retrospective*. Giles Radice's *Friends and Rivals: Crosland, Jenkins and Healey* relates Jenkins to Anthony

Crosland and Denis Healey. Peter G. Richards's *Parliament and Conscience* discusses the liberal reforms of the 1960s. The standard history of the SDP is *SDP: The Birth, Life, and Death of the Social Democratic Party* by Ivor Crewe and Anthony King. Both were supporters of the new party and encouraged the breakaway from Labour. But in their book they conclude that the failure of the SDP was inevitable.

Keith Joseph

Joseph is the only major figure of the Thatcher era not to have written his memoirs. But there is compensation in an outstanding biography, *Keith Joseph* by Andrew Denham and Mark Garnett. There is also much valuable material in biographies of Margaret Thatcher, particularly *Margaret Thatcher: The Authorized Biography* by Charles Moore, published in three volumes.

For an excoriating criticism of socialism, rivalling that of Joseph, Edmund Dell's *A Strange Eventful History: Democratic Socialism in Britain* emasculates, with equal fervour, Bevanite socialism, Jenkinsite social democracy, and the SDP.

Tony Benn

Benn is best studied in his nine volumes of diaries. They constitute a remarkable collection of source material – though the published diaries apparently contain only around 10 per cent of what is in the original diaries.[2] Benn's day-to-day diaries begin in 1940. There is in addition a fine biography, even if perhaps too favourable – *Tony Benn: A Biography* by Jad Adams.

---

2 Adams, *Tony Benn*, 397.

Nigel Farage

Nigel Farage has written three short volumes of memoirs – *Fighting Bull*, *Flying Free*, and *The Purple Revolution: The Year that Changed Everything*. There is also a good interim biography by the journalist Michael Crick, *One Party After Another: The Disruptive Life of Nigel Farage*. But the best way to understand Farage is to read two fine scholarly books on UKIP – the first *Revolt on the Right: Explaining Support for the Radical Right in Britain* by Robert Ford and Matthew Goodwin, the second *UKIP: Inside the Campaign to Redraw the Map of British Politics* by Matthew Goodwin and Caitlin Milazzo. There is also a good analysis of the 2016 referendum by Harold D. Clarke, Paul Whiteley, and Matthew Goodwin, titled *Why Britain Voted for Brexit: An Individual-Level Analysis of the 2016 Referendum Vote*.

Acknowledgements

I am grateful to the following kind friends who have read earlier drafts of this book and made valuable and constructive comments on it: Paul Bogdanor, Gareth Cadwallader, Heraclis Economides, Simon Lewis, Hugo Mascie-Taylor, Nancy Neville, Tom Otte, Sandy Sullivan, and Richard Tolkien. I am grateful also to Madeleine Sumption for checking my statistics on immigration and to John Barnes, Michael Crick, Iain Dale, and Dominic Lawson for answering queries.

I am especially grateful to Anthony Teasdale, not only for reading and commenting copiously on an earlier draft but for sharing with me over many years his wide and deep knowledge of the Conservative Party.

But, of course, responsibility for what I have written remains mine alone.

Nuffield College, Oxford kindly granted me permission to consult the late David Butler's oral interviews, a goldmine for researchers into recent British history, in the David Butler Archive. I want particularly to thank Emma Quinlan, assistant librarian at the college, for guiding me through the collection and, in doing so, saving me hours of work.

I would also like to thank the incomparable London Library, without whose facilities I would have been unable to write this book.

I should like to thank Harry Hall for commissioning the book and Jo Stimfield and Ed Doxey for the many helpful suggestions they made at the copy editing stage, suggestions which have greatly improved the book. I should also like to thank Daisy Wilkins.

But my greatest debt is to my wife, Sonia, who not only read an earlier draft and made valuable suggestions on it, but has sustained and encouraged me throughout.

Index